TRY XS SIGHTS
RISK-FREE WITH OUR:

# 30-DAY SATISFACTION GUARANTEE

## TEST AND EVALUATE XS SIGHTS
### IF YOU ARE DISSATISFIED WITH YOUR PURCHASE:

- Exchange the sights for a different available option
- Return the product for a refund

Sights that have been installed and test fired qualify for this program. Products must be purchased through **XSSIGHTS.COM** or a participating dealer partner.

For assistance email tech@xssights.com or call **(888) 744-4880**.

# AMERICAN HANDGUNNER DIY GUNS

## 2020 SPECIAL EDITION

**28 STAR WARS ARMORY**
**HOW TO MAKE AN IMPERIAL BLASTER ... THAT SHOOTS.**

# FEATURES

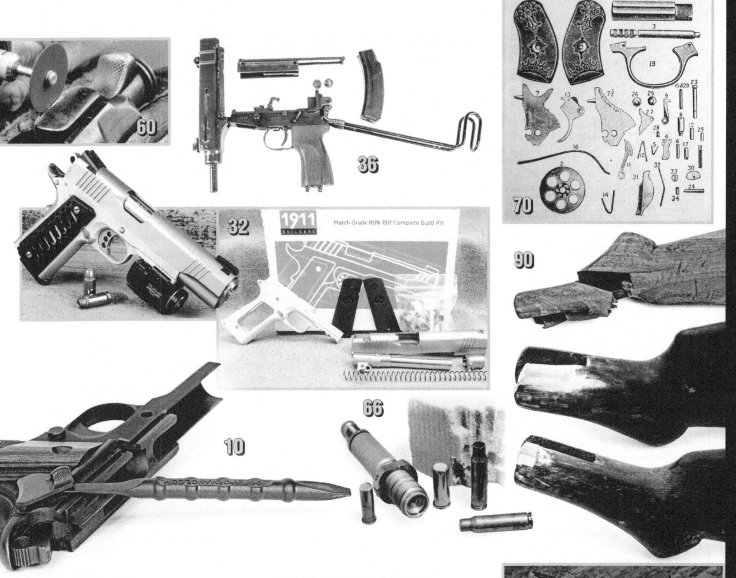

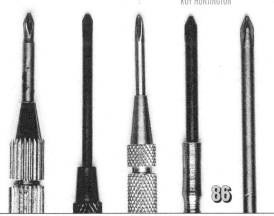

Partial numbers visible: 60, 36, 70, 32, 90, 10, 66, 44, 86

# RESOURCES

AMERICAN HANDGUNNER® Personal Defense DIY Guns Special Edition (ISSN 2161-2110) (ISBN: 978-1-7321327-7-1) is published bi-annually in January and July by Publishers' Development Corporation, 13741 Danielson St. Ste. A, Poway, CA 92064. Contributors submitting manuscripts, photographs or drawings do so at their own risk. Materials cannot be returned unless accompanied by sufficient postage. PAYMENT is for all world rights and will be made at rates current at the time of publication and will cover reproduction in any and all AMERICAN HANDGUNNER® editions or promotions. The act of mailing a manuscript constitutes the author's certification of originality of material. ADVERTISING RATES furnished on request. Reproduction or use of any portion of this magazine in any manner without written permission is prohibited. The opinions and recommendations expressed by individual authors within this magazine are not necessarily those of Publishers' Development Corporation. Copyright© 2019 by Publishers' Development Corporation. All rights reserved. SUBSCRIPTION PROBLEMS: For immediate action email subs@americanhandgunner.com, write Subscription Department, 13741 Danielson St. Ste. A, Poway, CA 92064 or call (866) 820-4045. POSTMASTER: Send address changes to AMERICAN HANDGUNNER® Personal Defense DIY Guns Special Edition, 13741 Danielson St. Ste. A, Poway, CA 92064.

## If only guns could talk ...

**From The Desk Of Tom McHale** — *Executive Editor*

Ever done anything supremely dumb? You know, one of those moves that makes you cringe when you think about it years later. If you haven't, I call fibbing or maybe unconscious denial because we all have at least some regrets. In this issue, and at great personal risk, I come clean with one of mine. I did so in the interest of learning — to help others avoid similar mistakes with their DIY gunsmithing projects. So be gentle, my boundless embarrassment is for the common good.

DIY gunsmithing can get a bad rap. Sure, if you don't know what you're doing, you probably don't want to make adjustments to the trigger or safety of a fine 1911. A valid point. On the other hand, there are lots of fixes and improvements one can make falling closer to the beginner end of the experience spectrum. We've got plenty of those in this Special Edition of *DIY Guns*.

Want to upgrade the trigger on your polymer pistol? No problem. We'll show you how. How about making your standard pistol shoot 1" groups? A semi-drop-in barrel job will do the job. Here's the best part: You won't even need a pile of expensive tools. Easy peasy. On the other hand, if you're looking for an excuse to add to your tool collection, we'll help you out with some recommendations.

If you're already an intermediate or advanced home gunsmith, never fear. We've got plenty of valuable tips and tricks in this issue for you too.

If you're feeling adventurous, consider making your own 1911 — from scratch! Will Dabbs, MD will show you how. You'll be surprised at what you can accomplish with kits and hand tools. If you've got tools and some know-how, be sure to check out "Barbecue on the Side." It's a story about turning a raw Wilson Combat compact slide and receiver into the social event 1911 of your dreams.

Speaking of Dr. Will, he cobbled up his childhood dream gun — an Imperial blaster right out of *Star Wars*. Except this one actually shoots — full auto. Did you expect any different from the new caretaker of *Handgunner*'s *Guncrank Diaries*?

Some of my favorite stories in the 2020 issue are resurrection tales. We've all got a wall hanger or beater gun that's seen better days. Heck, they may not even work. Whether yours are revolvers, surplus rifles or shotguns, we've included stories to help you bring that hot mess back into range or field condition. Heck, Frank Jardim even un-de-milled a Berthier rifle and converted it into a pristine blank firing replica. Cool stuff.

You're about to gain valuable pro tips on woodworking, metal working, parts fabrication, lathe and mill techniques, and even a bit of welding. There are even a couple of articles on how to make your own custom tools.

Now, get reading, then go hit the shop!

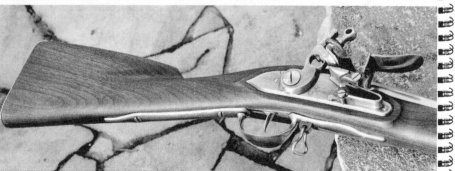

*Using the Stealth Arms Phantom Jig, you can build a 1911 from scratch. Here Will Dabbs, MD is cutting rails in the frame (left). Frank Jardim built this beautiful Charleville musket (below).*

## DIY GUNS

**CORPORATE OFFICERS** Thomas Hollander, Randy Moldé, Marjorie Young
**PUBLISHER** Roy Huntington

**Executive Editor** Tom McHale
**Associate Editors** Jenna Buckley, Jazz Jimenez
**Art Director** Jennifer Lewis
**Contributing Artist** Niki Ackermann
**Production Manager** Lori Robbins
**Digital Content Editor** Joe Kriz
**Website Manager** Lorinda Massey
**Staff Photographer** Joseph Novelozo
**Grammar Guru** Gwen Gunn

### CONTRIBUTING EDITORS

Jeremy D. Clough • Mark Hampton
Leonard Speckin • Garrett M. Baugher
Will Dabbs, MD • Ray Fleck • Tiger McKee
Frank Jardim • Greg Derr
David Freeman • Roger Smith

### FMG PUBLICATIONS

**SPECIAL EDITIONS** fmgpublications.com
Executive Editor: Tom McHale

**HANDGUNNER** americanhandgunner.com
Executive Editor: Tom McHale

**GUNS** gunsmagazine.com
Editor: Brent Wheat

**SHOOTING INDUSTRY** shootingindustry.com
Editor: Jade Moldae

**COP** americancopmagazine.com

NATIONAL AD SALES 800.537.3006
NORTH EAST Tom Vorel • tom.vorel@fmghq.com
SOUTH EAST Paula Iwanski • paula.iwanski@fmghq.com
WEST Delano Amaguin • delano.amaguin@fmghq.com
INTERNATIONAL Amy Tanguay • amy.tanguay@pubdev.com

**Online Traffic Manager:** Lori Robbins
TEL: 858.842.3934, lori.robbins@pubdev.com

## CUSTOMER SERVICE
www.americanhandgunner.com
EDITORIAL . . . . . . . . . . . . . . . . **800.458.4570**
Email: . . . . . . . . . . . . . . . . . editor@americanhandgunner.com
PRODUCTION . . . . . . . . . . . . . . **858.842.3934**
Email: . . . . . . . . . . . . . . . . . . . annuals@fmghq.com

PRODUCED IN THE U.S.A.

Jeremy D. Clough

# EVOLUTION GUN WORKS:

## Tools for professionals.

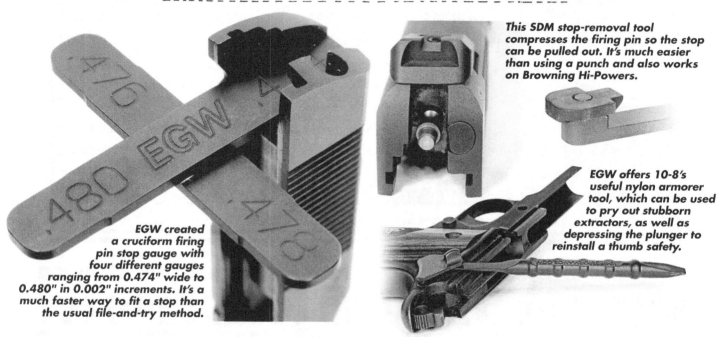

EGW created a cruciform firing pin stop gauge with four different gauges ranging from 0.474" wide to 0.480" in 0.002" increments. It's a much faster way to fit a stop than the usual file-and-try method.

This SDM stop-removal tool compresses the firing pin so the stop can be pulled out. It's much easier than using a punch and also works on Browning Hi-Powers.

EGW offers 10-8's useful nylon armorer tool, which can be used to pry out stubborn extractors, as well as depressing the plunger to reinstall a thumb safety.

**F**ounded in 1991 by George Smith, Evolution Gun Works (EGW) is a major aftermarket supplier of 1911 parts and produces OEM parts for many of the major gunmakers. EGW also offers an extensive line of gunsmithing tools.

Smith, who went to night school for Auto CAD (computer assisted design), CNC and Solid Works, also worked for Austin Behlert, a pistolsmith who did pioneering work making compact pistols out of large ones. With this background, it's no surprise many of the 'smithing tools he designed are for professionals. Designed to not only do the job well, but to do it quickly and efficiently.

### Firing Pin Particulars

The firing pin stop may not seem

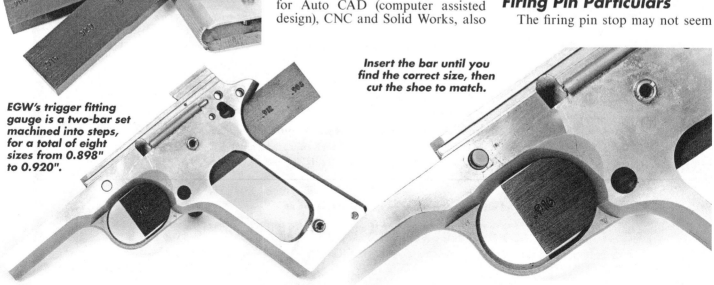

EGW's trigger fitting gauge is a two-bar set machined into steps, for a total of eight sizes from 0.898" to 0.920".

Insert the bar until you find the correct size, then cut the shoe to match.

EGW designed a plunger tube staking tool to fit in the well and has a clearance cut for the ejector. It comes with a spare tip and a Delrin nylon block to support the tube during staking.

like an important part, but it is. While it's rare, a loosely fitted stop can slide down out of place, locking up the gun. More commonly, since it holds the extractor in place, a loose stop can allow the extractor to "clock" or rotate in its tunnel. This changes the angle the extractor hook meets the case head, wreaking havoc with the gun's feeding cycle.

Recognizing the problem, EGW was among the first to offer an over-sized firing pin stop. The extra material allows you to fit it to your gun. Since the location of the channel in which the stop fits doesn't lend itself to using a dial caliper to measure it, EGW created a cruciform firing pin stop gauge with four different gauges. These range from 0.474" wide to 0.480" in 0.002" increments — a much faster way to fit a stop than the usual file-and-try method.

Since fitted parts are usually a little harder to get out, EGW also sells a neat stop removal tool made by SDM compressing the firing pin so the stop can be pulled out. It's much easier than using a punch, especially on Series 80 guns, and works on Browning Hi-Powers too.

EGW also sells the 10-8 Performance Armorer Tool, a reinforced nylon tool reminiscent of the Pachmayr Widget. It's used to pry out stubborn extractors as well as depressing the plunger to reinstall a thumb safety, both of which are easy ways to scratch your gun if you're using a metal tool.

## Measuring Up

As with the firing pin stop, when you're fitting a trigger, there's no great way to measure how tall the shoe needs to be. EGW's answer is a two-bar set machined into steps. Each bar measures four different heights, for a total of eight sizes from 0.898" to 0.920". Insert the bar until you find the correct size and cut the shoe to match.

EGW's staking tool comes with a Delrin nylon block to support the tube during staking without scratching it. It also has channels cut into it for traditional rounded tubes or machined ones with a more square profile.

EGW's barrel hood length gauge inserts between the breech face and the first locking lug in the slide, and has four separate gauges. Those two digits are in thousandths and should be added to 1.3".

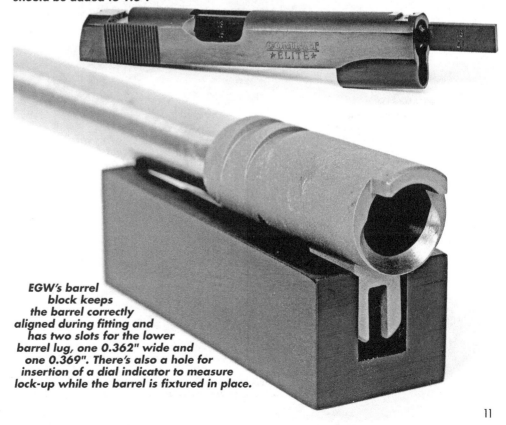

EGW's barrel block keeps the barrel correctly aligned during fitting and has two slots for the lower barrel lug, one 0.362" wide and one 0.369". There's also a hole for insertion of a dial indicator to measure lock-up while the barrel is fixtured in place.

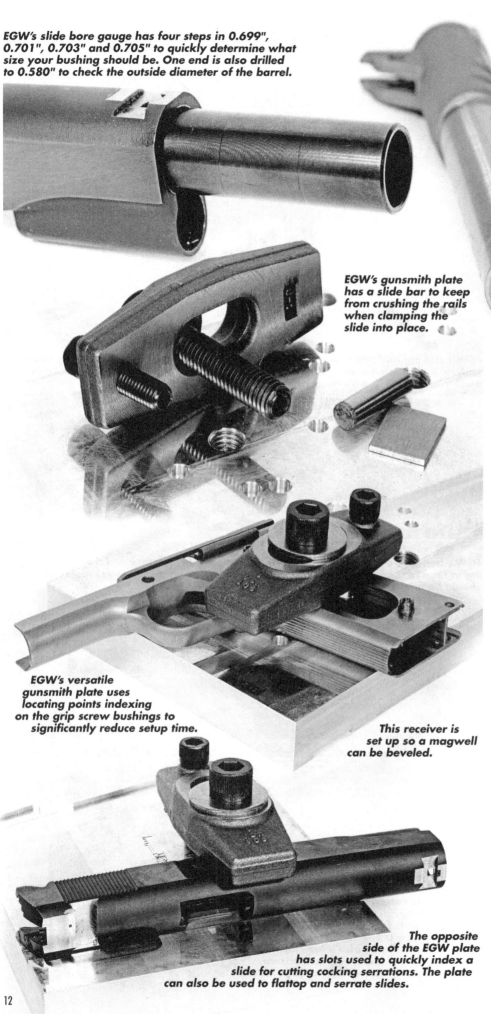

EGW's slide bore gauge has four steps in 0.699", 0.701", 0.703" and 0.705" to quickly determine what size your bushing should be. One end is also drilled to 0.580" to check the outside diameter of the barrel.

EGW's gunsmith plate has a slide bar to keep from crushing the rails when clamping the slide into place.

EGW's versatile gunsmith plate uses locating points indexing on the grip screw bushings to significantly reduce setup time.

This receiver is set up so a magwell can be beveled.

The opposite side of the EGW plate has slots used to quickly index a slide for cutting cocking serrations. The plate can also be used to flattop and serrate slides.

Staking in a plunger tube can be a bit tricky, because, well, it's a tube, and crushing or deforming it is a real possibility — ask me how I know. The rear staking leg is also located inside the magazine well, close to the ejector, making it difficult to get a tool in there. EGW designed a steel bar staking tool that fits in the well and has a clearance cut for the ejector. It also comes with a Delrin nylon block to support the tube during staking. The block has channels cut into it for traditional rounded tubes or machined ones with a more square profile.

Like the 10-8 tool, the Delrin block reduces the risk of scratching the tube, which is usually installed after refinishing so you don't spend the next several years with bluing salts leaching out from under it.

## Tight Fits

Barrel-fitting tools include a hood length gauge, a barrel-fitting block and a slide bore gauge. The hood tool inserts between the breech face and the first locking lug in the slide, a dimension not particularly easy to measure with a dial caliper. The tool has four separate gauges measuring from 1.313" to 1.321". Once you know the correct length, the sides and length of the hood can be cut to fit. The barrel block is used to keep the barrel correctly aligned without turning during fitting, which is critical.

I've used other designs, but the EGW is clearly beefier. It has two slots for the lower barrel lug, one 0.362" wide and one 0.369". There's also a hole for insertion of a dial indicator so the barrel lockup height can be measured while the barrel is fixtured in place.

The slide bore gauge is inserted into the front of the slide until it stops

*The clamps used with the plate come with a second bolt acting as a stop to help the clamp put even pressure on the slide or receiver it's holding. The plate also comes with a slide bar to keep from crushing the slide during clamping.*

on one of its four steps — 0.699", 0.701", 0.703" and 0.705". This provides a quick way of determining what size bushing you need to order or to what size you should cut the one you have. One end of the gauge is also drilled to 0.580" to check the outside diameter of the barrel.

## Fixtures And Cutters

The hardest part of doing machine work is usually fixturing. This can be especially hard on a pistol where a little too much pressure on a slide or receiver can mean major damage. Not only does EGW's gunsmith plate avoid the risk of damaging slides and frames, its use of indexing dowels, slots and pre-drilled holes indexing on the grip screw bushings significantly reduces set up time.

The versatile two-sided plate can hold slides for machining cocking serrations, top flats and opening ejection ports. It can also hold receivers for any number of operations like beveling mag wells and cutting feed ramps. It can either be clamped upright or laid down flat in the mill vise.

EGW also sells the cutters for many of these operations, including a neat double-ended carbide front dovetail cutter. It cuts 0.330" wide dovetails at either 60 or 65 degrees, accounting for two of the most popular front dovetails.

All of their tools and products are well thought out and of the highest quality. I simply can't recommend EGW enough if you're an aspiring gunsmith or a seasoned professional.

*For more info:*
*www.egwguns.com,*
*Ph: (212) 538-1012*

**70720**
Double End Carb Dove
Cutter .33 x 60 65

*EGW sells the cutters for many machining operations, including this neat double-ended carbide front dovetail cutter cutting 0.330" wide dovetails at either a 60- or 65-degree angle, accounting for two of the most popular front dovetails.*

You've Got a Friend in
**EGW**
Pennsylvania

*EGW also sells parts including barrel link kits, Colt ACE slide stops, grip and thumb safeties, mainspring housings, and much more.*

Jeremy D. Clough

# THE STORY BEHIND NOVAK SIGHTS

## Still going strong 4,000,000 sights later.

*Traditional M1911 front sights sat in a shallow recess in the slide and were peened in place.*

*One motivating factor behind the development of the Novak sights was the tiny traditional ones commonly found on 1911's.*

**M**ost people associate the name "Novak" with pistol sights, and there's a good reason. In addition to building Browning Hi-Powers for the FBI's Hostage Response Team (HRT), doing the lion's share of the design work on S&W's Third Generation series of pistols and serving as a consultant for many OEM manufacturers, Wayne Novak designed the most influential — and most copied — fixed rear sight ever put on a handgun. Named the Lo-Mount, it has appeared on factory pistols from most major handgun manufacturers and can be easily retrofitted onto the rest.

What many shooters don't know, though, is his influence on the front of the gun is where Novak sights started.

After graduating from Colorado School of Trades' gunsmithing program, where he specialized in high-end shotguns, Wayne accompanied fellow graduate Jack Mitchell on a visit to influential pistolsmith Armand Swenson. Wayne wound up working for Swenson for two years, during which he designed his first rear sight and learned the Swenson method for installing high-profile front sights: Machine a slot on the front of the slide, set a 0.125" wide blank in it and silver-braze it in place.

### Sights In Orbit

Traditionally, M1911 front sights sat in a very shallow half-moon recess in the slide, and a stem on the bottom of the sight (called a tenon) protruded through a hole in the bottom of the recess. Installing the sight required peening (also known as swaging) the tenon from the inside of the slide, spreading it out to lock the front sight in place.

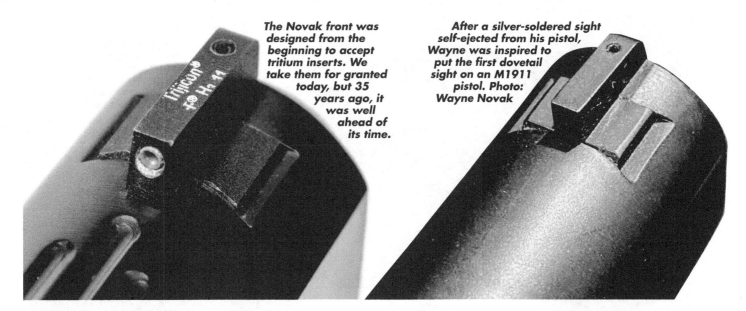

The Novak front was designed from the beginning to accept tritium inserts. We take them for granted today, but 35 years ago, it was well ahead of its time.

After a silver-soldered sight self-ejected from his pistol, Wayne was inspired to put the first dovetail sight on an M1911 pistol. Photo: Wayne Novak

No doubt this was adequate for the tiny front sights on original M1911's, but you also couldn't see them, which is why we have larger sights today. Unfortunately, as a sight gets larger, it's subject to much more inertia when the slide cycles at some 300 feet per second. The bigger a sight is, the more strain it puts on whatever holds it in place. Because of this, peened sights will eventually shoot loose, but are not likely to leave the gun.

Not so with silver-brazed front sights, as Wayne learned around 1984 while shooting one of his pistols that used a brazed mount. Although it had been fine for some 30,000 rounds, the sight simply disappeared, ejected into the ether when the gun went off.

Inspired by Ken Hackathorn's HK P7, which had a dovetail front sight, Wayne ordered a dovetail cutter from Brownells and shaped a new sight to fit that dovetail. Within a week or two he had it installed on an M1911, where he secured it with a roll pin to ensure even if the sight got loose it would not lose its zero.

The alert reader will notice the length of the front sight: It was designed from the beginning to accept tritium inserts — considered pioneering technology at the time. Wayne is quick to point out he's not the first person who created a pinned dovetail front sight. In addition to the P7, there was one on the 1900 model Luger, but he was the first to do it on an M1911, something we now take for granted.

*Although it had been fine for some 30,000 rounds, the sight simply disappeared, ejected into the ether when the gun went off.*

The Swenson method silver brazes the sight in a slot. It's clean, but may not last forever.

## Rear Sight Revolution

The rear sight was a bit more evolutionary. He had first created a sight

To install a front sight, mill a short, narrow flat on the slide top, cut the dovetail and drill a hole for the roll pin. You may need a dovetail file and sturdy drift.

Patented in 1985, the LoMount rear sight combines a snag-free ramp with a rear contour that matches the heel of the slide. Thirty-five years and some 4,000,000 sights later, it's the most influential rear sight ever put on a handgun.

To install a LoMount, machine a large flat with a 1/2" end mill, then cut the dovetail. Or you can ship just the slide to Novak's for installation.

for the S&W 745 with the distinctive ramp-like shape at the front that kept it from snagging. This morphed into the LoMount when Wayne contoured the rear of the sight (formerly square to create a bold sight picture) to match the heel of the slide. Virtually every wedge-shaped rear sight you've seen was inspired, either directly or indirectly, by this distinctive profile.

Other features include the shadowbox effect of the rear sighting surface drawing the eye to the rear notch. This hollowed out area also protects any tritium inserts, which, like the front sight, the LoMount was designed to accommodate. The sight body also tapers toward the front allowing a broader range of windage adjustment than a straight-bodied sight. In addition to the beefy dovetail, the sight is further secured by a sturdy hex screw.

There have been some minor changes through the years, including the creation of an adjustable LoMount, but the sight remains essentially the same as when it was designed and patented in 1985. Other variants include gold-bead fronts, fiber-optic inserts for both front and rear, suppressor-height sights and a variety of dovetail dimensions to retrofit guns that did not come with Novak sights. Since the LoMount is designed to be snag-free, there is no version available for the popular but dangerous sight-cocking technique.

## Machine Time

Installing sights on slides without dovetails requires some machining; instructions come in the sight package and are available on the Novak's web-

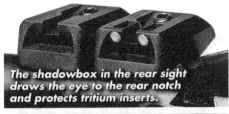

The shadowbox in the rear sight draws the eye to the rear notch and protects tritium inserts.

The first LoMount rear is on Wayne's personal BHP, which is similar to the guns he built for the FBI HRT. When the HRT later spec'd out a new pistol, they only asked for two things by name, one of which was a Novak LoMount. Photo: Wayne Novak

site. For the front sight, you mill a short, narrow flat on the slide top, locate and cut the dovetail and, once the front sight is installed, drill a hole for the roll pin.

To install the rear LoMount, you machine a large flat with a 1/2" end mill followed by locating and cutting the dovetail. Those without access to machine tools can ship just the slide to Novak's for installation, which usually has a quick (approximately one week) turnaround. Both the front and rear sight designs are so influential most non-retro M1911 pistols come with a front dovetail and many also have a rear dovetail either patterned after the Novak cut or very similar.

The popularity of those sight cuts is one measure of the influence of Novak sights. Another is when the FBI spec'd out their new HRT pistol to replace the Hi-Power, they only asked for two things by name: one was a Novak LoMount for which they even gave the part number. The United States Marine Corps also spec'd them on their M45 pistol, and is one of Wayne's proudest achievements.

A third measure is the number of sights sold. In the 35 or so years they've been around, Novak's has produced or licensed some 4,000,000 sights, not counting innumerable unauthorized copies.

For those who want the real thing, genuine Novak LoMount sights are CNC-machined from 4130 steel and are marked "Novak's." 🔫

*For more info:*
*www.novaksights.com,*
*Ph: (304) 428-2676*

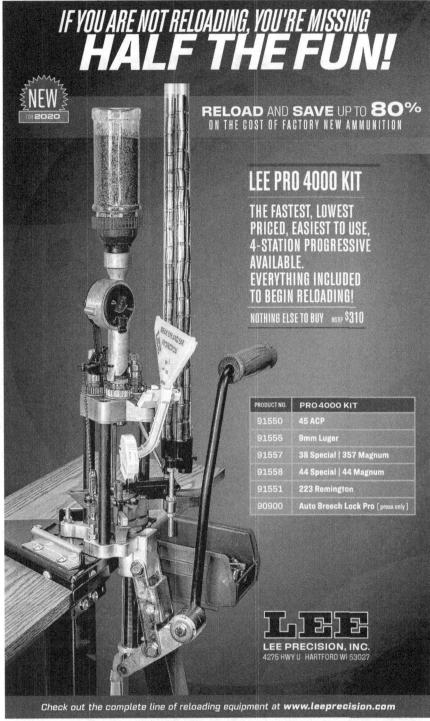

Tom McHale

# UPGRADE YOUR POLYMER PISTOL BARREL

## Make your off-the-rack service pistol a tack driver.

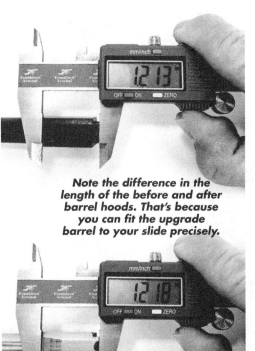

*Note the difference in the length of the before and after barrel hoods. That's because you can fit the upgrade barrel to your slide precisely.*

Today's production pistols are an amazing value when you think about it. With rare exception, for several hundred bucks you'll get a handgun guaranteed to be reliable and accurate. Modern computer-controlled machinery produces parts with tight tolerances we could only dream of just a few decades ago.

However, even with all the engineering marvels, companies still have to engineer a little bit of "slop" into parts specifications. Assembly teams must reach into a bin of barrels, pull one out and be sure it'll work with any given frame and slide. To ensure parts interoperability and compatibility with a near-infinite variety of ammunition, there's always got to be wiggle room.

### Before: Out-Of-The-Box Performance

If you want to improve the mechanical accuracy of a production pistol, the best thing you can do is fit an upgraded barrel. Doing this allows you to define the precise fit between barrel and slide. The more precise the fit, the more likely those two parts will return to the exact same positions from shot to shot. *Ipso facto e. pluribus unum*, you'll get better accuracy results.

The Smith & Wesson M&P 2.0 shown here is a solid production gun. It's flawless in terms of reliability and shoots more accurately than most users can hold. With a wide variety of factory ammo, the 25-yard, 5-shot groups ranged between 1.79" and 3.80". The overall average of 19 different groups with seven brands of ammo worked out to 2.86".

### Get Ready To Rumble

The good news is this DIY job is beginner-friendly. All you need are a few inexpensive hand tools, some of which you might already have. A bench vise makes the job much easier and more precise. If you don't have a fancy-schmancy gunsmith vise, no worries. Just tape two strips of alu-

*The S&W M&P 2.0 9mm was fine out of the box. Utterly reliable and more accurate than most can shoot. The Apex Semi-Drop-In Barrel upgrade makes it a tack driver.*

*For tools, this is all you really need. A pillar file, diamond hone, emery cloth and either Dykem marking fluid or a Sharpie pen.*

Make your garage vise gun-friendly by taping strips of aluminum (or other soft metal) to those rough jaws.

While hard to see, there is movement between the barrel and slide. As any part pulled from the barrel bin has to work with any slide, there is a bit of forgiveness built into both.

The vise modification allows you to hold steel parts stable without mucking up the finish.

minum to the inside of your regular vise. Being softer than steel, they won't butch-up your parts. The tape holding the aluminum in place offers an extra degree of scratch protection.

You'll also want some Dykem layout fluid, but if you don't have any or don't want to buy it, a Sharpie will do just as well. You'll want two items from a gunsmith-savvy store like Brownells: a narrow pillar hand file and an EZE-Lap Fine Diamond Hone and Stone. Last but not least, some 600-grit emery cloth will help you smooth everything out at the end. Oh, don't forget a spoonful of patience. As they say, it's easy to remove metal but hard to add it back.

After clearing all ammunition from the premises, field strip your pistol and degrease the new barrel and the slide.

## Put A Muzzle On It!

The Apex Semi Drop-in Barrel is manufactured to be "too big" in a couple of key places. The muzzle area of the barrel has excess metal around the 10 and 2 o'clock positions. You'll probably need to hone it down to achieve tight lockup at the muzzle end of the slide. Our goal is to remove metal (if necessary) until the barrel just barely fits into the slide. Depending on the tolerances of the fiery-end hole in the front of your slide, the replacement barrel may work as-is, so check before breaking out the diamond hone.

Apply some layout fluid around the barrel and lock it into position in your vise. Using the EZE-Lap hone, gently remove a bit of material from the 10 and 2 areas using a rocking motion so you don't create flat spots. The Dykem will guide your work, so reapply as needed. Go slow and check often. Like the subsequent steps, this fitting process is a balancing act between "just barely" fitting into

Remember, this process is a fine balancing act between tight tolerances and reliable function, so don't be discouraged if you experience some failures to go into battery at the range.

The muzzle end of Apex barrels are larger (on purpose) at the 10 and 2 o'clock positions. This allows you to remove just enough material to ensure a tight lockup with the muzzle end of the slide. The Dykem allows you to see exactly where steel is being removed.

Tom used this wide EZE-Lap Fine Diamond Hone and Stone in a rocking motion around the 10 and 2 o'clock areas to fit the muzzle.

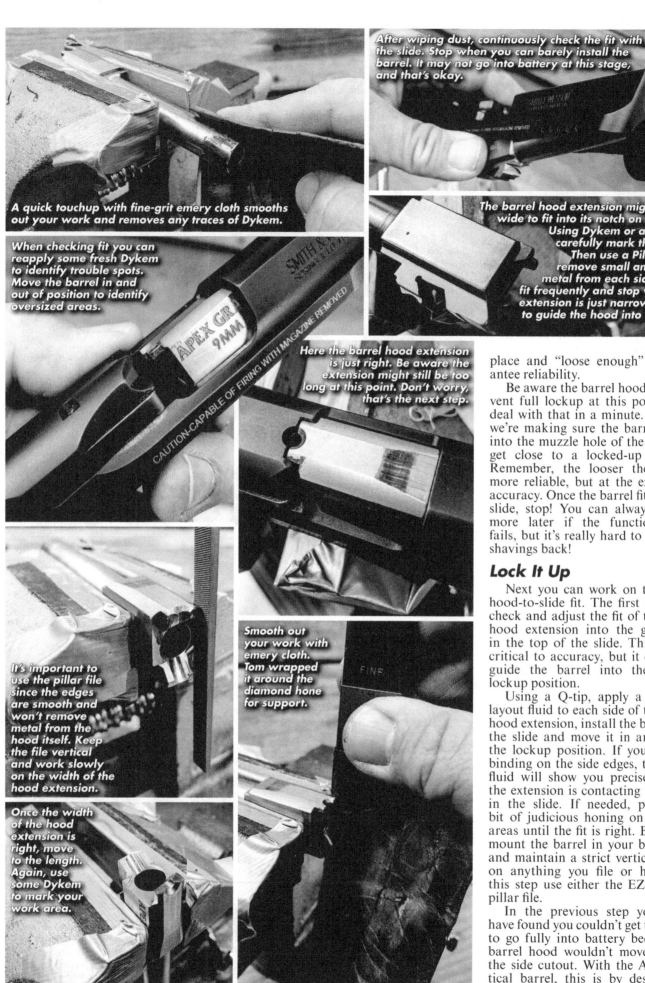

A quick touchup with fine-grit emery cloth smooths out your work and removes any traces of Dykem.

When checking fit you can reapply some fresh Dykem to identify trouble spots. Move the barrel in and out of position to identify oversized areas.

After wiping dust, continuously check the fit with the slide. Stop when you can barely install the barrel. It may not go into battery at this stage, and that's okay.

The barrel hood extension might be too wide to fit into its notch on the slide. Using Dykem or a Sharpie, carefully mark the edges. Then use a Pillar file to remove small amounts of metal from each side. Check fit frequently and stop when the extension is just narrow enough to guide the hood into the slide.

Here the barrel hood extension is just right. Be aware the extension might still be too long at this point. Don't worry, that's the next step.

It's important to use the pillar file since the edges are smooth and won't remove metal from the hood itself. Keep the file vertical and work slowly on the width of the hood extension.

Smooth out your work with emery cloth. Tom wrapped it around the diamond hone for support.

Once the width of the hood extension is right, move to the length. Again, use some Dykem to mark your work area.

place and "loose enough" to guarantee reliability.

Be aware the barrel hood may prevent full lockup at this point. We'll deal with that in a minute. For now, we're making sure the barrel can fit into the muzzle hole of the slide and get close to a locked-up position. Remember, the looser the fit, the more reliable, but at the expense of accuracy. Once the barrel fits into the slide, stop! You can always remove more later if the function check fails, but it's really hard to put those shavings back!

## Lock It Up

Next you can work on the barrel hood-to-slide fit. The first step is to check and adjust the fit of the barrel hood extension into the guide slot in the top of the slide. This fit isn't critical to accuracy, but it does help guide the barrel into the desired lockup position.

Using a Q-tip, apply a touch of layout fluid to each side of the barrel hood extension, install the barrel into the slide and move it in and out of the lockup position. If you feel any binding on the side edges, the layout fluid will show you precisely where the extension is contacting the notch in the slide. If needed, perform a bit of judicious honing on the edge areas until the fit is right. Be sure to mount the barrel in your bench vise and maintain a strict vertical profile on anything you file or hone. For this step use either the EZE-Lap or pillar file.

In the previous step you might have found you couldn't get the barrel to go fully into battery because the barrel hood wouldn't move up into the side cutout. With the Apex Tactical barrel, this is by design. The

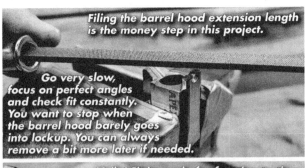
Filing the barrel hood extension length is the money step in this project.

Go very slow, focus on perfect angles and check fit constantly. You want to stop when the barrel hood barely goes into lockup. You can always remove a bit more later if needed.

The Apex barrel also has a fitting pad on the bottom to control vertical play. Tom didn't have to adjust this, but if your slide won't close properly, you might have to remove some material from this area.

The goal of all this fit fine tuning is to make sure the barrel locks up to the slide tightly at the breech and muzzle ends.

Voila! Fit is ready for function testing.

To test final fit, reassemble the pistol with the recoil spring in place and without the magazine. Allow the slide to ease forward with light pressure. If you can press it into battery with light-to-moderate thumb pressure, you're ready for range testing. Remember, in normal operation the recoil motion will slam the slide closed, so it's okay if it requires a bit of pressure.

The finished product ready for the range.

Tom prefers to accuracy test using a handgun scope mounted with this UM Tactical adapter. It allows error-free sighting and removes human eyesight completely from the equation.

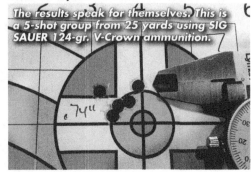
The results speak for themselves. This is a 5-shot group from 25 yards using SIG SAUER 124-gr. V-Crown ammunition.

hood is too long, so you can file it down to the exact length required for your particular slide. What we're trying to achieve here is a near-exact fit with no excess back-and-forth play between the barrel and slide when in lockup. In the pistol shown here, I measured about 9/1,000ths of an inch of slop with the factory barrel.

As you might have guessed, it's time to break out the Dykem again. Apply a bit to the rear surfaces of the barrel hood. When you try to lock up the barrel, move it up and down against the slide and you'll see where there is excess contact. I find it easier to mount the barrel vertically in the vise for this filing operation.

Using the narrow pillar file, gently stroke across the high areas identified by the layout fluid. Take extra care to maintain a level stroke. It's also a good idea to reverse the barrel after each couple of passes. This is where patience is important. Less is more, so remove the barrel and check fit frequently, after each couple of light file passes.

When you can insert the barrel into full lockup position with only light finger pressure, you're done — at least for now. There should also be no front-to-back play. If we did things right, we eliminated that movement.

## Final Fitting

The Apex Semi Drop-In Barrel includes one more fitting area. There is a fitting pad on the bottom of the barrel lug which is used to adjust vertical play. In most cases, you won't have to adjust this. To check, apply a bit of layout fluid to the lug and check the vertical fit by assembling the frame, recoil spring, barrel and slide. Be sure to wipe down all parts to remove metal shavings and grit. If everything goes back together normally, it's time for final fit testing.

With the pistol fully assembled, except magazine and ammo, of course, slowly allow the slide to close. To get the pistol into battery, you should only have to apply light pressure with your thumb on the back of the slide. When you're shooting, there will be plenty of recoil spring force driving the barrel and slide into battery, so a little resistance is okay.

Last but not least, it's time to test on the range. Remember, this process is a fine balancing act between tight tolerances and reliable function, so don't be discouraged if you experience some failures to go into battery at the range. If you're having trouble figuring out exactly which area is too tight, just apply a bit of layout fluid or use a Sharpie on relevant barrel hood and lug areas before you shoot. If needed, you can always take a bit more metal from the high spots.

When you get fit and function nailed, do a little smoothing work on the filed areas with 600-grit (or higher) sandpaper or emery cloth to polish any rough spots.

## My Results

That's it! Job well done! Now head back to the range and check your accuracy improvement. I suspect you'll be pleasantly surprised. I was when I performed this gem of an upgrade. After fitting the Apex Tactical Semi Drop-in Barrel, 25-yard, 5-shot groups shrank to a range of 0.74" to 2.41". That "big" group was an outlier. Every other group was well under 2", with the average falling below 1.5". I'll take it.

*For more info: www.apextactical.com*

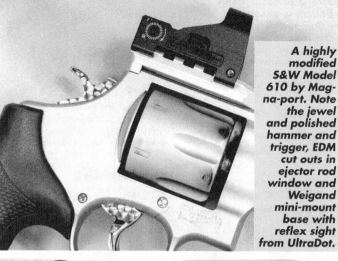

A highly modified S&W Model 610 by Magna-port. Note the jewel and polished hammer and trigger, EDM cut outs in ejector rod window and Weigand mini-mount base with reflex sight from UltraDot.

Muzzlebrakes come in a variety of designs. Mark finds them to be lifesavers on big-caliber handguns.

A Lovell scope mount and rings on a Freedom Arms Model 83.

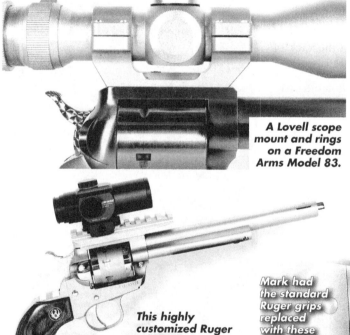

This highly customized Ruger Single-7 by Mag-na-port is topped by an UltraDot sight with a Weigand Machine And Design base.

Mark had the standard Ruger grips replaced with these Gary Reeder Corian grips.

Mark likes red dots on hunting revolvers. Here's one of his UltraDot configurations.

**Mark Hampton**

# HUNTING HANDGUN HOT RODS

## Should you customize your hunter?

So ... you purchased a new handgun and are ready to hit the woods. Is it field ready right out of the box? Or should you consider a few modifications to enhance the performance, accuracy and enjoyment of your handgun?

### For Want Of A Trigger

The first and most important customization is a good trigger. A trigger with a heavy pull and lots of creep makes consistent accuracy much more difficult to achieve. I don't enjoy "fighting" a heavy trigger. A good trigger is an asset to most any shooter — it takes a lot of work out of the equation.

Every shooter may define "a good trigger" differently. For me, a good trigger breaks clean and crisp, with no creep and with no gritty feel. On most of my revolvers, the trigger breaks around 3 lbs. or less. This works well for me, and I can shoot during cold weather and still be safe. On single-shot handguns, I prefer a trigger pull of 2 lbs. or fewer. Single-shot handguns like the T/C Encore, Nosler NCH and custom XPs and handguns of similar design are scary accurate — a good trigger helps with consistent, precise shot placement.

For over 30 years I have been sending revolvers to Mag-na-port International for action and trigger jobs. Today, Ken Kelly continues in his father's footsteps with top-notch gunsmithing there. Recently I sent Ken several revolvers for tune-ups and they all came back with great triggers. Without a quality trigger, everything else is just window dressing.

### Get A Grip

We handgunners come in all different

sizes and shapes, so grips are often one of the first modifications considered — it's impossible for firearm manufacturers to provide a one-size-fits-all. Changing grips to properly fit your hand can improve your comfort level — and your shooting. I have a Ruger Super Blackhawk Bisley Hunter in .41 Mag. The factory grips just didn't feel right, and as a result I didn't enjoy shooting this revolver. I reached out to Gary Reeder and he was kind enough to fit a set of Corian grips to this stainless revolver. Boy, did they make a difference! And they look great to boot. Gary Reeder Guns offers many other custom-revolver embellishments including maxi-throat, deep-dish crown and action job. He's an avid handgun hunter and knows what works.

Certain grips can also help manage heavy recoil better. Some shooters prefer finger groove, or combat-style grips. Perhaps rubber grips will best serve your intended purpose, or maybe some high-end Turkish walnut sure to impress your friends. Textured or finely checkered grips may help with sweaty palms. Choosing the right grip to properly fit your hand and purpose will definitely be an asset.

For single-shot handguns such as the T/C, changing forends can also be beneficial. There are several aftermarket options available in a variety of shapes and styles. I prefer a forearm 2" wide as it rides nicely in a bag or backpack.

## What You Can't See ...

Sights are another area for modification consideration. If you're still enjoying iron sights, you may want to consider switching out front and rear sights for easy target acquisition. Perhaps you need a taller front sight, patridge with gold bead or bright colored insert. Depending on your eyes, barrel length and shooting application, different blade widths may make sense.

I'm past iron sights at this stage of life, so I lean toward optics. For revolvers and semi-autos, reflex sights are common on today's hunting handguns. With a little practice, you can get on-target mighty fast. Red dots come in different sizes from 1 MOA to 8 MOA. For more precise shooting, the smaller the dot size the better. Remember, a 3 MOA dot will cover 3" at 100 yards. For hunting in the woods where shots normally occur inside of 100 yards, the red dot sight is very practical. I've been using UltraDot sights, both tube and reflex models, on revolvers and semi-autos with satisfactory results. Trijicon and Leupold also provide quality reflex sights.

Some handgunners prefer scopes over the red dots. Your planned hunting endeavor will determine the best power level. A straight 2X scope is fine for woods hunting. If you're likely to encounter long shots in open country, you'll appreciate higher magnification. I've been shooting Leupold's 2.5-8x for many years. It's a great optic for many types of hunting. Leave it on 2.5x for close-range opportunities or crank up the power for longer pokes. Burris also makes a 2-7x and a 3-12x scope, both are fine optics for hunting.

While we're discussing optics, proper mounts and rings are a must. Many of my handguns use Weigand Machine And Design mounts and rings. Warne mounts and rings are another source for quality mounting gear. SSK Industries' T'SOB mount is tough as nails and will withstand brutal recoil. I refuse to mount a good optic in a cheap base mount and rings — it makes no sense. I'm in the process of installing a Leupold scope on a Freedom Arms Model 83. A Lovell mount with integrated rings will secure the optic and will not shake loose regardless of how many heavy loads it endures.

## Recoil Reduction

Another modification I frequently choose involves recoil management. The older I get the less I enjoy brutal recoil — it's just a reality I embrace. Many of my revolvers have the Mag-na-port process which reduces felt recoil and tames muzzle rise. Lately I've been pleased with the dual-trapezoidal porting. For single shots, muzzlebrakes come in many flavors. The side-dis-

**Mark replaced the T/C Encore factory forend with this custom model. He prefers the wide versions for stability on rests.**

**This T'SOB base from SSK Industries is built like a tank. The scope is rock-solid in three Weigand rings.**

charge versions seem to be the most effective on many of my single-shot handguns. I know what you're thinking — those darn muzzlebrakes are loud! You're correct. I never shoot any handgun, even when hunting, without hearing protection.

Today's muzzlebrakes are impressive. I have an H-S Precision bolt-action handgun chambered in .270 WSM. With a side-discharge muzzlebrake, I can shoot this handgun one-handed with little felt recoil. The pistol even wears a riflescope! Some shooters don't consider muzzlebrakes accessories, but necessities.

## Cosmetics

Different finishes are another modification to consider. You might like color case-hardening, or maybe you're more attached to high-luster blue. Others might gravitate to a matte or stainless finish. Mag-na-port offers a beautiful velvet hone finish for stainless steel firearms. There is a plethora of options for Cerakote, Duracoat or Gun-Kote finishes. The Encore in .375 JDJ I own has seen a tremendous amount of use and abuse — it's a working gun for sure. To hide the years of maltreatment, I had a camo finish applied. It's different, unique and looks cool in the jungle.

Other alterations or conversions may include smoothing internal parts, timing work, combat trigger conversions, adding an oversize locking base pin, reaming cylinder throats, change hammer, jewel and polish trigger and hammer and re-chamber to name just a few. It's up to each individual shooter what you need or want.

Before diving into custom gun work, be sure to spend enough time with your handgun to get a feel for what you specifically want or need. Consider your goals and intended use for that gun. Heck, you may shoot the gun and not have a need for any custom work. There is a world of options to consider, and half the fun is figuring out what's best for your particular situation. 🔫

*For more info:*
*www.magnaport.com,*
*www.sskindustries.com,*
*www.reedercustomguns.com*

**Leonard Speckin**

# THE PROBLEM WITH LUGER SIGHTS — AND THE EASY FIX

*Leonard's Luger is a nice 1918 model but he was always frustrated by the terrible stock sights! Plus they are sighted in for a point of impact at 75 yards — hardly handy!*

*Leonard was able to come up with a solution to the sight issue by adapting a modern brass-bead sight by re-cutting the dovetails on the sight.*

If you've been frustrated by the old-school sight picture and "too-high" point of impact of your Luger, you're not suffering alone, trust me! It's fixable, but the problem is most don't want to destroy the originality of these firearms by installing adjustable sights — or filing rear notches. The options for the Luger shooter today are not plentiful. They were manufactured and targeted at the factory to a point of impact at 75 meters with German issue military ammunition. Most of us who enjoy shooting a Luger don't shoot targets at 75 meters, but likely enjoy shooting cans, watermelons or bull's-eye targets at 25 yards or less.

Most Lugers, in my experience, shoot much too high at 25 yards with original sights. Windage adjustment, however, isn't a problem since the front sight can be drifted right or left. The height of the front sight is the problem. The obvious solution is to drift out the front sight, install a higher front sight and solve the problem. Keep the original front sight and nothing has been irrevocably changed.

Where to get a higher front sight? This was my problem. I have a Luger I enjoy shooting. It's all original with matching numbers and a perfect bore. It's on its third incarnation, however. The chamber date is 1918, but closer inspection ahead of the 1918 date discloses faint markings showing it was at one time a double-date Luger with a reissue date of 1920. In all probability mine is a Luger refurbished after World War I in 1920 and reissued to a German police department. At some later date, it was then recalled from the police department, rebuilt, the 1920 date mostly removed and then reissued either to another police unit or the German army. It has had three lives but functions perfectly and never jams.

## Metal Work

Having the machines and the skill — and with no other choice — I made a higher front sight. Brownells offers a standard European 24-degree milling cutter, duplicating the Luger barrel/sight dovetail. I used the cutter in my vertical mill to cut a matching dovetail on my experimental sight. The original front sight has two tapers, back to front and top to bottom. I made the sight and installed it. The short story is it worked. However when filed down to achieve the right point of impact, the thickness of the tapers changes. The more the sight is filed down the thicker the taper becomes.

These two tapers must then be filed to achieve the original taper ratios so the front sight will present the sight picture in the rear sight as originally designed. A lot of work there. Additionally, I find the original Luger front sight awkward to use. It's difficult to acquire a consistent sight picture from shot to shot. For many years I was a handgun competition shooter and accuracy is important to me. I had read the Luger was inherently accurate, and in Europe had been extensively used in competition — with special sights. I laid the project aside for some thinking. There had to be a better, easier way to adjust

*The stock Luger rear is a shallow "V", non-adjustable and difficult to use well with the stock front inverted "V" arrangement. Leonard's solution allows a nice bead to rest in the "V" rear.*

these Lugers to shoot to a certain point of impact.

About a year later I was perusing the 1939 Stoeger catalog where, right in front of me was a full-page ad for King Modern Gun Sights. In this advertisement was a King conversion for the Luger pistol involving altering the rear sight notch and installing a new improved bead front sight. The result was a nice conversion but it significantly and permanently altered the barrel and rear toggle link containing the rear V-notch sight. So it was a no-go idea for me.

In the lower left corner of the page was an innocuous listing for a Luger front sight, also having a bead. It could be installed simply by drifting out the military front sight and installing the bead sight — nothing is changed. Good morning, Lenny boy! As I age these flashes of brilliance come less and less. They never were overwhelming, so when they do occur I cherish them.

## Presto!

On the preceding page of the catalog was a Marble's ad offering a 1/16" bead front sight for the Luger pistol. Then, on another page was a picture of this sight, the No. 27. The whole solution suddenly became obvious. A 1/16" bead will fit perfectly into the V-notch of the Luger rear sight. Think about English express double rifles and their classic dangerous game sights. What do they have as sights for quick target acquisition? A bead front sight and a V-notch rear. A round object fits into a V-notch naturally. Consider V-blocks used in machining to hold round stock.

But alas, King Gunsight went out of business after World War II so ordering a sight is impossible. The Redfield and Lyman catalogs also listed 1/16" bead sights for the Luger pistol. These pre-war sight manufacturers were on to something. This is why I previously mentioned there were no options "today." It was very easy in 1939. Just order the sight from the King Gun Sight Company, Stoeger, Redfield, Lyman or Marble and you were in business. Unfortunately, this sight is no longer offered by any of these companies.

The problem became what was the height of this elusive sight? To frame this

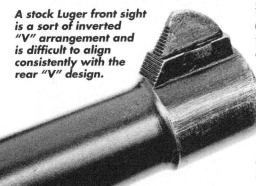

A stock Luger front sight is a sort of inverted "V" arrangement and is difficult to align consistently with the rear "V" design.

This is 25 yards, off-hand, with the new sights. Call it 97-5X. The "misses" were what Leonard calls his "age ring" shots. He thinks in a rest all 10 shots would have been in the X-ring. Lugers can shoot, indeed.

question simply I had to determine the correct height of a 1/16" bead front sight installed in an original Luger dovetail that would shoot a certain weight bullet to the point of impact at 25 yards. At first blush this sounds like a tough nut to crack because even variations of 0.005" will change the point of impact.

By chance I found a 1/16" bead rifle sight in my junk drawer. I set it up in my mill and using Brownells' cutter I re-cut the sight's standard American dovetail to duplicate the dovetail in the Luger barrel. I then cut the bead portion off at the base, drilled and tapped two small holes in the base and made shims to allow adjustment of the bead's height. Stay with me here.

I could then mount the bead portion onto the base, place a shim under it and secure it with the two screws. At the end I had an adjustable 1/16" bead front sight. By firing it and adding or subtracting shims I could determine the correct height of the front bead sight on my Luger to place its shots on target at 25 yards. And it worked perfectly.

## Performance

The sight picture with that 1/16" bead was crystal clear. Firing the Luger with different shim heights established the correct height of 0.931" from the bottom of the barrel to the top of the sight when using Winchester 115-gr. factory ammunition. I ordered two different rifle sights from Williams Gunsight, both with white beads: 0.375" and 0.406" heights with a 0.250" width. Shooting experiments with the adjustable shim sight showed a height of 0.931" above the bottom of the barrel should put the bullet where I want it. I then re-cut one of these new sights to set the top of the bead 0.931" above the bottom of the barrel and installed it in my Luger.

Much to my delight, it shoots to the point of aim at 25 yards with a six o'clock hold, furnishing a clear, repeatable sight picture both fast and easy

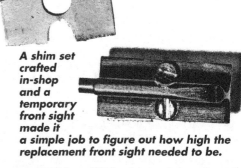

A shim set crafted in-shop and a temporary front sight made it a simple job to figure out how high the replacement front sight needed to be.

to acquire. With those sights Luger's inherent reputation for accuracy was reaffirmed. It shoots as closely as you can hold it. Those old pistolsmiths at King Gun Sight, Redfield and Marble had it right.

## Can You Do It?

Shot placement could vary according to the load used, especially the bullet weight. The sight height listed here is for my eyes and the ammunition I used and might be a tad different for you. It's a good start, however, and you can fine-tune it if needed.

I realize most shooters don't have vertical mills. However the task of re-cutting the dovetail on a rifle sight to fit the Luger barrel dovetail would be easy for most gunsmiths. Once the mill is set up for the job, two or three different heights could be made to accommodate different bullet weights and individual sight picture anomalies. The sights can be ordered from many sources including Williams Gun Sight, Brownells, Midway and others. The cost for each sight is about $14 and the cost of machining probably would be minimal. This is not much expense to tune your Luger so it will shoot exactly where you want it, with your load, while also providing a clear, repeatable sight picture.

This 10-round target was shot by me at 25 yards with the 1918 Luger, free standing, using a two-hand hold. The score is 97-5X. Not bad for a pistol originally made in 1918. The 4-shot hole in the X-ring is where the pistol is shooting and is testimony to its accuracy. If the target had been fired from a machine rest I would wager all 10 shots would have made one jagged hole in the X-ring. The shots outside the X-ring are what I call my "age rings." The bead sight clearly brought out the accuracy of these fascinating pistols.

Enjoy that Luger! They were made to shoot. ⌐

Garrett M. Baugher

# INSTALLING SKINNER SIGHTS

## An easy upgrade for your favorite rifle.

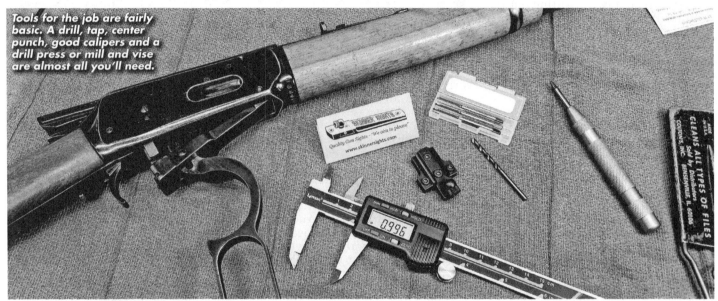

Tools for the job are fairly basic. A drill, tap, center punch, good calipers and a drill press or mill and vise are almost all you'll need.

The rear sight was a fixed open sight with limited adjustment or precision. Garrett found them hard to use accurately.

A few precise measurements scribed in layout fluid show Garrett exactly where to drill holes. A Sharpie pen works in place of the Dykem layout fluid too.

Starting with a "center drill" is important if you have one to ensure accurate hole placement. Otherwise, punch a prick-mark and use a small drill with just a small portion sticking out from the chuck so it doesn't flex.

everal months ago I came across a sweet deal on a Winchester 94 lever action in .30-30 and just couldn't resist taking the old girl home. When I hit the range I was less than thrilled. While I could ring steel out to about 50 yards, I didn't get the performance I was expecting from a rifle with such a legendary reputation. I wanted so badly to fall head over heels for this American beauty, but unless something changed it just wasn't gonna happen.

Thanks to the worldwide web it's now easier than ever to turn a black sheep of a shooter into an all-time favorite. At one time or another we've all felt the hankering to change-out sights on a rifle or handgun. Most, though, never tackle what can actually be a simple, fun afternoon project. Now don't be frightened off by phrases like "drill and tap" or "file to size." With a little patience and attention to detail it's easier than it sounds. Keep in mind most of these techniques will apply to other sights on other guns. Drifting a front sight out of a dovetail is pretty universal,

but there are ways to do it right, and ways to mess it up.

Lots of folks make great after-market sights for the cowboy classics, but my all-time favorite for rugged reliability and ease of use are Skinner sights. Their sights are outrageously simple, rock solid, intuitive, handsome and made in America.

### Getting Started

In the case of the 94 I had to drill and tap two small holes in the rear of the receiver rails. You'll need at least a good drill press to do this sort of thing (a milling machine is even better because it's more precise). Don't even think about using a handheld drill. Since the sights are held in place with screws, we will need to cut threads in the holes using an appropriate tap.

A good drill-press vise or machinist vise is also a must for drilling. Before clamping the receiver into the vise, you'll want to apply several layers of masking tape to both sides to avoid marring the gun's finish. Keep in mind, this technique of "drill and tap" works in other instances where you need threaded holes. Just apply the same methods.

After removing the bolt in the 94, I applied machinist layout fluid so I could see my marks without leaving scratches. You can also use a Sharpie pen, or other marker.

When measuring you'll want to use calipers, and take your time. Even the Harbor Freight $10 calipers are fine for things like this. Measure twice — or maybe 10 times — before you mark and drill. I started with the sight to find out how far apart the center of the holes are, then marked corresponding spots on the receiver. Before every step I would check my accuracy by setting the sight on the receiver to make sure everything would line up properly. After dimpling the center of the holes with a center punch, it's time to make some chips.

## Drilling And Tapping

This is the hardest — or scariest — part, but it's really quite simple if you just take your time. Set up your receiver in the vise so the holes you're drilling are perpendicular to the top of the receiver. A simple small machinist's square will do just fine. Chuck-up your twist drill in the machine you're using and push it in far enough so it's "short." A long small-diameter drill can flex.

Once the drill is lined up over one of the dimples you made earlier, clamp everything down. You don't want anything to suddenly move when you go to drill a hole. Most drill presses have a travel stop that can be set to ensure you don't drill too far. If your machine isn't so equipped, you can use a piece of tape on the drill bit as a reference. We only needed about 0.125" depth in this case.

Take your time setting everything up — once you start drilling there's no going back. Use high RPMs and sort of "peck" at it, touching to drill a tad, backing out, touching the drill in again, etc. Use plenty of lubricant too. There's dedicated cutting oils but even good old WD40 would work. I like to use one of those "cans of air" you use to dust computer keyboards, to clear chips. Once drilling is done in one hole — *don't move the vise.* We are perfectly lined up to tap the hole.

Since our hole is shallow we'll use what's called a "bottoming tap" for this operation so the threads go all the way down. If using a drill press it's easy enough to chuck the tap into the machine and using a little downward pressure, turn the chuck by hand, making sure to back the tap frequently to avoid binding on the chips. I like to use a little shop-made tapping fixture (picture at the top right of this page), but use what you've got.

If you feel any resistance — *stop!* You don't want to break a tap in the top of your receiver. Ouch. For plenty of examples of how to do thread, jump onto YouTube and you'll see hundreds of "how to tap" videos. I'd also practice on a piece of mild scrap steel a few times. Taps can be found online or at some of the better inventoried box stores. Companies like Brownells or Midway have dedicated "gunsmithing" taps in the correct sizes.

So there you have it, one hole drilled and tapped. Just repeat for the other side. Mounting the sight is easy (once you clean out the screw holes) using the screws and wrenches that came with the sight.

## Half Way There

Use a brass or nylon punch and light taps of a hammer to drift out the front and rear factory sights from left to right. Sometimes you can get away with using the original front sight, but mine has seen 50 years of hard use and needed upgrading.

If the replacement sight doesn't seat in place with a few taps on the brass punch, use a triangular file to begin to remove material from the angled sides of the dovetail on the sight. Don't remove material from the bottom of the sight. You want to file the sight, not the dovetail in the rifle.

File a little, check the fit and repeat. Go slow, checking your progress often. Remember, you can remove a little more metal, but you can't put it back on unless you're a talented TIG welder! I like to use the file to lightly deburr the dovetail in the barrel if it needs it. Once the sight seats properly it's time to hit the range and get sighted in.

## Presto

Starting at 25 yards, a couple of initial shots showed my new sights required very little adjustment. Soon I was ringing an 8" steel plate at 100 yards with ease. I almost couldn't believe how much fun I was having with the same rifle that had been so frustrating before. I left the range with a grin on my face, pride in my chest and a newfound love for this old cowboy gun.

This is a relatively simple project to tackle if you take your time and keep your wits about you. Once finished, chances are good it will lend new life to a project gun you've been wanting to upgrade. 🔫

*For more info:*
*www.skinnersights.com,*
*www.midwayusa.com,*
*www.brownells.com,*
*www.harborfreight.com*

*After drilling to depth with a #31 drill to fit the needed tap, a shop-made fixture is used to start the tap cutting the threads. The fixture allows the tap to be turned while being held in the chuck of the mill or drill press.*

*Once the holes are cleaned up, installing the sight is only a matter of lining up the holes and dropping in the screws. This is made easy because Skinner sights come with the necessary wrenches.*

*Garrett ordered a plug to fill the rear factory dovetail. Fitting it only takes a file and a little patience as they are oversized.*

*The original front sight was worse for wear showing dings and dents. The new brass-beaded front sight is a much needed improvement and shows beautifully in the new rear aperture.*

*The Skinner sights are installed, offering a fully adjustable rear. They don't interfere with empty case ejection either. Initial shooting showed them easy to zero, and their clear sight picture helped improve accuracy significantly.*

# THE ULTIMATE MOVIE GUN

**Will Dabbs, MD**

## DIY BlasTech E-11 Stormtrooper Blaster.

*The BlasTech DLT-19 heavy blaster rifle was actually a minimally modified German MG34 machine gun.*

**A** disclaimer is in order: *Star Wars* is a pretty serious thing for me. In 1977 I was 11 years old. I recall even today the playground chatter about some incredibly cool new space movie. The bad guy was some big black dude in a space suit. My mental image was Kareem Abdul-Jabbar wearing Neil Armstrong's clear plexiglass NASA helmet. Then I actually saw the film.

I sat in the front row in a tiny theater in Brookhaven, Miss., gleefully ensconced between a brace of cousins. Were I to do the same today I'd likely suffer the sort of neck cramp that might actually kill me. Back then, however, I was much more flexible.

At the conclusion of the final credits, I sat amidst a massive pool of unseemly drool. My heart raced, and my breath came in shallow gasps. I involuntarily rose to my feet amidst a sea of similarly mesmerized grade schoolers, held a skinny fist aloft and shouted, "As God as my witness, someday I will bodge together an Imperial blaster of my own!"

In truth, I didn't actually say that. However, the seeds planted that fateful day did indeed spark a lifelong quest. Several decades of toil later, I am proud to admit my gun collection does actually include a genuine BlasTech E-11 stormtrooper blaster. Here is how it came to be.

### Backstory

Firearms are an integral part of the modern cinema experience. To paraphrase the Terminator, "It is in our nature to destroy ourselves." In no place is the axiom better manifest than in the ubiquitous weapons used to entertain us.

The two coolest movie guns of all time — the M41 pulse rifle from Alien alongside the BlasTech E-11 stormtrooper blaster from Star Wars.

The E-11 and DLT-19 were the two most common Imperial small arms in use by the elite stormtroopers.

## Technical Particulars

The E-11 blasters used in *Star Wars* and *The Empire Strikes Back* crafted from fully operational Sterling SMGs. These weapons were modified to cycle with blanks and can be seen ejecting empty cases during certain action sequences. Luke and Leia struggling to cross the chasm in the Death Star is a good place to start if you're geeky enough to want to see it for yourself. The muzzle flash and report gave the special effects folks a starting point and served as cues for the actors.

By the time *Return of the Jedi* came along, the state of the movie-making art had advanced to the point where the blasters no longer needed to produce a muzzle flash. As a result, the props used for this film were crafted from Japanese-made non-firing Model Gun Corporation Sterlings. The technical details were similar, though not identical for all the blasters used in these three films.

The basic L2A3 Sterling chassis was left unmolested. Bapty armourers added cooling fins along the ventilated barrel shroud and affixed a periscope of the sort used in Lend-Lease M4 Sherman tanks atop the receiver. Some blasters included a small non-functional battery pack, while others did not. All the blasters were fitted with stubby magazines.

## Raw Material

I started my build with a semi-auto Wiselite Sterling. These guns were sold by Century Arms for a time, though they have not been in the Century catalog for years. As I have my own 07/02 manufacturer's FFL, I registered the gun as a post-sample machine gun and converted it to full auto using an original British surplus Sterling parts kit. For those of you who might be tempted to stop reading at this point, fret not. Should you wish to build a blaster of your own, the raw material is still available to do so legally and relatively easily.

Surplus Sterling SMG parts kits, raw barrels, semi-auto conversion parts and

*Star Wars* was actually a fairly iffy thing. United Artists, Universal and Disney all rejected the project as excessively weird. I bet they feel pretty freaking stupid right about now.

20th Century Fox eventually agreed to produce the movie. The film was an unprecedented gamble for the studio and went over its $8 million budget by $2 million before it debuted. *Star Wars* is now recognized as the second-highest grossing film in North America (behind *Gone with the Wind*) and the fourth-highest grossing movie of all time. In 1977 there were 60 American theaters that ran nothing but *Star Wars* on every screen for a full year.

Per the original screenplay, Luke Skywalker was to be Luke Starkiller. Kurt Russell, Sylvester Stallone, Christopher Walken, Al Pacino, Bill Murray and Steve Martin were all considered for the role of Han Solo before Harrison Ford made the final cut. Jodie Foster turned down Princess Leia's flowing white robes due

to previous commitments. Alec Guinness was the only member of the cast who thought the film would be a success.

The studio work for the movie was undertaken in London, so the weapons used were drawn from the guns available in Europe in the 1970s. According to the backstory, BlasTech was the primary manufacturer of Imperial small arms. The BlasTech DLT-19 wielded by stormtroopers on Tatooine and by Chewbacca on the Death Star was a minimally modified German MG34 machine gun. The scant rails included on the barrel shroud were actually just metal drawer runners purchased from a hardware store down the street from Bapty and Co., the company that supplied the weapons for the film.

The ballistic star of the movie, however, was the BlasTech E-11 stormtrooper blaster. Crafted from British Army-issue L2A3 Sterling submachine guns, the E-11 became a sci-fi icon. This weapon became my grail.

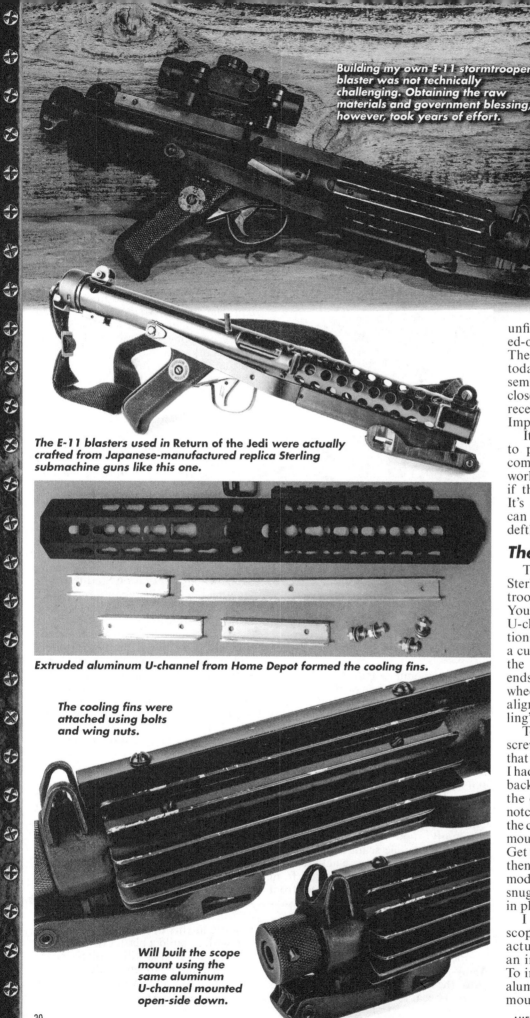

*Building my own E-11 stormtrooper blaster was not technically challenging. Obtaining the raw materials and government blessing, however, took years of effort.*

**The E-11 blasters used in *Return of the Jedi* were actually crafted from Japanese-manufactured replica Sterling submachine guns like this one.**

**Extruded aluminum U-channel from Home Depot formed the cooling fins.**

**The cooling fins were attached using bolts and wing nuts.**

**Will built the scope mount using the same aluminum U-channel mounted open-side down.**

unfinished receiver tubes with bonded-on templates are all available online. The easiest way to build a host gun today is to finish out the weapon as a semi-auto pistol. Weld the stock in the closed position before completing the receiver and you avoid any unfortunate Imperial entanglements.

It takes a little mechanical talent to pull this off, but I have honestly completed tougher builds in my home workshop. Get some professional help if the welding seems overly daunting. It's simply breathtaking what you can accomplish with a Dremel tool deftly wielded.

## The Transformation

The actual conversion from L2A3 Sterling SMG into BlasTech E-11 stormtrooper blaster is fairly straightforward. Your local Home Depot sells aluminum U-channel stock. I measured the sections to length and cut them down using a cutoff wheel on a table saw. I dressed the edges by hand and rounded the ends using a bench grinder and sanding wheel. I then sighted my screw holes to align with the cooling holes in the Sterling's barrel shroud.

To set the fins in place I used machine screws and butterfly nuts reversed such that the nuts rode inside the barrel shroud. I had to cut the wings of the butterfly nuts back just a bit to get them to fit through the cooling holes, and I ground little notches to help them fit snugly. Attaching the cooling fins is conceptually similar to mounting accessories on an M-LOK rail. Get the cooling fin assembly in place and then tighten the machine screws into the modified butterfly nuts until everything is snug. A little thread locker keeps things in place.

I didn't have a Sherman tank periscope handy, and I wanted this rig to actually work. I therefore substituted an inexpensive NC Star red dot sight. To improvise a mount, I used the same aluminum U-channel stock, but this time mounted it with the open side down. I

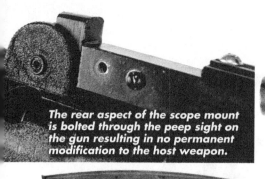

The rear aspect of the scope mount is bolted through the peep sight on the gun resulting in no permanent modification to the host weapon.

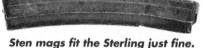

Sten mags fit the Sterling just fine. This is what Will used as a basis for his stormtrooper conversion.

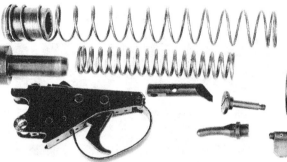

Semi-auto Sterling entrails are still available online should you wish to build a legal Sterling pistol.

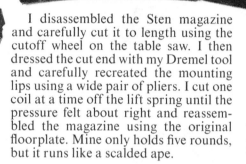

The original 34-round Sterling magazine sports a roller bearing follower and is arguably the finest ammunition magazine ever contrived.

Our E-11 stormtrooper blaster runs just fine with the large 34-round magazine if you can stomach the aesthetics.

didn't want to permanently modify the host gun, so I bodged together an adaptor to secure the back end of this assembly to the rear sight.

The front end is held in place with a butterfly nut in the manner of the cooling fins. With the base in place, I secured some aluminum scope rail harvested from my parts box. Degrease everything, spray it with flat black engine block paint from your local Auto Zone and cook the gun per the instructions on the can. The resulting finish will outlive you.

The 34-round box magazine used with the Sterling submachine gun is an object of undeniable engineering beauty, and I could not bring myself to cut one up for this project. This device sports an elegant curve and a unique roller bearing follower. Fun fact: Sten magazines will actually fit and feed in the Sterling. Sten mags were cheap as tent pegs when I built this gun, so I gladly sacrificed an old beater example to the cause.

I disassembled the Sten magazine and carefully cut it to length using the cutoff wheel on the table saw. I then dressed the cut end with my Dremel tool and carefully recreated the mounting lips using a wide pair of pliers. I cut one coil at a time off the lift spring until the pressure felt about right and reassembled the magazine using the original floorplate. Mine only holds five rounds, but it runs like a scalded ape.

## It Is Alive!

Friends, you simply have not lived until you stroll out onto a public firing range packing an operational *Star Wars* blaster. This thing will reliably get you a seat at the cool kids' table anyplace two or more gun nerds are gathered. Expect a crowd as soon as you slide it out of its case.

The stubby little magazine doesn't last very long on full auto, but the gun still runs the big sort if you can stomach the aesthetic dissonance. My version

fires from the open bolt via advanced primer ignition. A semi-auto build will fire from the closed bolt. I don't think I've ever had a stoppage with my blaster.

How accurate is this thing, might you ask? Who cares? It's a freaking *Star Wars* blaster. Even if it couldn't hit the broadside of a bantha at half a parsec (not a real measure of a weapon's innate accuracy potential) it wouldn't matter. Every time I have ever run this gun in a crowd everybody stares at the blaster, not the target.

In reality, the gun remains just as effective as the host Sterling. The rate of fire is sedate, and the ergonomics are first rate. Shallow grooves cut into the surface of the bolt channel grime away for reliable function. It would take the strength of a Wookiee to run the gun pistol-fashion like they do in the film, but my E-11 blaster would fill a room with pain should it ever be called upon to do so.

## Ruminations

It took literally decades of scrounging, some rarefied government licenses and a not insubstantial investment to contrive my BlasTech E-11 stormtrooper blaster. However, it no longer matters how geeky I was in high school or how tough it might have been to get dates.

Clarification: "Getting dates wasn't tough at all." The Author.

Further clarification: "Oh yes, it was. Have you seen a picture of this guy?" The Author's Wife.

Now I'm very nearly cool. Packing an operational BlasTech E-11 Imperial-issue stormtrooper blaster will do that for a guy.

My friends, you simply have not lived until you stroll onto a public shooting range packing a fully operational full auto E-11 stormtrooper blaster.

Will Dabbs, MD

# HANDCRAFTING A LEGEND

## Build your own 1911 pistol at home.

**"W**hatcha' packing?" I live in the Deep South. I get that question a lot. I reached under my scrubs and carefully extracted my custom-built aluminum-framed 1911 pistol. I dropped the magazine, cleared the gun and handed it butt-first to my buddy. He checked the action himself, pointed the gun at an outside wall and took its measure. He was obviously impressed with the pistol's modest weight and superlative feel.

*Before embarking on this project it's necessary to ask yourself if you are awesome enough to carry a sterile unmarked 1911 you built. If the answer to this question is "yes" then, by all means, proceed.*

"Check out the markings," I baited shamelessly. But there are no markings. Nothing. Nada. Zilch. The gun is as bare as Lady Godiva out for an evening ride.

"How did you get this?" he asked incredulously.

"I used to be a spy," I lied.

My wife tells me I would be taken more seriously if I would stop intentionally misleading people. It's indeed true I've never technically been a spy. However, I have contrived my own sterile 1911 pistol at home. So long as you build the gun yourself for personal use, there is no federal legal requirement to put a serial number or identifying markings on it at all. The entire process is just ridiculously cool.

### A Bit Of Legal Background

To build a firearm for commercial sale in America requires a fairly onerous license from the government. The paperwork and financial outlay are not insubstantial, and the inspections and subsequent oversight are thorough. However, if you have a clean record and want to build an otherwise legal firearm solely for personal use, you need not even tell Uncle Sam about it. You cannot conjure up a machine gun or thermonuclear bomb, but if you want to make yourself a pistol, then have at it. The rub has been in the past this was a fairly tool-intensive undertaking.

The government establishes the threshold for completion at 80%. This determination is both arbitrary and impossible to quantify accurately. Less than 80% frame blanks can be sold through the mail like any other inert trinket from Amazon. More than 80% finished, and the frame becomes a firearm requiring transfer through a Federal Firearms License holder. In the case of the 1911 frame, BATF has established two criteria.

The simplest of the two involves a frame lacking the frame-rail cuts, barrel-seat machining and hammer and sear pin holes. Where previously it took an expensive milling machine to perform these operations, nowadays the Phantom Jig from Stealth Arms and parts available from 1911 Builders will let you knock these chores out with nothing fancier than a drill press and a shop vise.

### Sundry Details

The folks at 1911 Builders offer parts kits for scads of different 1911 pistols. Frames can be had with or without dustcover rails in either aluminum or stainless-steel versions. They sell basic frames in Government, Commander, Officer or double-stack configurations. If you cannot find the type of gun you want on their website, you are just too picky.

There are 17 different combinations by my count. You can craft your own stubby bobtail carry gun or build a full-

The Stealth Arms Phantom Jig cuts the frame rails as well as a CNC mill might.

> So long as you build the gun yourself for personal use, there is no federal legal requirement to put a serial number or identifying markings on it at all. The entire process is just ridiculously cool.

sized double-stack hand howitzer to keep tucked in your bedside table. All of their parts are top quality, and the satisfaction derived from customizing a gun to fit your unique personality is remarkable. Here's how it works.

## The Stealth Arms Phantom Jig

Every now and again you happen upon some human contrivance that just knocks your socks off. Such is the manifest mechanical virtuosity of the Phantom Jig from Stealth Arms. Wow, but this thing is cool.

The first order of business is to bore the hammer and sear pin holes. The jig clamps rigidly around the frame and locates these two holes perfectly. The instructions included with the device will walk you through the process. Buying a cheap box-store drill press makes this easy, and you still have a drill press at the end of the exercise. The jig is essentially infinitely reusable.

The Phantom Jig affixes to the unfinished 1911 frame and guides a manually driven carbide cutter to cut the slide rails and barrel seat precisely. First you secure the assembly in a standard shop vise. A sliding shuttle holds the cutter, and an adjustment knob controls the depth. Grasp the handle and slide it along its track so the cutter removes a sliver of material about half the thickness of aluminum foil.

Lubricate the mechanism generously throughout. Turn the knob to lower the

*1911 Builders offers everything needed to build your own 1911 pistol at home except sights — and it can be shipped right to you.*

cutter by an increment before taking another pass. In short order you have the rails formed as precisely as though they were cut on a mill. The process is a bit time consuming but is not difficult.

I built my 1911 on an aluminum frame. Aluminum is obviously softer than steel and subsequently much easier to cut. The Phantom Jig will cut a steel frame as well, but expect the process to be a bit more onerous.

You then reorient the Phantom Jig to the top of the frame to cut the barrel seat. The same device guides both pro-

cesses. In this phase the apparatus slides on your newly cut frame rails. I found cutting the barrel seat to be a bit more challenging than the side rails, but not by much. Be thorough and meticulous, and the professional nature of the results will amaze you.

My daughter and I finished out our aluminum 1911 frame in an afternoon. I used my shopworn drill press for the hammer and sear holes. I crafted the three frame cuts using nothing more than the Phantom Jig and a shop vise bolted to my workbench. It was all surprisingly easy.

Like most mechanical things, the limiting factor is patience. Cut gently and check the fit regularly. Taking material

5A
STEALTH ARMS
1911 PHANTOM JIG

*The Phantom Jig, shown here disassembled, will transform an 80% frame into a functioning and reliable firearm.*

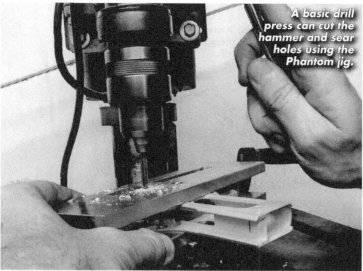

A basic drill press can cut the hammer and sear holes using the Phantom jig.

The sliding shuttle on the Phantom Jig gradually cuts the frame rails one sliver at a time. Be patient and the results will amaze you.

Check the fit as you go along.

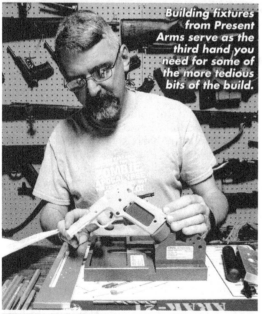

Building fixtures from Present Arms serve as the third hand you need for some of the more tedious bits of the build.

Skeletonized black grips amp up the cool factor. A flat, checkered mainspring housing provides a solid grip.

away is easy. Putting it back is hard. The end result is as professional as it would be from a respected factory.

## Assembling A 1911 Pistol

Assembling the 1911 pistol is involved, but not terribly difficult. The internet is awash in helpful tutorials, and YouTube will let you watch other people do it well. You'll need a punch or three, a small non-marring hammer and some basic tools to go along with a smidgeon of institutional knowledge. We used a set of building fixtures from Present Arms, which kept everything going smoothly.

The Present Arms fixtures are milled from a robust non-marring polymer. They are designed to keep everything in place and provide the third hand you need to get through some of the difficult bits. The build can be undertaken without this device, but the Present Arms fixtures make the process easier.

The internal mechanism is intuitive so long as you have some familiarity with it. Read up on the details or check out YouTube before you get started. You'll also need to drill a 1/8" hole to retain the ejector, but this chore is painless with a drill press.

Compressing the hammer spring into its housing is undeniably onerous. However, you can use the vise to hold the assembly in place while you fret with it. We placed a small ball bearing over the top when compressing the spring to push the plunger low enough to get the cross pin started. Wear safety glasses lest this powerful spring slips its bonds. A cool eye patch might help you get dates, but you would inevitably lament the loss of your depth perception.

You'll need to provide your own sights, and we opted for the TRUGLO TFX sort. TFX stands for Tritium Fiber-Optic Extreme. These reasonably priced aftermarket sights will maximize the effectiveness of your new handheld howitzer.

Fiber optic inserts funnel light to where you need it under daylight conditions. Radioactive Swiss-made Tritium inserts illuminate the same fiber optic tubes in the dark. These steel sights are all but indestructible and greatly enhance the effectiveness of most any tactical handgun, whether it's built at home or bought in a store.

## Tweaking The Details

The slide-to-frame fit feels like greased glass, and the crisp single-action trigger is simply divine. I had to buff the safety a smidge with my Dremel tool to get it to fit, but everything else was plug and play. There are a lot of really capable artisans out there customizing 1911 pistols. With 1911 Builders you can taste some of the same sweetness yourself at home. Building this gun from scratch gave me a familiarity with its entrails I never could have appreciated otherwise.

The back of the slide overhung the frame by just a bit when everything was done. I could have left this in place without adversely affecting function, but the aesthetics would have just eaten at me. I gently laid the back of the completed slide against my bench grinder to true it up, and then polished the rough spots with my Dremel tool. The unique geometry gives my home-built gun a little character.

I found some black skeletonized grips through an online auction which perfectly complement the racy silver of the base gun. Check out the pictures. Even Chuck Schumer would think this gun looked cool.

## Light It Up

Despite the fact I built this thing from a pile of parts, function and

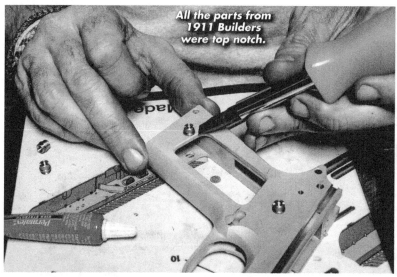

All the parts from 1911 Builders were top notch.

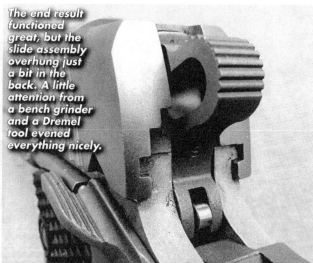

The end result functioned great, but the slide assembly overhung just a bit in the back. A little attention from a bench grinder and a Dremel tool evened everything nicely.

lockup were tight from the get-go. Reliability was 100% with three different brands of ammunition and the gun shot beautifully straight. Maintenance is a snap once you literally know every single piece of the gun inside and out.

The resulting pistol is light enough for concealed carry and accepts any standard accessory on its railed dustcover. The slide/frame interface is stainless steel on aluminum so keep the gun lubed well with quality gun oil until it breaks in to prevent any galling of the rail surfaces. I was blown away how well this home-built pistol looked and shot.

The manual of arms is foundational dogma for most American gun nerds. Magazines drop away cleanly, and the controls are crisp and positive. The responsive single-action trigger sets the standard for everything else.

## Ruminations

It does indeed require a little mechanical aptitude to pull this project off. However, a polished end result really is more a function of patience than skill. Take your time and don't rush anything. This build is well within the reach of anyone even reasonably handy with tools.

You do need a small drill press, but not for long. You can borrow somebody else's or just buy a cheap one: Amazon has one for $75 with free shipping. A drill press takes up very little shop space, and you'll use it for lots of other stuff eventually.

Legally building a sterile firearm with no markings or serial number adds mystique to any collection. The gun actually shoots as well as a high-end 1911. The total price, including the Phantom Jig, is comparable to a mid-range commercial 1911 pistol. You could even get together with a few like-minded friends and share a jig.

There are no federal restrictions on building one of these guns at home for personal use, though local laws may adversely impact the project. If you live in a free state, there is immense satisfaction in conjuring, shooting and carrying a top-flight 1911 you crafted at home. You don't even have to be a spy to build one. 🔫

*For more info:*
*www.1911builders.com,*
*www.stealtharms.net,*
*www.presentarmsinc.com,*
*www.truglo.com,*
*www.streamlight.com,*
*www.silencerco.com*

Go look in the mirror. If what you see seems sufficiently awesome to rock an unmarked gun as cool as this one, then 1911 Builders and Stealth Arms can get you there.

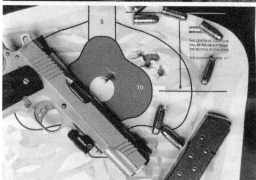

This 15-meter group is not too shabby for a gun Will built himself from scratch.

Will loves a good factory handgun at least as much as the next rabid gun nerd, but a 1911 you build yourself has so much more character.

Will Dabbs, MD

# DIY CZECH VZ. 61 SKORPION

## An adorable .32-caliber fistful of dynamite.

I n 1959 a Czech weapons designer named Miroslav Rybar, along with a few others, contrived a remarkably charming little machine pistol. Released for service in 1961 and designated the *Samopal vzor 61 or Vz. 61 Skorpion*, this extraordinary SMG occupied a unique niche. The Czechs employed the Vz. 61 as a personal defense weapon to arm aviators, armor crewmen, truck drivers, special forces and the like. International terrorists adored the tiny gun for its compact footprint and prodigious firepower.

*The Czech Vz. 61 Skorpion is one of the smallest production automatic weapons ever contrived. Enterprising American shooters can now build a legal semi-auto version of this Cold War classic.*

Despite being chambered for the .32 ACP cartridge, a state-of-the-art round in 1929, the Vz. 61 still had much to commend it. Featuring an overhung bolt conceptually similar to the Uzi or MAC10, the Vz. 61 packed a great deal of chaos into an absolutely tiny chassis. The gun fed from either 10- or 20-round magazines and typically rode about in a holster. Subsequent variants were produced in 9x18mm Makarov, .380 ACP and 9mm Parabellum. The gun was also produced under license in Yugoslavia,

and roughly 200,000 copies rolled off the lines before production ceased in 1979.

In years past, private ownership of a Vz. 61 Skorpion would have been literally unimaginable. Nowadays, thanks to Recon Ordnance you can buy a pre-built handgun version without a stock, or build your own from parts. Always on the lookout for a cool gun-bodging project, we ordered a semi-auto receiver and demilled kit along with a few ancillary parts and went to town.

## Technical Details

The Vz. 61 Skorpion fires from the unlocked blowback position. The .32 ACP round is so anemic it doesn't require a great deal of mass to keep the bolt closed at the beginning of the firing cycle. The subsequent bolt travel, however, is exceptionally short. On the original full-auto versions, this means the gun would otherwise naturally cycle at a blistering rate. The Czechs' solution to this quandary was a novel counterweight rate reducer built into the pistol grip. As these full-auto parts are not required on American civilian guns, they are omitted from the kits.

The steel semi-auto receivers are made in the U.S. and are superbly well executed. They come without the stock-mounting fixture of the originals. There is an adaptor should you wish to register the gun as a short-barreled rifle and install the tiny stock. Recon Ordnance sells the stock adaptors as well. My kit also came with the slagged original receiver that was rendered well and truly useless.

My parts kit was clearly harvested from a new unfired gun and came with a couple of spare magazines and a gimpy leather holster. The new receiver is fin-

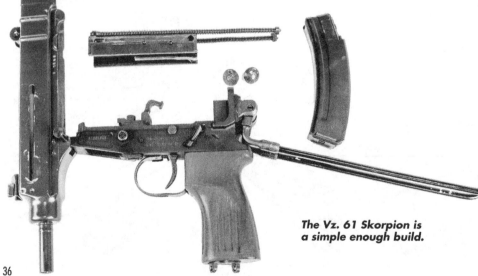

*The Vz. 61 Skorpion is a simple enough build.*

The steel receiver around which the Vz. 61 is built is an exceptionally well-executed component.

The Vz. 61 Skorpion occupies a similar tactical niche as the American MAC-11 .380 ACP submachine gun.

ished in a deep, rich-gray Parkerizing. The upper receiver that came with the kit has an odd light-gray paint-on finish. With everything laid out and cataloged, it was time to get to work.

## The Build

Quite a number of DIY builds like this involve modifying old parts or require a bunch of tedious welding. In the case of the Vz. 61 Skorpion, you just drop the parts in place. There are no instructions, but anybody with a modicum of mechanical inclination can figure out the details. There's only one way everything will fit together.

You can find an exploded schematic at www.gunpartscorp.com. Should you get flummoxed, there is always the miracle of YouTube. The build didn't require any special tools and took me maybe an hour to complete. If you've ever built an AR, you can pull this off.

The buttstock presents a unique dilemma. There's nothing innately immoral about leaving the stock off and building the gun as a pistol. However, I wanted something as close to the originals as possible. It meant registering the gun as a short-barreled rifle. The instructions for the Form 1 to do this at home are available on the BATF website, but the process is not for the faint of heart. Expect the better part of a year for processing.

My receiver was already drilled and tapped for a drop-in stock adaptor. I've read some aren't. In this case, you can do the drilling and tapping with a drill press if you're careful. Welding the adaptor in place would be an option as well.

Yet another option would be to install the stock in the folded position and pin or weld it in place, thereby preserving the gun's handgun status. This approach avoids any registration requirements but can potentially interfere with disassembly of the gun. This would, however, produce a pistol that looks like the factory SMG. I suspect some enterprising soul could figure out a way to permanently restrict the stock such that it would open just far enough to facilitate disassembly, but no further.

## How Does She Run?

The diminutive .32 ACP chambering is all but recoilless. The original SMG fires from the closed bolt by means of an internal hammer, and the bolt locks to the rear on the last round fired. To put the gun back into action just swap out the magazines, give the bolt actuator ears on the sides of the gun a little snatch and let the bolt close under spring pressure.

The selector is one-sided and easily accessed by the right thumb when firing right-handed. Left-handed people are naturally screwed, but they should be used to that by now. Placing the gun on safe also locks the bolt in place. A little plunger on the left bottom of the gun can be used to manually lock the bolt to the rear if desired.

The tiny buttstock pops over the front sight ears to secure it in the closed position. To deploy the stock, give it a little snatch and fold it up, over and back. It will lock in place on its own accord. To

Will's Skorpion includes a flip-adjustable rear sight with 75- and 150-meter settings.

The new semi-auto receiver lacks the mounting hardware for the folding buttstock, but the adaptor Recon Ordnance offers works like a champ.

*The folding stock on the Vz. 61 is lyrically small yet still marks an improvement over the pistol not otherwise equipped.*

*The gun's entrails are conceptually similar to those of an AR-15. Using an exploded parts diagram found online, Will assembled the gun in about an hour.*

*The Vz. 61 ejects straight out the top. Both the full-auto SMG and the semi-auto pistol version fire from the closed bolt via a conventional hammer.*

*In the original SMG there is a brilliant mechanical rate reducer built into the pistol grip. These superfluous parts are not included in the demilled parts kits.*

*Twin rigid ejectors affixed to the frame ensure reliable vertical extraction and ejection.*

*The bolt on the Vz. 61 is overhung and telescoping like the Uzi or MAC-10.*

collapse the stock, just give the base a little squeeze and it will release to fold.

With the stock folded, the Vz. 61 Skorpion shoots like a front-heavy, underpowered handgun. The manual of arms is intuitive, and the gun runs quickly enough. The magazine release is a handy button on the side of the receiver. With the stock extended, the gun acquires a different personality.

The stock is way too short, no matter how you slice it. However, like the arm braces so popular these days, it does give the shooter a handy spot against which to rest the arm or cheek. In this sense it is not philosophically unlike the collapsible stock on the .380 ACP MAC11 submachine gun. The Skorpion stock is a fairly wretched piece of kit, but it does provide better stability than the same gun not thusly equipped.

The closed-bolt design is indeed pleasantly accurate and controllable. On the full-auto gun, the cyclic rate runs around 850 rounds per minute. I have had the privilege of running a full-auto Skorpion once and found it to be surprisingly comfortable and effective on rock-and-roll. It's worth mentioning the gun ejects its empty cases vertically and tends to drop them on top of the shooter's head.

## Ruminations

Just face it. There is absolutely no tactical reason to add a Czech Vz. 61 Skorpion to your gun collection. The little .32 ACP round carries less than half the power of a pedestrian 9mm Parabellum, and there is nothing the semi-auto Vz. 61 will do a GLOCK 17 won't do better. But the Vz. 61 has some undeniable sex appeal.

Cute as a button, though tactically worthless compared to more modern

The .32 ACP cartridge is a fairly anemic round for serious social use. From left to right we have the .32 ACP, the .380 ACP, the 9mm Parabellum and the .45 ACP.

The gun breaks open in the manner of an American M4.

The Vz. 61 Skorpion is lyrically small and arguably the most easily portable SMG ever produced.

iron, the Vz .61 Skorpion hearkens back to a different era. Tiny, concealable and mean as a snake in the wrong hands, the Vz. 61 retains a following among terrorist types even today. The list of nefarious organizations that kept the little gun in inventory is a rogues' gallery of ne'er-do-wells.

The Irish Republican Army was an enthusiastic recipient, likely via their Libyan benefactors. The Italian Red Brigades used a Skorpion to off the unfortunate Italian former prime minister Aldo Moro in 1978. In the 1990s the *Gang de Roubaix* used several Skorpions to spread mayhem across France. Swedish police lost track of 50 copies in 2017 that had been imported in a deactivated state from Slovakia and were subsequently reactivated for the purpose of criminal mischief.

I honestly like mine simply because it looks so darn awesome. Thank the Good Lord the Cold War remained cold, and we never had to face down the Warsaw Pact in the Fulda Gap and elsewhere. As a result, the Czech Vz. 61 Skorpion remains little more than a nifty novelty in the more rarefied American gun collections today. Tiny, brilliant, adorable and fairly worthless at anything but bad-breath range, the Vz. 61 Skorpion is nonetheless a tiny fistful of awesome.

*For more info: www.reconord.com*

**Ray Fleck**

# INSTALLING A RED DOT SIGHT ON A MODEL 92

## The DIY way!

I needed to test the ammo in the picture with this gun. The intent was to use it for acquiring a deer for the freezer. A "strictly business" proposition I do yearly. As the title indicates, I can no longer see iron sights well enough to reliably hit a deer in the small part of it I want to hit. I like to be as precise as possible to put them down fast. And, this .44 Special doesn't have a lot of built-in stopping power. To be ethical, I need to hit in the lungs/heart — with no error. Before modern bullets — like the HoneyBadger from Black Hills — I would not have considered .44 Special up to the task.

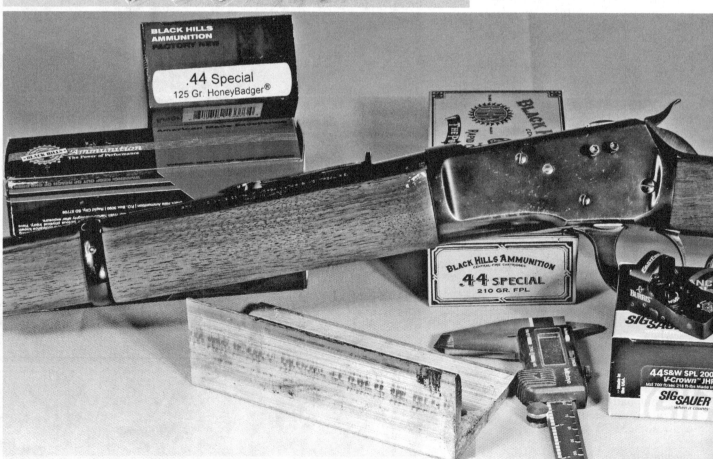

Old-school layout is made easier if you make drawings before you start cutting. The holes on the side of the Browning 92 were a non-factory addition. Ray determined the distance between hole centers by putting screws in the holes and then measuring both the inside and outside distance between the threads on the screws. Averaging the results from the inside and the outside distances was "close enough." Ray said the two sets of holes were added for customized sight height. (Ha! The real reason for the four holes is because Ray didn't allow for clearance above the hammer! — Editor)

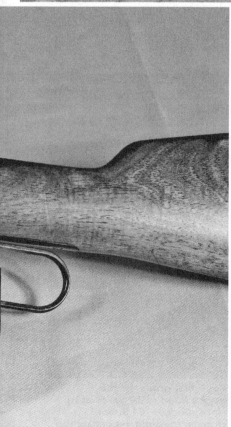

Aluminum is good for a project like this because it's soft, light and easy to work with. However, soft material is also bad for a project like this because threaded holes are easy to strip during assembly. Ray used aluminum he had on hand due to bad planning — as in no planning since this was a rush job. Ray used slightly undersized tap drills for the screw size selected and used a good industrial lubricant (the green goop in the picture with the tap) during the tapping operation.

If you don't have experience with free-hand tapping, practice making threaded holes in scrap first. The time spent will eliminate lots of language not permitted in polite company. High quality taps will also reduce the use of expletives. Coughing up for good quality (expensive) blades for the saw also lowers the angst. You can make straighter cuts with less effort.

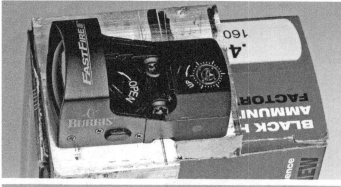

The screws mounting the sight were selected to be long enough to take full advantage of the material thickness to mitigate stripped threads. Having a selection of screws facilitates this as the screws coming with the sight are short. They normally go into a thin aluminum mount having steel threaded inserts.

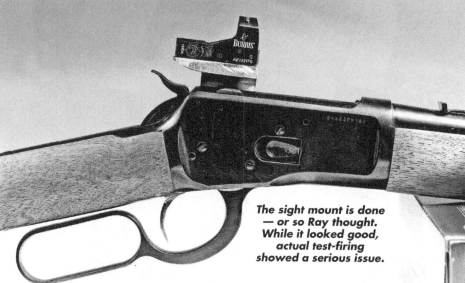

The sight mount is done — or so Ray thought. While it looked good, actual test-firing showed a serious issue.

As with any prototype, there will be issues. In this case, the issue was ejecting brass hitting the delicate glass lens of the sight. This is not Ray's first rodeo of this type and he'd put a protector over the lens for testing "just in case" as he said. Ray used his cell phone's slow-motion video to capture the brass being ejected from the gun. It let him see he needed to add a case deflector to the gun. Using the slow-motion video is a handy trick to solve lots of function-related issues.

The gun is ready to go. The final version of the brass deflector turned out to be a lot simpler than the first deflector idea. Ray had put two holes in the mount for long screws. The two long screws would be the structure for mounting a flat deflector plate. However, just to "see," Ray tested where the brass went with one screw where the deflector is now. The empty case went forward and Ray realized he didn't need a flat plate. The screw was then replaced with aluminum stand-offs.

For the distances I plan to shoot, a scope is just a lot more sight than I need. And, it's too heavy and clumsy on a light rifle like this one. A red dot sight was the perfect solution. The catch was no one makes a mount for this kind of sight for my old Browning B92. My goal was to create something recoil-sensitive low upper-body strength shooters can use to take deer at responsible distances. I need the red dot because I simply can't see well any longer. Less experienced shooters will find it easier to stay on-target, making hunting more fun and a clean kill more likely.

I put my "former engineer's brain" to work on this, and wanted to be able to use simple tools and materials to craft the mount. When I was finished, I felt anyone with even modest tool skills should be able to attempt something like this. You could modify the design to fit the gun you might have too.

I thought the best way to show how I did this is to simply show it step by step. The concept is simple and I think you might find it fun and practical to tackle a simple project like this for your own needs. The end-result allowed me to shoot tight groups at the 50- to 75-yard range I usually take a deer.

*For more info:*
*www.black-hills.com,*
*www.sigsauer.com*

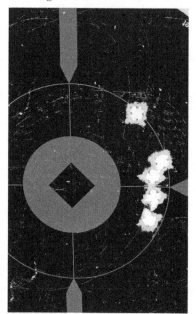

Ray's first group off the truck's hood at 50 yards using HoneyBadger .44 Special showed the sight/mount combo delivered the goods! Ray said vertical stringing is his own fault.

# GUNS MAGAZINE®

## 1-YEAR PRINT SUBSCRIPTION

**ONLY $24.95!**

### FREE
2019 Digital Download
with your paid order

Call (866) 820-4045 • www.fmgpubs.com

M-F 8am-3pm PST ($64.95 outside U.S.)
P.O. Box 509094, San Diego, CA 92150

**Tiger McKee**

# BUILDING A MODEL 10 RAT ROD!

## Get busy — but don't try for perfection!

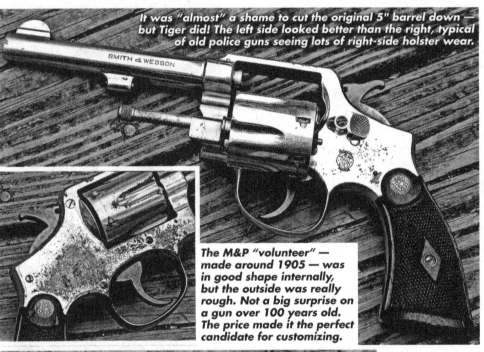

It was "almost" a shame to cut the original 5" barrel down — but Tiger did! The left side looked better than the right, typical of old police guns seeing lots of right-side holster wear.

The M&P "volunteer" — made around 1905 — was in good shape internally, but the outside was really rough. Not a big surprise on a gun over 100 years old. The price made it the perfect candidate for customizing.

The rear portion of the frame's grip is cut down to a round butt shape, matching the stocks. The front of the grip is left as is, and the stocks are cut out to fit the front of the grip. A rotary tool and patience are mandatory. Measure three times, cut a little, sand and check fit. Repeat as necessary. After fitting I stipple the stocks using a wood burner.

I'm a DIY guy. I've always "figgered" if someone else can do something — so can I. My work may not be as pretty, but there's pride in doing something yourself. Several years ago I started customizing S&W revolvers, focusing on K-Frame models. I began with small tasks, like bobbing the hammer, and eventually I was picking rough-looking volunteers to convert into what I call "Choppers."

My favorite revolver is the S&W Model 13 with a 3" barrel and round butt — the old FBI gun. These are hard to find and usually expensive, and it's a shame to modify one of them. My solution is to take a 4" pistol with square butt — think Model 10 or 13 — which are readily available and affordable. I then chop them down to 3" round butt pistols. My inspiration is the original chopped motorcycles of the '50s and '60s. You took a big heavy bike and cut everything off that wasn't absolutely necessary, making it lightweight, easy to handle and faster.

After building several Choppers for friends, which funded more gunsmith adventures, I decided to build a lightweight version using an early K-Frame with the thin tapered barrel.

### Raw Material

October 2017, my buddy Jimmy at Scottsboro Gun & Pawn — best gun shop in the world and 30 minutes from home — notifies me they received a shipment of "evidence" guns sold off by a police department. "We've got lots of revolvers," he says. On my next day off I head into town to visit.

They have some nice revolvers, too nice for what I need. But, over to the side is a rough looking M&P .38 Special, a pre Model 10, with a 5" barrel, square butt and an ugly nickel finish. According to the serial number it was built around 1905 or so. Mechanically it's sound, and a perfect candidate for a chopper with a $250 price I can afford. I take it home and shove it into the safe.

When it was time to begin the build, the first thing is to strip it down for cleaning and inspection. It looks good, especially for a gun over 100 years old.

I mark the barrel at 3", which works out perfectly with the factory lettering on the side of the barrel. I add another 1/8" for insurance and give it the "chop" — cutting off 2" of barrel and the front sight. It's done, the point of no return. I am fully committed.

## Serious Work

I bead blast the frame to get off as much nickel as possible. You never know what to expect when blasting nickel, so it's a good surprise when most of it comes off cleanly, leaving a great finish to work with.

Next I cut down the grip to make it a "round" butt. I say "round" but it's really partly round and partly square. I cut and contour the rear strap of the frame to fit the round butt stocks. The front of the frame is untouched and the round butt stocks are modified to fit the frame.

For Choppers, I use Precision Gun Specialties "Hideout" stocks. With a little reshaping these stocks fit my hand perfectly and the injection-molded nylon can be stippled with a wood burner or soldering iron. The rear of the frame grip is stippled using a hammer and punch. This adds texture for control and matches the stippling on the stocks.

In the old days many fighting revolvers had the front of the trigger guard narrowed to make it easier to slip your finger onto the trigger. I take it a little further by blending the frame into the thinned guard and "melting" the frame in other areas, rounding off a bunch of the sharper edges. Older guns often have nicks and scratches on these edges, so this gives you a better feeling pistol while improving the look.

Time to work the internals, plus the hammer and trigger. The internals are in great shape, so all that's necessary is light polishing to smooth everything. If you're considering doing any of this type of work, get Kuhnhausen's *S&W Shop Manual.* Tuning a revolver requires much more than just changing springs. This book has the details on improving the S&W J-, K- and N-Frames.

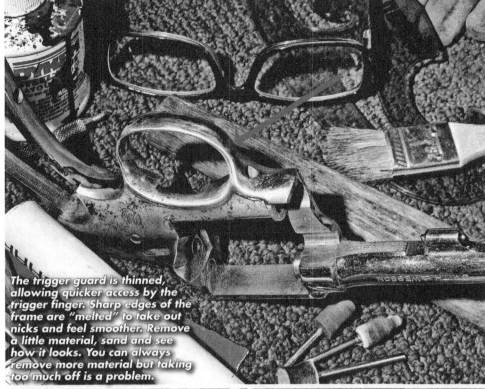

The trigger guard is thinned, allowing quicker access by the trigger finger. Sharp edges of the frame are "melted" to take out nicks and feel smoother. Remove a little material, sand and see how it looks. You can always remove more material but taking too much off is a problem.

Bobbing the hammer is the way to go for a defensive revolver. The hammer spur can catch in clothing, and all defensive revolver work is DAO anyway. Tiger also removed the serrations from the trigger, and put a nice radius on the front edges so the finger slides smoothly on the trigger as it's stroked.

Crowning and putting a chamfer on the barrel is simple as long as you have the right tools.

It looks good and improves accuracy. Everything you need, for any caliber, is available from Brownells.

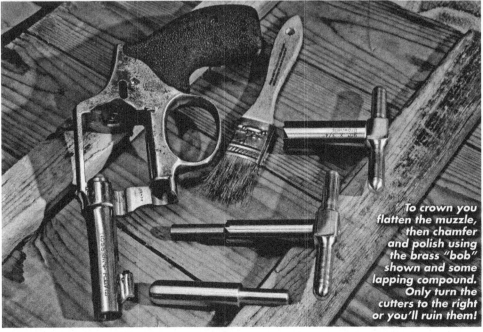

To crown you flatten the muzzle, then chamfer and polish using the brass "bob" shown and some lapping compound. Only turn the cutters to the right or you'll ruin them!

The milling machine from the Little Machine Shop, Grizzly or others, is a great tool for the hobby gunsmith. They're not that big — especially a tabletop model, or expensive, and it allows you to make almost anything. Tiger considers it one of the best investments he's ever made and uses it all the time.

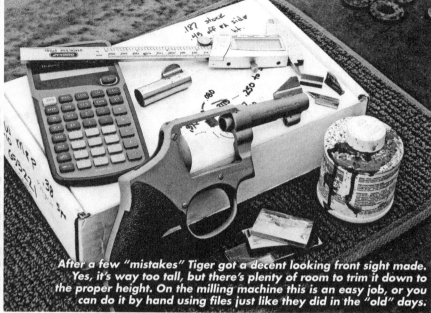

After a few "mistakes" Tiger got a decent looking front sight made. Yes, it's way too tall, but there's plenty of room to trim it down to the proper height. On the milling machine this is an easy job, or you can do it by hand using files just like they did in the "old" days.

Every build Tiger tries something new, and this one is no different. One of the new skills required on this build is silver soldering. The front sight jig from Brownells keeps everything held in place during soldering. Tiger was surprised how good the results looked after only a little practice.

The M&P Chopper is assembled and ready for test firing and zeroing the front sight. The "raw" look is actually cool, and reminds me of a rat rod — a hotrod assembled from a variety of parts without concern for how it looks. The focus for Tiger is function and performance.

The final zero at 7 yards from a standing, off-hand position, is a little high, which is what Tiger likes for defensive work. For final testing he fired from 60 yards. He held on the "belt buckle," focused on the front sight and stroked the trigger. Happiness is the sound of a solid "ding" from the plate. Now he knows how much to trim off the top of the sight.

I don't change out any of the springs in this pistol. You can get a trigger too light, causing ignition problems, especially with the harder primers found in less expensive practice ammo. Plus, I'm not a trigger snob when it comes to weight. I'm looking for a smooth trigger action, both in the stroke and reset, and reliable ignition with any ammo. Smoothing the action and using factory weight springs is the way to go, or at least I think so.

A fighting pistol must have a bobbed hammer. All the spur does is hang up on your clothing, plus all defensive revolver work is DA-only. I also polish the face of the trigger to remove any serrations as well as sand and move the bevel on the front edges — I like a smooth trigger. I also blue the hammer and trigger with Birchwood Casey Super Blue. The key to cold bluing, or any type of finishing, is preparation and following the instructions. Take your time, prep properly and you'll get good results.

## Sight Work

I could buy a replacement sight, but this is "custom" work, meaning making one from scratch. Time for some work with the milling machine. "Milling machine," you say, "Don't have one of those." Then I recommend visiting the Little Machine Shop on Grizzly Tools' website. Both offer affordable table and benchtop machines that handily do just about anything a hobby gunsmith needs. I use mine constantly, saving many hours of filing/sanding, and it makes my work look a lot better.

Designing a front sight is easy. The hard part is determining what order or sequence to make your cuts. I'm still learning machine work so often in the middle of the work, I realize the sequence is wrong. After a few experiments — some people call them "mistakes" — I

The "finished" project — still needing a finish — actually looks pretty good. Tiger likes the rat-rod, or neo-tribal look, especially with the contrast between the blasted frame and barrel and the parts still having some nickel coating. At some point he'll probably apply a finish — or maybe not. For now he's going to carry, shoot and enjoy it.

During testing and zeroing Tiger tried different loaders, especially speed loaders, to ensure they clear the stocks. The pistol looks good, fits the hand well and shoots plenty accurately.

If you're going to work on S&W revolvers you'll need Kuhnhausen's S&W Shop Manual. This has the details needed to restore or modify a Smith. You'll also need a few specialty tools. The proper screwdrivers, or bits, are mandatory, ensuring you don't ruin the screws.

get it right. The new sight is nothing fancy but will do the job, and it fits the look of the pistol. I'm not sure yet what the "look" is, but the cool thing about a DIY is often the look is sort of revealed during the build.

Crowning and chamfering the muzzle is easy as long as you have the right tools like handles, pilots and cutters. The pilot goes into the handle, the cutter goes onto the pilot and the pilot goes into the barrel, keeping everything straight. Apply a little cutting oil and give the handle a few twists (to the right only!) to square the muzzle. Swap-out cutters and repeat to chamfer. This part is *almost* fool proof.

To attach the new front sight, I need to learn how to silver solder. It looks mystifying, but I've never let it stop me. I watch videos on the 'net, which are not very helpful. I read about it in my old gunsmith books too so in theory I know what I'm trying to accomplish. I "google" Editor Roy from *American Handgunner* to ask him questions and get advice on what supplies to order from Brownells. Finally, I decide it can't be put off any longer. It's time to solder.

To practice I use one of the "mistake" sights and some tubing. The hardest part is indexing the sight on the round barrel, getting everything straight. On Roy's advice I get a Brownells sight jig to hold things in place. After testing I determine that yes, silver soldering is an art and it's messy, but it's not difficult to achieve decent results. I'm also surprised at how strong it is, especially considering the solder and flux used only has to be at 475 degrees to flow and "weld."

I assemble the pistol for test firing and zeroing the front sight, determining what height it needs to be. And it's always a good idea to test drive something before putting in the time required to apply a final finish to the metal.

The lightweight Chopper looks cool, and more importantly feels great in-hand. The trigger is at 9 lbs., smooth and crisp. Final weight of the pistol is 29 oz., unloaded — 5 oz. less than my 3" Model 13 with a heavy barrel and round butt. Now if I can just get time to actually shoot it.

## Test-Fire Time

It's only the third day of summer but already blazing and muggy here in Kirbytown, Alafrickinbama. It's also the first Saturday in a long time I haven't been teaching, so it's a perfect day to test fire the new Chopper-version M&P.

I know the front sight is way high. No surprise the first shots at seven yards are about 18" low. But it goes bang with every stroke of the trigger. To determine sight height I use blue tape on the sight, providing me with an exact point of hold. After a few groups and adjusting the tape, I find a good zero. Final testing occurs at 60 yards. It's ringing the plate so I'm calling it good. Now it's just a matter of cutting the sight down to the right height.

I'm pleased with the build. It shoots great, is accurate and looks bitchin'. The only thing left is to disassemble and put a nice finish on it.

Or not.

I kinda' like the "rat rod" look. I think for now I'll just clean it, carry and shoot it. Maybe along the way it will let me know what color it wants to be.

## Words Of Encouragement

"Perfection" is the enemy of progress. The only way to learn how to do something is repetition. If you attempt "perfect" you'll never finish anything. Remember, it's only a failure if you stop trying. As long as you're learning from your mistakes you're making progress. As I tell students, "If you're not making

mistakes you're not doing it right." At some point you say, "That's good enough," and complete your work. Enjoy the experience, knowing the next one will be better.

Take your time. My first revolver took me about a year and a half. I started by learning how to take it apart and putting it back together, learning how it works. Small modifications came first, and after each of those I reassemble to test fire. Eventually I got it right, then immediately found another pistol to work on.

With every build I was adding new skills and the necessary tools. Plus, I have a personal connection with each gun, something you don't get when you buy a pistol or have someone build it for you. It feels good when you explain, "Oh, yes, I built that."

Start out small and slow, take your time and don't expect perfection. This way you'll be pleased, amazed and proud once you're done. Speaking of, now it's time to think about my next "Kirbytown Kustom." 🔫

*For more info: www.brownells.com, www.precisiongunspecialties.com, www.littlemachineshop.com, www.grizzly.com*

Jeremy D. Clough

# LESS FUN THAN IT SOUNDS

## Converting a Winchester M12 to a 1918-style riot gun.

*The same gun, minus the paint and a few inches of barrel, plus 40 hours of work and a round trip to Turnbull Restoration.*

*A new magazine plug and stainless front bead finished out the muzzle end. Note the difference between the barrel and mag tube, finished at 400 grit and rust blued, and the other parts that are 600 grit charcoal blued.*

*The camouflaging was thorough — and included the wood. Unfortunately, it also covered a fair amount of pitting.*

**W**inchester's Model 12 should require no introduction, but for those of us who grew up with Mossbergs, Benellis and the omnipresent Remington 870 as the combat shotguns *du jour*, perhaps a little intro is in order.

### Fearsome History

Introduced in 1912, the pump gun that would come to be known as the "perfect repeater," was a refinement of John Browning's legendary Model 1897. Not the first pump-action shotgun, it is no doubt the iconic one. The '97 Winchester cut a broad swath through history, not least of all during the trench warfare of WWI. When the average infantryman was armed with a bolt-action rifle, one can imagine the ferocity of a close-range volley by a line of doughboys armed with repeaters firing nine pellets of 00 buck

*The riot-gun version of the M12 arrived in 1918, too late to provide much service in the trenches as did Winchester's 1897. It did appear in WWII and Vietnam, as well as in the hands of countless law enforcement agencies.*

every time they ran the pump. Lacking a disconnect, the '97 will slamfire if you keep your finger on the trigger. The volume of fire was tremendous.

It made enough of an impression for the Germans to complain using such a barbaric weapon was a war crime, much the way the British viewed shotguns during the American Revolution. One wonders if the Kaiser's men let the clouds of their mustard gas pass before they drafted the complaint, but that's neither here nor there. The point is, the '97 proved the devastating effect to which a scattergun could be put. The Thomas C. Johnson-designed Model 12 was built on the '97 with a much

simpler mechanism (it has about a dozen fewer parts), eliminating the fearsome reciprocating bolt of the '97 and exposed hammer. It did retain the clever takedown mechanism found on some '97's.

Arriving too late to see widespread use in the trenches, the M12 nonetheless served in WWII and Vietnam, and was widely loved as a sporting gun, with some two million produced. For those who shoot SASS, it's also one of only two pump shotguns allowed in Wild Bunch, having been allowed in over the objection that, unlike all other SASS guns, its concealed hammer makes it impossible to tell at a glance whether it's safe.

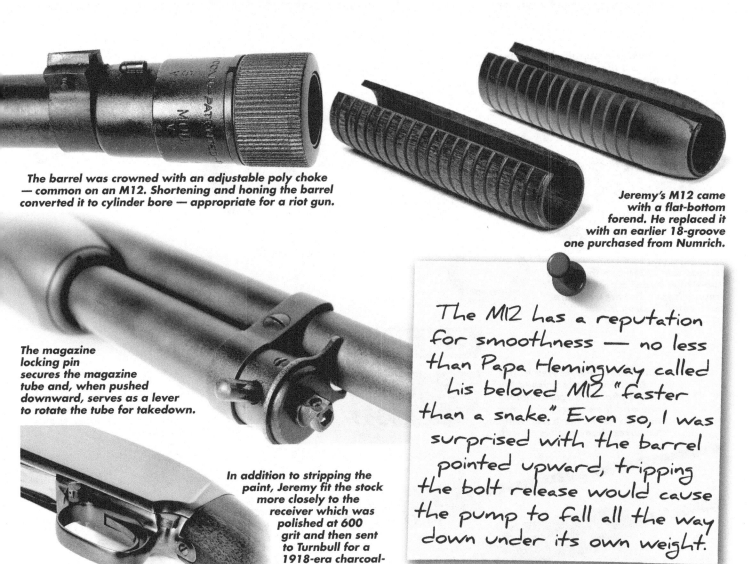

The barrel was crowned with an adjustable poly choke — common on an M12. Shortening and honing the barrel converted it to cylinder bore — appropriate for a riot gun.

Jeremy's M12 came with a flat-bottom forend. He replaced it with an earlier 18-groove one purchased from Numrich.

The magazine locking pin secures the magazine tube and, when pushed downward, serves as a lever to rotate the tube for takedown.

In addition to stripping the paint, Jeremy fit the stock more closely to the receiver which was polished at 600 grit and then sent to Turnbull for a 1918-era charcoal-blue finish.

The M12 has a reputation for smoothness — no less than Papa Hemingway called his beloved M12 "faster than a snake." Even so, I was surprised with the barrel pointed upward, tripping the bolt release would cause the pump to fall all the way down under its own weight.

This M12 was made in 1947. Since then, it was modified for use as a turkey gun, complete with added-on sights and a green painted finish. The spare barrel/pump assembly is for home defense.

While the gun itself was introduced in 1912, the riot version came along in 1918. For clarity, "riot gun" usually means a defensive shotgun with a shortish barrel (20") and a long magazine tube, while a "trench gun" features a heat shield and bayonet lug. The trench gun usually has a heavier barrel profile.

## Before: Utilitarian And Slick

My M12 came as a package with two barrel/pump assemblies (only one of which was numbered to the gun). The matching barrel was a bit over 28" long and crowned with an adjustable poly choke and a set of colored rifle-type sights. Apparently set up for turkey hunting, the gun had been sprayed green in unfortunately thorough fashion, including all the major metal parts visible on the outside and the wood. Perhaps fine for its intended purpose, I had other plans.

The M12 has a reputation for smoothness — no less than Papa Hemingway called his beloved M12 "faster than a snake." Even so, I was surprised with the barrel pointed upward, tripping the bolt release would cause the pump to fall all the way down under its own weight. Shooting it before the rebuild, I timed

my double taps to see how fast I could fire two rounds. My best time clocked in at 0.28 seconds.

## Let's Get Started

Since my interest is early-defensive guns, I chose to covert this sporting M12 to a 1918-style riot gun. The first step was to find out what one looked like, which meant hours of combing through books, including a reprinted Winchester catalog. I also put in a call to Doug Turnbull, who was kind enough to tell me not only what bluing should have been applied, but at what grit the metal should be polished. Usually knowing is half the battle, but in the case of polishing, "knowing" is the on-ramp to 40 hours of hand-cramping labor. More on that later …

An M12 takedown is easy. Push the magazine locking pin downward and use it as a lever to rotate the magazine tube 90 degrees counterclockwise as viewed from the muzzle end, then pull the magazine tube forward. Make sure the pump is all the way forward and rotate the barrel/pump assembly 90 degrees counterclockwise, then pull it forward to separate it from its interrupted threads in the receiver. Further disassembly is

Brownells supplied the facing reamer used to square off the muzzle after cutting. Note the pilot bushing: They're available in more than one size, so measure your barrel to get the correct one.

It's possible to remove the action side-sleeve screw cap without this Brownells tool, but the odds are good you'll destroy it.

Bottle-brush-style Flex Hones from Brownells finished the bore; a slightly larger chamber hone and then coarse and finer finish hones for the bore. Using the correct honing oil is critical.

Jeremy used a reamer to lengthen the forcing cone, helping reduce shot deformation. Brushing the Dykem onto the reamer shows where it's cutting.

*Removing the barrel from the receiver extension turned out to be one of the hardest parts, and an operation where it's easy to damage the gun. Before I turned the barrel free, I recruited a barrel vice, strap wrench, oxy-acetylene torch and a friend.*

too complicated to list here. I strongly suggest a manual and an illustrated parts list, as well as bagging and tagging the small parts and springs as the gun comes apart.

Removing the barrel from the receiver extension turned out to be one of the hardest parts, and an operation where it's easy to damage the gun. Before I turned the barrel free, I recruited a barrel vice, strap wrench, oxy-acetylene torch and a friend.

## Barrel Work

Since the barrel should be 20" I measured (using the correct method of inserting a rod down the barrel to the breechface) and then cut the barrel to length with a hacksaw. Then I squared it off using a facing reamer from Brownells I ran in a drill press. Instead of replacing the long gone bead front sight with a brass one, which would be correct, I chose a 0.130" diameter stainless bead from Brownells. Before drilling and tapping the hole, I leveled the barrel in the mill. While the job could be done in a drill press, or perhaps even very carefully by hand, if you have access to a mill, it's a much better choice to get the hole perfectly vertical and in the right place.

With the barrel off, I re-reamed the forcing cone, lengthening it slightly and then honed the bore, both of which can reduce shot deformation. With a bottle brush-style Flex Hone from Brownells to create a mirror-like finish in the bore, I used three different hones: a slightly larger chamber hone to smooth out the work done on the forcing cone, and then a Medium-Coarse and Fine finish hone for the bore. After applying liberal doses of the proprietary Flex Hone oil to soak the hone, I chucked one end in a 3/8" hand drill and then ran the hone in and out of the barrel to create a fine, cross-hatched polish. Take your time, use plenty of oil and start from the chamber if possible.

## Polishing And Bluing Blues

This was the end of the easy part. While hot blue was correct for my gun's 1947-era serial number range, the more attractive early finish used in the 1910s required a much finer level of metal finishing. The barrel and magazine tube were finished at 400 grit with a rust blue,

while all other exposed parts were 600 grit and received a charcoal blue.

Also called "carbona blue," it's the same finish applied to early M1911 pistols such as the 1912-style Colt I built last year in these pages. As with the Colt, I did the metal preparation before sending the gun to Turnbull Restoration for bluing and reassembly. Doug Turnbull is the acknowledged master of period-correct finishes, so if you want it done right, and done beautifully, that's where it goes.

Thanks to the tenacity of the green paint, I resorted to bead blasting the larger pieces of the gun with 800-grit media and then began the long, tedious

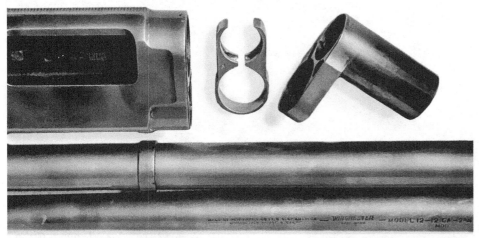

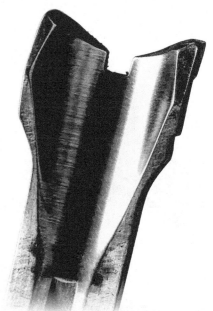

Whatever the spray-on finish was, it was tenacious. Jeremy resorted to a bead blast cabinet full of 800-grit media to remove it.

A swivel countersunk into the butt left a hole too deep to fill. Instead Jeremy milled a slot for the military-style sling swivel that came on M12 trench guns and was optional on riot guns.

The carrier after removing the rough machining marks and hand polishing to 1,000 grit. As with any other polishing, the sandpaper has to be backed with something hard — Jeremy used the wooden plug from the magazine tube.

The receiver after the pits were removed — one gouge remains, which was too deep to remove without weakening the receiver. It took 220-, 320-, 400- and 600-grit paper to prepare it for bluing.

polishing process during which I discovered the pitting underneath. This was in addition to the inevitable dents found in a 70-year-old working gun, including a couple of gouges too deep to remove without weakening the metal. I would have preferred to have the surface flawless, but it's just part of the gun's story.

In addition to polishing out any damage, part of the challenge of finishing a later gun to an earlier, higher-gloss finish is the gun was never so finely finished to begin with, so you can expect the entire gun to be covered with coarser polishing and tooling marks to remove.

For those who haven't had the pleasure, the art in polishing isn't making the part shiny, it's keeping the flat parts flat without ripples, the curved parts at the same curvature and all the various angles and curves meeting in a straight line. So, removing a pit or the striations from an earlier, coarser finish doesn't mean you polish the one part until the marks disappear, it means you bring the entire surface of the part down to the bottom of the mark, all the while maintaining the original shape. For this gun, it meant listening to dozens of hours of podcasts while I wore out innumerable

sheets of sandpaper, splitting a few fingertips in the process.

## Woodwork And Parts

The same level of work was applied to the buttstock I fit to the metal and freed of dents using the same technique as on the steel and correct grit of sandpaper backed by a hard surface such as a file. With the buttstock, I started at 220 and worked down to 600 to prepare it for final finishing by Turnbull, who also did the final fitting of the wood to a new hard plastic buttplate, since I just couldn't get the green off the original one.

There were other parts to replace as well. My M12 came with a flat-bottom forend I replaced with an earlier 18-groove one purchased from Numrich. Depending on who you believe, the slimmer 18-groove forend either appeared in 1919 (as per Dave Riffle's book on the M12), or was found on all riot guns (Poyer's *U.S. Winchester Trench and Riot Guns*). Other parts I ordered from Numrich included a replacement for a broken firing pin (M12's are famous for this); an action slide handle retaining spring missing on my gun; a trigger pin to replace the bent one I found inside and a breech bolt retaining lever I damaged

while trying to drive out its particularly stubborn retaining pin. New hammer and magazine springs also seemed like a good idea.

And that wasn't all: A former owner had installed sling swivels (this was a turkey gun, remember?) in both the walnut buttstock and the magazine plug, which required replacing the plug. The butt was a different question, though, since the generic swivel had been countersunk, leaving a hole too deep to fill. Instead, I located a correct military-style

*To keep the gun safe and sound, Galco sent a field-grade breakdown case; it fit the M12 quite nicely.*

*Depending on who you believe, the slimmer 18-groove forend either appeared in 1919 (as per Dave Riffle's book on the M12) or was found on all riot guns (Poyer's U.S. Winchester Trench and Riot Guns).*

*The brilliance of the takedown system is the adjustable locking collar, held in place by this toothed retainer and can be turned to adjust for wear in the barrel/receiver lockup.*

*Like most other parts of the M12, the sling swivel had to be polished to 600 grit prior to being charcoal blued.*

sling swivel assembly and after carefully measuring it with dial calipers, used a 1/2" end mill to cut the correct size slot to inlet it into the butt. While M12 riot guns did not come with those (trench guns did), they were an option and were sometimes added at the arsenal.

## A New 1918 Riot Gun

After carefully bubble-wrapping all the parts and paying an exorbitant shipping tab to get them to Turnbull, it came home well packaged in a hard case. The wood I had rendered into its pale natural color by all the sanding was now stained in a reddish-brown, dull-oil military finish. The metal parts are an even black so shiny it almost looks like it's dripping, so much so when you take the gun in a firing position, you can see the reflection down the top of the receiver. An

*After removing the green paint from the stock, Jeremy used sandpaper backed by a large file and oak dowel to fit the stock to the receiver.*

*Even the buttplate had its share of green paint. Turnbull Restoration ended up replacing it.*

alert eye will notice a slight difference in shade between the rust bluing on the barrel and mag tube and the charcoal blue of parts such as the magazine band, but you have to look for it.

It's so pretty I don't want to use it — I don't even want to load it — because I know the inevitable scratches and dents will mar the fine finish. But things are meant to be used, and those scars, like the ones too deep for me to take out, will just become another part of this gun's story. I could always polish it again, but then again no, that part was a lot less fun than it sounds.

*For more info:*
*www.brownells.com,*
*www.galcogunleather.com,*
*www.gunpartscorp.com,*
*www.turnbullrestoration.com*

Frank Jardim

# BUILD A PEDERSOLI CHARLEVILLE MUSKET

## The muzzleloader that won the Revolutionary War.

Located in Italy's northern gun-making region, family-owned-and-operated Davide Pedersoli & Company takes great pride in the quality of their historic replica firearms. Nobody makes as many different muzzleloaders. European competitive marksmen win lots of medals with them too. They're exceptionally well made and show admirable dedication to historic accuracy.

Their pricing reflects that quality, but if you have a moderate amount of skill you can save over 20% by buying their guns in kit form and building them yourself. The retail on the factory-finished musket in this story is $1,595, while the kit is only $1,275. This isn't something likely to be found at the local gun shop, but you or your hometown dealer can order anything in the Pedersoli online catalog from IFG (Italian Firearms Group) that imports, distributes and services Pedersoli products. If IFG doesn't have it in stock, it will be on the next inbound container.

### A Beginner/ Intermediate Project

One of the best features of Pedersoli kits is you need not be an expert to finish them into beautiful guns. They are perfect for beginners because all the stock inletting, fitting and even some finishing is done at the factory. The guns arrive dry-fit (completely assembled with the stock fully inlet and every part in its correct position).

By starting with a dry-fit gun, you cut out the most challenging and anxious aspect of the build. Most people haven't built, or even seen, enough Charleville muskets to know the exact location of the rear barrel band, trigger guard, etc. When you start a Pedersoli kit, you jump ahead to the inspection stage and double-check their work instead of going through the sometimes-lengthy process of researching, locating and then adjusting the inletting and fit of each part yourself.

On kits from lesser brands, you should always be suspect of the inletting, hole locations and stock geometry. Expect everything to be a little off and some things to be *a lot* off. Is the time you spend correcting those issues on lower-priced kits worth it? That's for you to decide. You need to be a much more competent craftsman to get the cheaper kits to come out nice.

This Charleville's walnut stock was 95% finished, remaining a little beefy from rear barrel band to butt. Most of the remaining work was focused there. It's important to note where the three barrel bands fit, the stock was already at its correct final size. I noticed this during my dry-fit inspection. Take care when stock sanding to avoid reducing these areas any further, or you could end up with loose bands. Mark their edges on the stock with a sharp pencil so you can see where not to sand.

This kit also had the difficult metal polishing of the lock and trigger guard already done, and the barrel nearly so.

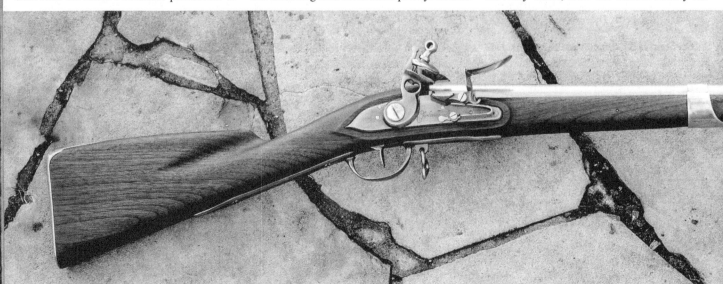

The rest of the metal parts were cast and needed the mold sprues filed off. You'll also need to do some fine shaping with files and sequential hand polishing with 100-, 150-, 220-, 360-, 400-, 500- and 600-grit sandpaper or emery cloth to give them that rust-resistant, armory-bright look. Back when this was state-of-the-art military issue, the troops used a regular issue of fine brick dust to keep them polished.

## Frank's Custom Design

If I'd made this kit to match the factory finished guns, it would have taken two weekends of my full attention. However, I had something else in mind, and it's the beauty of a kit-built gun. You can modify them into precisely the gun you want. I wanted to make a gun that had the look of surviving examples with provenance to the American Revolution.

During the Revolution, the French government sold or otherwise provided the American cause with approximately 200,000 muskets. Most were older French muskets of at least six different obsolete patterns held in storage at their military arsenals. While these guns were obsolete from the French point of view, they were the equal or better of the British Brown Bess musket, and the Americans needed them badly.

Regardless of the actual French military model nomenclature or the actual arsenal of their manufacture, the Americans called the French muskets "Charlevilles" after one of the arsenals that made them. Besides the standard models, the French sent repaired and partially upgraded muskets sharing characteristics of two or more models.

In fact, from the looks of surviving historical examples, it appears they frequently varied in the minor details of their furniture, particularly triggers, trigger guards, front barrel bands and bayonet lug location. I think this is because the guns of this era were all essentially handmade and it's the result

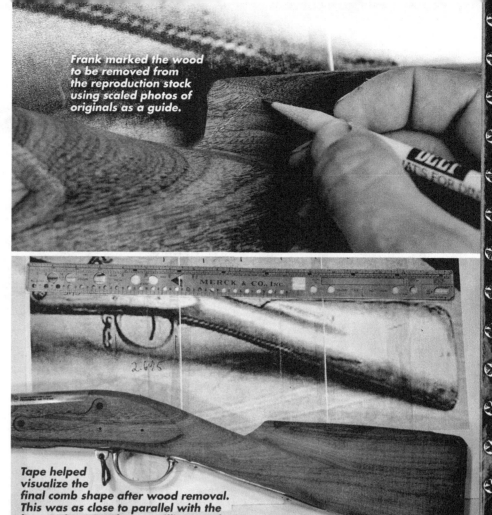

Frank marked the wood to be removed from the reproduction stock using scaled photos of originals as a guide.

Tape helped visualize the final comb shape after wood removal. This was as close to parallel with the bore axis as Frank was willing to take it.

Tap out the trigger and sling swivel pins from the outside with a punch. Driving them from the inside out could chip the wood in the last place you want — where it shows!

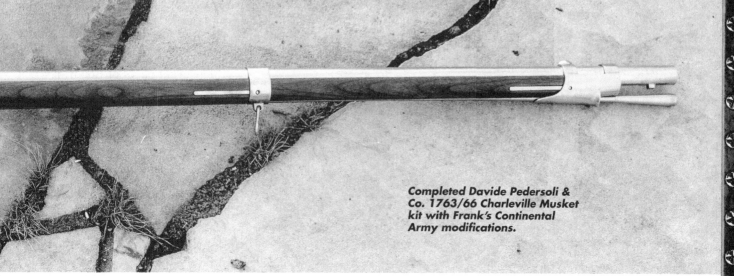

Completed Davide Pedersoli & Co. 1763/66 Charleville Musket kit with Frank's Continental Army modifications.

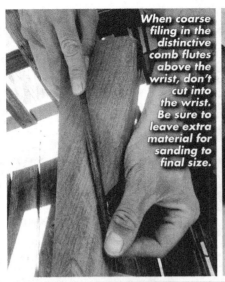

When coarse filing in the distinctive comb flutes above the wrist, don't cut into the wrist. Be sure to leave extra material for sanding to final size.

Using photos as a guide, Frank marked the wood to remove from the point of the comb to get the correct "spear point" geometry.

Frank used 80-grit emery cloth to take down excess wood to match the tang.

Brownells' Hard-Cut Curl Scraper Set is useful for inletting and general stock shaping. Frank is using it here to shave away excess around the lock area.

when six different models' parts are combined. However, one characteristic was reasonably consistent: the general geometry of the buttstock.

## Fact Finding

To research this Revolutionary War Charleville build, I studied photographs and descriptions of 15 reportedly original muskets from excellent to relic condition and inspected one in very fine condition in a local museum collection. With a sampling this small, I wouldn't bet my life on my conclusions, but it appeared nearly all the original guns had very similar buttstocks that differed significantly from the Pedersoli replica.

The replica has a long, high, upward-angled, square-nosed comb. The original Revolutionary War Charlevilles had shorter, lower, level combs with a sloping nose. Unlike the replica, the top of the original combs ran parallel — or close to parallel — to the axis of the barrel, and the butt was deeply fluted on each side of the comb above the wrist. Sometimes this fluting ran 3/4 the length of the comb.

I asked Stefano Pedersoli about this and learned their replica was based on research done by the respected French military arms historian Jean Boudriot. Pedersoli kindly sent me copies of the relevant pages of Boudriot's 1961 book *Armes a Feu Francaises Modeles Reglementaires*. Their stock matched the illustration perfectly.

Pedersoli observed the earlier model French muskets had combs similar to those I was finding in my research. I don't feel I can offer a definitive answer to explain why nearly all the original examples I found differed from Boudriot's drawing of the 1766 model. It could be any number of things, starting with too small a study sample to post-war modification while in American military arsenals.

It's fine to sand across the grain when rough shaping, but leave extra material and go with the grain when you get over 100-grit abrasive.

The time to glue in a chip is immediately after it's discovered. Wipe off excess glue, clamp it and let it dry before you resume sanding.

You can use a file to get close to the right metal-to-wood fit, then use a sanding block and sandpaper for the final adjustment.

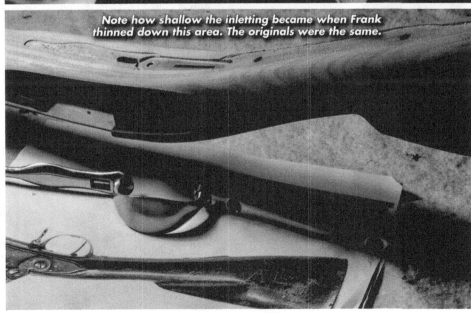

Note how shallow the inletting became when Frank thinned down this area. The originals were the same.

It's tough to tell what's happened to a gun over the course of 250 years, even when you can hold it in your hands. In any case, I decided to copy the geometry of the best original Revolutionary War muskets found in my research. Fortunately, there's plenty of wood on the semi-finished stock of the kit to work with.

## Woodwork First!

When building the kit, it makes sense to start with the wood because you can go back and work on the metal parts while the stock finish is drying. Begin by studying the assembled gun and make note of where wood needs to be removed. I enlarged pictures of the original stocks as close to full scale as I could with a photocopier and laid a straight edge over them to understand the geometry. Then I transferred my findings onto the beefy buttstock of the replica and started marking the areas to be removed.

Carefully remove all metal work from the stock except for the buttplate and put the parts in the original box so you don't lose them. Set up to work where dust won't be a problem and you have plenty of room because the stock is long! Have a few clamps and scraps of smooth board to hold the stock steady so you can work on it. I often make holding fixtures out of scrap wood to clamp the stocks securely without damaging them. Without the metal attached, the stock is fragile and must be handled carefully.

Since wood can't be put back after you take it away, I was very conservative when carving, filing and sanding away material. Check your work more often than you think you should, and keep the example photographs in sight at all times while working.

## Stock Work ...

To more closely match my chosen original, the stock needed thinning

Frank finished and sealed the stock by wet-sanding with Birchwood Casey Genuine Oil (tung oil) and 320-, 400-, 500- and 600-grit sandpaper to fill the grain. Let it dry a day between applications.

Steel parts in the raw have a coarse finish from casting.

above and below the lock, thinning of the wrist and an extensive reshaping of the buttstock, comb and buttplate. I completed all of my rough wood removal for shaping work on the heavy wood of the wrist and butt using 36- and 50-grit sandpaper and coarse files. Then I finished close to the final shape with 80-grit sandpaper. It's easy to take off too much with abrasives so rough. You may want to work with 80-grit paper alone for the sake of caution.

I began by shaving a thin triangular slice off the top of the comb's nose, tapering rearward to the tang of the buttplate. This gave the comb a slightly humpback look, which I observed on some original guns. To get the comb perfectly parallel to the barrel axis would have required re-inletting the buttplate so the upper tang was parallel with the barrel. It was more trouble than it was worth.

On the bottom of the buttstock I shaved off about 2mm from the trigger to the buttplate, reducing the trigger guard inletting to a shallow 0.5 mm like

the original guns. Then I cut back the comb's nose to match the sloping angle of the original. I ended up moving the nose back another 10mm after ruminating on my photos of original stocks.

I cut the comb flutes on either side in two stages too, first with a coarse file and then with 80-grit sandpaper wrapped around a 1/2" dowel. Files and sandpaper this coarse really hog out material fast, so again I advocate caution and frequent inspection. Leave enough material for final shaping. You must also take great care to remove material only from the comb. Don't drift down into the wrist area of the stock. The fluting is all above the wrist line.

Eventually, I extended my flutes halfway down the butt. I cut the nose of the comb to a triangular point that looked surprisingly abrupt, like a spear point, when viewed from the top. This pointed comb nose and the deep fluting were the hardest part of the buttstock geometry to understand from photos alone. If you were to cut through the stock comb vertically and look at the

As he shaped the wood first, Frank had to file the edge of the buttplate back to match the stock.

Clean your file with a card file often so chips don't get stuck in it and scar your work. A little chip can do a lot of damage to the surface.

Sanding the casting lines off the trigger is a job for 80-grit sandpaper.

The barrel is the easiest part to final polish to armory bright since it's nearly there as delivered.

Frank found there was room to lower the tang a little more in the stock by deepening the inletting directly under it, but unless you're ready to grind down the bottom of the priming pan, you can't go far because the flash hole will be too low.

severed end, it would resemble a number "8" with the flutes pinching the top from the bottom. This shape actually made for an excellent grip. At the time, the French were world leaders in arms development.

## Moving Forward

On the top of the stock, above the lock where the barrel tang fit, I used a "shoeshine" technique and 100-grit emery cloth to quickly get the wood down to the tang. Later, I noticed the barrel wasn't fully seated in the channel and the tang inletting was holding it up. I removed another 0.5mm to lower it and reduce the gun's thickness through the lock area. I might have reduced it another 1mm with more tang inletting, but it would put the touch hole below the priming pan. I would then have to grind out the bottom of the pan to fully expose the hole. This didn't seem worth the trouble.

I sanded the bottom of the forend until the inletting for the front of the trigger guard was only 0.5mm deep and tapered it up to the pencil line marking the back of the rear barrel band — my "no sand-zone." With the basic upper and lower limits of the stock geometry now set, I focused on sanding the outside edges of these flat borders to the correct radii and shaping the wrist and lock areas using traditional curl scrapers and sandpaper.

The Brownells Hard Fit Curl Scraper Set I used included three flat and three round scrapers of increasing size. They can slice away a sliver of wood thinner than a piece of paper, and the big handles improve your control. Sometimes they cut better in one direction along the wood's surface than they do the other. Though intended for inletting, I found them very helpful in stock shaping prior to sanding with 80-grit paper.

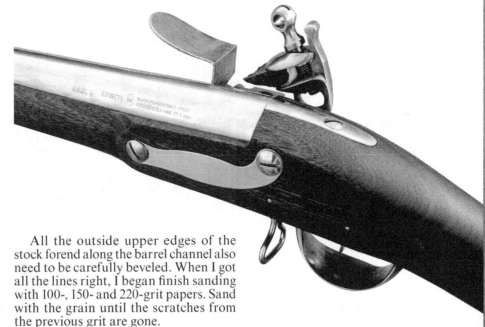

All the outside upper edges of the stock forend along the barrel channel also need to be carefully beveled. When I got all the lines right, I began finish sanding with 100-, 150- and 220-grit papers. Sand with the grain until the scratches from the previous grit are gone.

## Finishing Touches

When done, wipe the stock with water and let it dry to raise the grain. When dry, the surface will feel like fine sandpaper and is ready for oiling with tung oil.

To seal wood on military guns, I prefer Birchwood Casey's Genuine Oil. This high-quality tung oil is quicker to apply, more durable and more easily touched up than boiled-linseed oil. I wet-sanded the oil on the wood with 320-, 400-, 500- and finally 600-grit sandpaper, allowing the slurry to dry, fill in and seal the grain. The result is a low-sheen, military, rubbed-oil finish. Dispose of the oily rags outside because they can spontaneously combust.

## Metalwork

There aren't many metal parts to finish on this kit. The more involved work is cleaning up and polishing the casting marks off the buttplate, trigger, trigger plate, sling swivel loops and the barrel bands. The barrel and barrel-band springs needed only some work with 400- and 500-grit sandpaper before a final polish on the buffing wheel.

Steel is a lot harder to work than brass, and I resorted to the delicate use of a Dremel tool to get the porous-looking cast surface finish smoothed out fast. After that, I used files and progressively finer sandpaper just like working on the wood.

The only fine-tuning required on the metal parts was a slight enlargement of the middle band retaining spring hole with a round file, a slight beveling on the back inner edge of all the bands so they install without catching and gouging the stock (especially the rear band) and reshaping of the buttplate.

The material shaved off the bottom of the buttstock left about 2mm of buttplate hanging in the breeze that had to be cut off; filed to match the correct profile of the wood buttstock; filed again along its edge to a uniform 1mm thickness and finally again filed to slope the edge up to a crown at the centerline as it was originally.

Once all the reshaping I was willing to do was complete, I was quite satisfied with the overall look of the piece. It was now unique among modern reproduction Charlevilles, much like the originals seem to have been. However, unlike the mixed bag of fine and flawed European arms that made it to the desperate empty hands of Continental soldiers 240 years ago, this Pedersoli is of known excellent quality. 🔫

*For more info:*
*www.italianfirearmsgroup.com,*
*Ph: (800) 450-1852;*
*www.davide-pedersoli.com;*
*www.brownells.com,*
*Ph: (800) 741-0015*

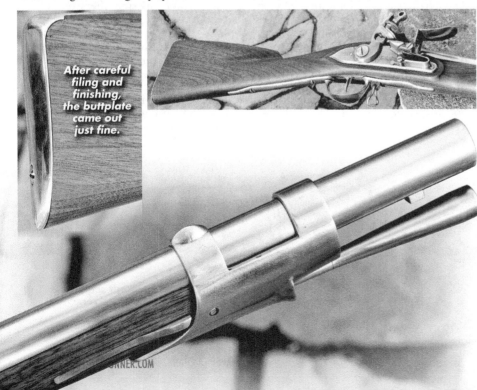

After careful filing and finishing, the buttplate came out just fine.

**Frank Jardim**

# DEMILLED SURPLUS RIFLE? NO PROBLEM!

## New life for a World War I wall hanger.

Last summer Century Arms International bought the entire inventory of Springfield Sporters. Peers and former rivals, both companies gained prominence importing military surplus arms in the early 1960s. The Springfield Sporters inventory was a treasure trove of guns and parts. Now Century's Surplus division is in the process of reposting the hundreds of parts and firearms, including bolt actions of nearly every description. The massive inventory haul includes 60 years of odds and ends, most of which hadn't been offered for sale in decades. Some are collector gems, others diamonds in the rough, and some ... well, just rough. While scrolling through the latest Century Surplus listings on their website, I discovered a neat, but demilitarized, French, World War I Berthier. I snatched it up for $275. Decent condition, shooter-grade Berthier carbines commonly sell for around $475.

### The Berthier Story

First generation smokeless powder bolt actions are fascinating thanks to the diversity of their design — especially the Berthier. A French railroad engineer working in Algeria in the late 19th century designed it for use by the French Colonial troops. The 3-shot, clip-fed, Berthier was economical to make and simpler to operate and maintain than the 11-shot Lebel rifle with tubular magazine issued to regular French Army troops.

The Berthier was better than the Lebel in terms of balance and lighter weight. The urgent need for weapons to arm millions of French troops during World War I resulted in huge numbers being issued despite its one major flaw. When most military bolt actions had at least a 5-round capacity, the Berthier had only its 3-shot clip. By 1917 capacity was increased to five shots with a simple modification.

After the war, surplus Berthiers seem to have circled the globe, but France retained a large number of them in reserve into World War II. After France capitulated to the Nazis, many Berthiers were issued to occupying German troops. Photographs of the era show the guns also ended up in the hands of the French Resistance, creating peculiar situations where both sides could be shooting at each other with the same weapons. My son has become very interested in the history of the French resistance, and I bought this demilled carbine for him to use in his educational displays about the Maquis. I hoped to restore it to safely shoot blanks.

### Before ...

The Century Surplus team does a great job of photographing the guns and the enlarged photos showed a fairly clean carbine missing the front barrel band, oxy-acetylene welds securing the bolt in the receiver in two places and six holes drilled in the top of the barrel, one of which might have cut into the chamber area. Assuming good chamber, unobstructed barrel and complete internals, restoring this gun to function with blanks looked like a three-phase job. I'd need to cut the welds to free the action,

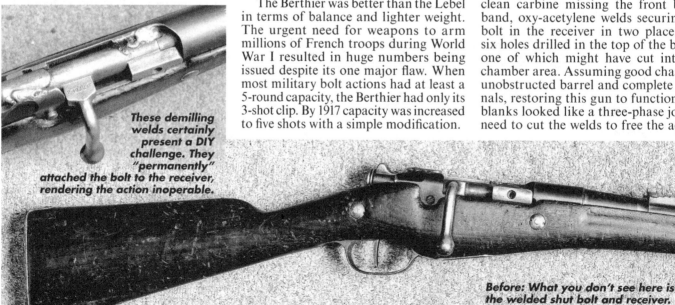

These demilling welds certainly present a DIY challenge. They "permanently" attached the bolt to the receiver, rendering the action inoperable.

Before: What you don't see here is the welded shut bolt and receiver.

In some cases, the demilling weld interfered with original parts and Frank had to add new metal.

The first step to convert this rifle to fire blanks is to cut through the welds, doing minimal damage to the bolt and receiver.

repair the holes in the barrel and refinish the bare spots with cold blue.

The only expensive tool I planned to use was a MIG welder. Arguably, the job could be done fine without welding for the cost of a couple replacement parts. If you want to use MIG welding for repairs but don't want to buy a machine, you might get the work done at a local shop.

When the carbine arrived, I found the cocking knob was also welded to the receiver, but the weld was cracked and the knob wiggled freely. The crack did most of the work for me when it came to grinding it free with my Dremel tool. The firing pin was obviously missing, and the going rate for those is around $30, so I made a new one on my lathe. It was a pretty easy pin to turn, but that process is a story in itself for the next issue of *DIY*.

### Removing Welds

I began the project by cutting through and grinding away the old welds to free the bolt. This required a variable speed Dremel tool with abrasive cutting discs and tiny grinding wheels of various shapes, the most useful being the cylindrical and cone-shaped ones. Welds are hard and they'll dull your steel cutters, so I recommend you use only abrasives.

Cutting welds is delicate work for a steady hand and best done in excellent light. Don't rush the tool, especially the tiny abrasive cutting wheels, or you are likely to break them. Safety glasses are a must for this work. Economy should guide your cutting decisions; it's easier to take metal away than to add it. Always sacrifice metal on the easily replaced or repaired parts. To use a maritime disaster analogy, "women, children and receivers in the lifeboat first."

If the welds were really deep, I planned to cut and grind the bolt away from the receiver. The worst-case scenarios would be buying a replacement bolt for $80 to $100 or welding the damage to the old parts and grinding and filing them back to size. Though this was not the case with my carbine, sometimes the demilling welder will carelessly melt away parts of the receiver that show. Rather than leave it a mess, consider replacing the lost metal with an additional bead of weld to restore the receiver's contours before you start cutting the action open.

There's really no telling how deep the weld bead penetrated into the parts so, if possible, trim away the bead in layers rather than just cutting straight down. You're less likely to over-cut that way.

"Restoring this gun to function with blanks looked like a three-phase job. I'd need to cut the welds to free the action, repair the holes in the barrel and refinish the bare spots with cold blue."

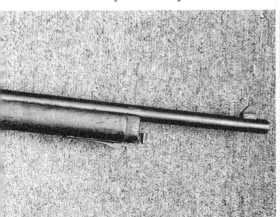

After Frank added a weld bead he had to file some parts back to original dimensions.

To fill holes in the barrel, Frank chose to enlarge and thread the holes, later to be filled with plug cap screw and weld beads.

"The welder who demilled this carbine must have liked guns, because he used a light hand."

By using the plug cap screw approach, Frank ensured the finished barrel would be free of obstructions in case some future owner tried to fire live ammunition.

Frank removed the sights to minimize risk of them getting welded on permanently. Note the "moats" he cut around the plug cap screws to allow for a more stable weld bead.

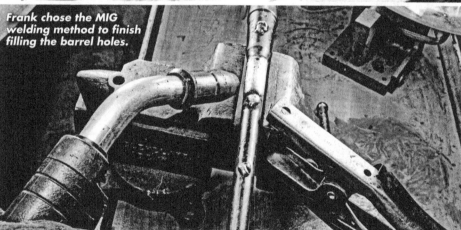

Frank chose the MIG welding method to finish filling the barrel holes.

Also, give the parts a solid whack with a non-marring rubber or dead-blow mallet from time to time, and you might get lucky and crack the weld all the way through.

Around the bolt head, it was prudent to make gradual, shallow, vertical cuts parallel to the inner wall of the receiver and then grind the bead down in layers toward the bolt. The weld cracked just short of all the way through and I had minimal cleanup to do on the bolt body and head. Had I not ground a little too deeply on the round surface of the bolt body, you'd have never been able to tell the bolt was welded.

## Virtues Of MIG Welding

On the rear cocking piece, the weld connecting it to the right side of the receiver was only about 1/8" deep and I freed it with single deep cut straight down. I repaired the long, thin slice from the cocking piece with a bead of weld.

In all cases, when adding metal, I recommend MIG welding over all other techniques with the possible exception of TIG welding which has advantages in certain delicate operations. MIG welding localizes better and introduces a lot less heat into the metal overall, reducing the risk of interfering with the

Be sure to use a hand file, and not a Dremel tool, to smooth out the welded sections.

Once the rough barrel work was complete, Frank was able to re-solder the sights back in place.

Be sure to remove excess solder because it will not take bluing.

The hot iron and wet rag technique helped to raise some of those old knocks and dings from the stock.

original heat treatment. This is especially true with larger parts. Heat sinks — as simple as a wet rag near the welding area — help draw away damaging heat. Gas welding is the last method you want to use because it dumps loads of heat into the surrounding metal.

The welder who demilled this carbine must have liked guns, because he used a light hand. The obviously discolored part of the heat-affected area in the receiver was pretty small. I wouldn't be surprised if this receiver was still suitable for live ammo.

The hardest part of MIG welding is getting started in the right spot while trying to see through the dark protective eye shade. An auto-darkening helmet is helpful, but I've found flooding the work with light from several portable lights using conventional 100-watt or brighter bulbs is adequate to find the starting point and help me see where the weld bead is going.

### Repairing The Barrel

I could have plugged the barrel holes quickly by adding a loop of weld bead to the walls of each hole until they were bridged with molten metal. However, this method might have caused some obstruction in the bore. A partial barrel obstruction isn't an issue with blanks, but a live round could cause a burst barrel with potentially deadly consequences. By keeping the barrel clear, I've done my part to protect a future owner who lacks the sense to check the bore.

A clear bore is also easier to keep clean, and in a clean barrel the depressions where my plugs were fitted are easy to spot. Typically, the bores of these guns are dark and pitted from the corrosive priming in military ammo of olden times. Ironically, this demilled carbine rifle had a perfect bore, making the barrel repairs especially easy to spot.

An alternative means of plugging the barrel holes without obstructing the bore is to thread them with a hand tap, deburr the inside of the hole and install some Grade 5 cap screws with red Loctite thread locker, cut the heads off and file the stubs flush to match the exterior contour of the barrel.

The barrel gets thinner the closer you get to the muzzle, so you'll want to cut the ends of the plugs with a concave relief to get maximum thread contact in the hole. Do this by looking through the bore as you install the bolt until the end protrudes enough to bridge the hole completely. Mark the orientation of the bolt on the head by drawing a line across it in line with the bore. Then remove the marked bolt and use a Dremel tool to grind a concave relief on the tip large enough to clear the grooves of the rifling. Use a bullet as a gauge when making this relief. Thread it back in the hole to check the clearance. It might take a couple tries to get it perfect.

My barrel repair combined both weld and plug techniques with a few refinements. I installed the plug over the chamber area, so it protruded slightly into the chamber. Close inspection with a spent case chambered showed the hole was centered at the point where the chamber ended, and the throat began. A slight depression there presented no issues with crimped nose blanks, but I wasn't sure if the edge of the neck of a full-length blank wouldn't expand into a depression and get stuck. To err on the safe side, I cut the bottom of this plug to extend about 0.003" into the chamber, intending to ream out the excess. It turned out reaming was unnecessary. The chamber had fairly generous tolerances; full-length blanks chambered and extracted perfectly.

Since I was welding my threaded plugs in, I didn't use a thread locker to

install them. To ensure a good, deep, weld bead, I cut a shallow trough around the plug stubs (like a little moat) so the MIG wire could hit the bottom without first hitting the sides, and completely fill it in from the bottom up. I left the beads high, took the gross excess down with a bench grinder and did the final shaping to contour with a smooth cut mill file. For finishing on a straight, long surface like the barrel or the top edge of a receiver, don't even think of using a Dremel tool. That's work for a good sharp file.

### Take Care Of The Sights

On this project, I also unsoldered the front and rear sights because they were too close to the holes and I stood a good chance of accidentally welding them on. A propane torch and wooden block to knock them free handled the removal. Heat is bad for springs, so before applying any heat to the rear sight base, I removed the sight spring so it wouldn't lose its temper. I also marked the barrel with two punch marks to make re-indexing it easier. I left the solder on the parts because it makes re-attaching them easier.

If you can sweat copper plumbing together, you can re-install soldered sights — the process is the same. Apply flux on both parts, heat evenly, apply solder opposite the heat until it's drawn in the joint, let it cool and clean any excess carefully with files if it's heavy and sandpaper or steel wool where it's not. Since solder is a lot softer than steel, it's fairly easy to clean off. You will need to clean it off because it won't take bluing.

### Cold Bluing

With my metal work complete, it was time to look at final finishing. There was still plenty of good blue on the receiver, but the barrel was polished bright. On a valuable shooting gun, I'd have cleaned

Old repairs exposed lighter shaded wood once Frank cleaned the stock. On the right is the finished product after Frank color matched the stain.

Birchwood Casey's water-based stain can be diluted to create different shades.

A tung oil treatment finished the wood renovation.

Frank's son is making good use of this restored, blank-firing Berthier as a Maquis in reenactments.

it all to bare metal and rust-blued it. This salvaged wall hanger didn't warrant that degree of effort, so I turned to a vintage classic, Brownells' Oxpho-Blue in cream form. It's easy to apply using cotton balls, stays where you want it and doesn't mind a little oil or rust on the surface. Wearing rubber gloves and eye protection, rub the first coat in for a few minutes until the metal darkens. Then wipe the excess and allow it to dry on the metal. When dry, burnish lightly with 00 steel wool or coarse cloth, which removes a bit of the bluing and then apply another coat. The more coats, the darker and deeper the color.

If the metal is visibly spotted with rust or patina, as it was on my trigger guard, it will show through the bluing. The subtle spotting reminded me of the black leopards of the Yucatan, sacred creatures to the ancient Maya who called them *Ballam* in their language. Unfortunately, that wasn't what I was going for.

To un-*Ballam* my parts, I scrubbed them a few minutes with steel wool dipped in Birchwood Casey Blue and Rust Remover and got them close to the white. This is a mild acid, so you need to give the parts a good cold-water rinse and dry them before you do anything else with them. Don't leave the acid on the metal. On the acid-cleaned, unpolished surface, the bluing looked great.

## Stock Rejuvenation 101

The walnut stock was in decent shape, showing the usual, and sometimes inexplicably intricate spliced-in repairs done

Note the newly functional action.

at the French arsenals. It wasn't my intention, nor was it possible, to restore the well-used wood to new condition, but it could stand some cleanup. To this end, I stripped off the hardware in preparation. Those weird, two hole or notch, spanner head-style screws were common on guns of this era. To remove them use snap ring pliers, or better still, modify a screwdriver tip with a file to fit the holes closely.

With the wood denuded of steel, I gave it a vigorous scrub-brushing in the tub with hot water and dish-washing detergent until the rinse water went from black to clear. I removed some of the dents with a steam iron and damp cloth. The deeper war wounds, the gouges and cuts, were there to stay. When dry, I was surprised the grain wasn't even raised, but yikes ... the spliced-in replacement parts of the stock were a lighter colored wood that contrasted glaringly with the original walnut.

I remedied the unforeseen color-match problem by blending the light and dark wood together with water-based Birchwood Casey Walnut Stain. Simply dilute this stain with water to match the desired intensity. Repeated coats, drying in between, also results in a darker color. I brushed on the undiluted stain in the light areas and wiped on highly diluted stain in the dark areas. Though not a perfect match, it was as good as it was ever done. The final finishing with three coats of Birchwood Casey's Genuine Oil sealed it and left the wood with a good military oiled-finish look. Genuine Oil is a high-quality tung oil product and seals better with less work than boiled linseed oil. My efforts took half a century off the stock.

The final touches were polishing the clip release, trigger and bolt until they were shiny bright, contrasting with the blued receiver. My son didn't think it was the same gun. Though the project materials only cost about $50 from Brownells, and a dollar worth of cap screws from the hardware store, I had two weekends

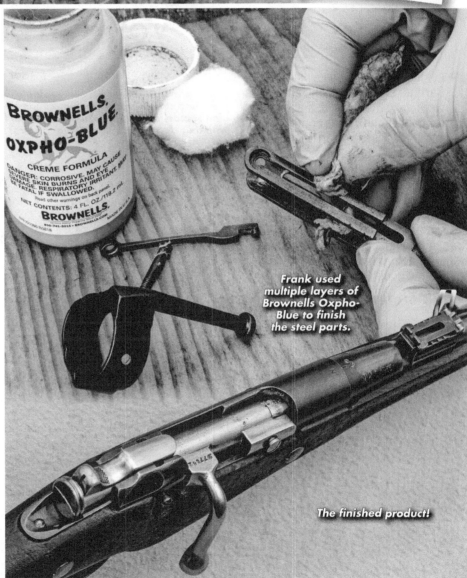

Frank used multiple layers of Brownells Oxpho-Blue to finish the steel parts.

The finished product!

of free time invested in making this relic into a good-looking blank gun. Some might not think it was worth the effort, but I look at it as solid practice for restoration of a really valuable gun, like an NFA-registered deactivated war trophy (DEWAT) machine gun. Restoring this little carbine was also a sound move in light of its intended use in World War II reenacts. The wear and tear it takes in the field won't destroy the collector value of the antique. My son tells me it was worth the trouble for just the "wow factor" it generates when people see it.

Frank Jardim

# WANTED: BLANKS IN OBSOLETE CALIBERS

## Making your own blank cartridges is easier than you think.

Seeking blanks for my newly restored Berthier carbine, I discovered there were none to be found; those blanks probably hadn't been commercially loaded since World War II. I suspect the national Berthier blank supply was wastefully dissipated in the decades following Hollywood's various inferior remakes of Paramount Pictures' 1939 original masterpiece, *Beau Geste*. Taking the "damned die hard" approach of the French Foreign Legionnaires, I vowed I would somehow find an economical way to load my own blanks!

### Blank Engineering

I soon learned loading blank ammunition isn't an arcane craft, but it does require some special tools and sometimes a little imagination. Guns are designed to work with full-length live cartridges; feeding and function problems can emerge

*The case mouth rolling die secures the wadding in blanks without a star crimp. These blanks can be reloaded almost indefinitely. The wadding is floral foam capped with thin chipboard disc cut from a spiral notebook cover.*

when you try to adapt ammo to blanks. Revolvers, single shots and break-open actions will digest anything sized for the chamber, but every other operating system often requires experimentation.

The simplest blanks use a standard case charged with powder and then wadded or star-crimped at the nose to keep the powder inside the case, insulate it from moisture and provide some momentary back-pressure for the powder to fully burn. Without back-pressure, much of the powder would go unburned and just get shot out of the barrel. A tightly wadded or star-crimped nose blank

*The Berthier carbine worked well with both star-crimped and wadded blanks. Graf & Sons was the source for the rare 8x50mm brass.*

*The Lyman Brass Smith Ideal single-stage press and classic 55 powder measure, along with the RCBS hand-priming tool, were great for loading small runs of wadded blanks with new brass. Star-crimped blanks need to pass through both dies to get a tight seal at the nose.*

**Hornady's Blank Cartridge die set makes wadded, roll-crimped blanks with any cases whose necks are less than 0.592" and star-crimped blanks on any cases with necks less than 0.62". Anybody need .600 Nitro Express blanks?**

is also significantly louder than one that isn't.

## Feeding And Function

Both wadded and star-crimped blanks can feed in autoloaders, but the star-crimped blanks are generally more reliable. The rounded nose mimics the ogive of a bullet, which helps it find its way in the chamber. Wadded blanks often have the case mouth slightly rounded over to retain the wadding. It also helps reduce the chance of them hanging up on the feed ramp or chamber mouth. The wadded blank case mouth looks a little like what you would get if you let an orangutan run empty cases through your reloading press with the roll crimping die set too low. In fact, you can crimp wadded blanks in precisely this manner.

A common problem with using standard cases for blanks is they may be too short to feed reliably. A longer case of the same base dimensions to get the blank cartridge's length closer to the live round's is often the solution. For example, you can make 9x19mm and .45 ACP blanks from crimped 9mm and .45 Winchester Magnum cases.

## Powder Power

You can also charge blanks with black or smokeless powder. Fast-burning smokeless powders like Alliant Powder's Red Dot, Unique or Bullseye are the ideal choice.

When you want a lot of smoke with your bang (say you're staging a reenactment of the gunfight at the O.K. Corral for the entertainment of local youngsters) black powder is the way to go. However, all the cleanup and safety requirements for black powder still apply. You don't need the precision of a metering powder measure, but if you want to use one it must be a special non-static model. Lyman makes their famous 55 measure with an aluminum reservoir (instead of plastic) for just this purpose.

In solving my 8x50mm Lebel blank problem, I discovered the perfect tool for making blanks of any caliber, and the ideal resource for brass in similarly obsolete vintage calibers.

Hornady offers a new Blank Cartridge custom grade die set, including both a star-crimp nose die and wadded nose die adjustable for cases from .22 to .45 caliber. The two dies work in sequence to make star-crimped blanks. The wadding die adds the final squeeze to close off the nose of the star-crimp, sealing in the powder so you can waterproof it with a dab of nail polish.

## Got Brass?

Dies won't get you anywhere without brass, and the wellspring of weird, obsolete and metric brass is Graf & Sons Inc. in Missouri. They started in 1957 and quickly grew into a one-stop-shop for just about everything shooters could need — except the guns. When it comes to handloading, they really are the authority they claim to be with several thousand products in stock spanning major and minor brands at competitive prices. If it's for handloading, and Graf & Sons doesn't have it, it may not exist. They're especially proud of providing shooters with the things nobody else has. Like new brass for 8x50mm Lebel, 6.5mm Japanese, 8x56R Hungarian Mannlicher, 9x57mm Mauser, .43 Egyptian, 7.62 Russian Na-

**Want to reenact the 1939 Paramount Pictures masterpiece Beau Geste from the comfort of home? Try loading your own blanks. Gary Cooper putting some pre-war supply of 8mm Lebel blanks to good use in Beau Geste.**

gant revolver, 9mm Browning Long and 8x22mm Japanese Nambu to name just a few. Their prices are very reasonable, if not outright bargains.

The Lebel brass from Graf & Sons cost $0.66 a case for a 50-count bag, and can be reloaded many times if you use the wadding method and have a set of Lee dies to resize the neck. Star-crimping tends to cut into the neck, and though the cases can be straightened and reused, the more often you do it the greater the danger of a fragment of brass blowing off the neck and becoming a dangerous projectile.

A blank fired at a sheet of paper 15' away shouldn't leave a mark on it. My charge of 15 grains of Unique fired by a Winchester large rifle primer made a realistic report and passed the paper test. I used green floral foam, packed tight against the powder with a wooden dowel and capped with disc of thin (0.0115" thick), slick faced cardboard from a typical spiral notebook cover. The foam seems to evaporate and the disc doesn't go far.

Got a rare firearm begging to shoot blanks? You can make your own. Just take care to avoid use of anything that might become an unintended projectile.

*For more info: www.grafs.com, Ph: (800) 531-2666*

**Frank Jardim**

# OH S*&%!!! I BROKE MY RAMROD!

## How to replace that essential part.

If you're into traditional muzzleloader shooting, eventually you're going to break a wooden ramrod. In fact, you'll probably break several. This sort of thing wasn't unheard of back in the olden times either. Many, if not most, antique guns aren't sporting their original rammer, if they have one at all. Unlike shooters on the ragged edge of civilization 150 or more years ago, nobody's life is on the line while you whittle a new rammer from a hickory branch. Now let's get past our shame and on to fixing that busted rod.

### Avoidance Tips

Start with an ounce of prevention. You should have a polymer or fiberglass back-up rod with your shooting kit at all times. As a traditionalist, you naturally don't want to be seen with these nigh-invulnerable, modern abominations, but when you break your period-correct wooden rod, your whole shooting outing won't come to an end with you nervously driving home with a charge and ball stuck in the barrel.

Next, follow correct loading procedures. Don't patch your balls so crazy-tight they're hard to push down even a clean bore. Use a good patch lube to keep fouling soft and grease away. Use a ball starter. Clean the bore before the fouling gets so heavy you have to exert Herculean effort to ram the ball home. Finally, grip the ramrod no more than a few inches above the bore to minimize the flexing that will break it. If, despite all the care, you break it anyway, you'll have to cobble together a new one.

### Hickory Rocks

Unless the broken rod is an antique, forget about gluing it. A glued rod isn't safe to use. You did a lot of flexing to break it and it let go at the weakest point dictated by physics. You might have weakened it badly in another place. Get a brand-new hardwood wooden rod of the appropriate length and diameter. Home Depot isn't the place to shop for this particular item.

Hickory has long been the preferred wood for ramrods for its strength and flexibility. You can find hickory rods at primitive shows locally or order them from several vendors. Usually you need to order a few at a time because the shipping will cost more than the rod. That's okay because spares come in handy. Dixie Gun Works will sell you four, straight-grained, 48"-long hickory rods cut from kiln-dried, American hickory slats in any of four diameters for less than $20 including shipping. While you're at it, get some fiberglass ramrods too. Those sell for about five bucks a pair.

Ideally, you want a piece of wood as straight as possible. Dixie's hickory rods start out that way, but as with any wood, as it absorbs humidity from the air, it has a tendency to bend. You can

*Carefully salvage the old end caps off your ramrod if it has them. The caps on this Pedersoli rifle were pinned on.*

flex them a little to take the bowing out, but don't get carried away. Once you seal the surface of the wood, any future bowing will be minimized.

### Making A New Ramrod

Ramrods come in normal dowel sizes. What diameter you need depends on the caliber and the inside diameter of ramrod thimbles. You can probably load a .50-cal. patched ball with a 7/16" rod, but you won't get it through the thimbles. Up to .36 caliber will usually use a 5/16" rod; .40 caliber can be 5/16" or 3/8"; .50 caliber is usually 3/8"; and .54 to .58 caliber can use 3/8" or 7/16".

You'll want to make the new rod with the metal end caps salvaged from your old one. Install the cap that goes inside the thimbles first. This cap is a smaller diameter than the cap used for ramming home the ball and often has a threaded hole for a ball puller or cleaning jag. The ends of wooden ramrods are rebated to fit snug inside the end caps. Caps are attached with glue, a pin or both. If yours uses a pin, drive it out with a nail or punch before you try to pull off the cap. You may have to dig out the old wood with a drill bit if it's glued in.

If the rod fragment survived removal of the cap, use it to mark the depth of the rebating on the new rod by rolling the new rod under a sharp blade at the correct spot. Don't go too deep. Shave back just enough wood, evenly around the circumference for a snug fit. Apply epoxy, like J-B Weld, and fit the cap. Wipe off any excess epoxy immediately and inspect the cap to ensure it's on straight and let the epoxy dry. If you took off a little too much wood, the epoxy will take up the extra space and hold the cap solid.

If the cap is secured with a pin, wait for the epoxy to dry before you drill the hole. Do it by hand, with a bit slightly smaller than the pin. Hold the drill bit square and plumb with the hole and

With caps, you can use your old rod as a guide to cutting and rebating the tips of the new rod. Start with the end that goes through thimbles. You won't need a wood lathe for this job.

Remove just enough wood from the diameter for a snug fit. Epoxy will hold it tight and fill any gaps.

Drill pin holes undersized and halfway through each side to meet in the middle. It's best done by hand. This tool is just the chuck from an old "egg-beater" style manual drill.

Fully install the ramrod inside its channel in the gunstock before you use the front end cap to mark the rebating line and overall length. If you don't seat it all the way, the rod will come up short!

Once Frank had the correct rebating line, he added the necessary length to fit inside the end cap and marked the cut. Measure twice, cut once.

Three coats of Birchwood Casey Genuine Oil (tung oil) was enough to seal the wood and prevent warpage.

drill only halfway from each side, so you meet somewhere in the middle. If perfection escapes you, J-B Weld will fill the wandering path of your drill bit as solidly as the wood itself.

## Length Matters

The new ramrod needs to be exactly the same length as the original one, but length may be hard to judge with a broken rod, especially if it broke in two spots. That's why we installed the inner cap first. When the inner end cap of the rod is dry and secured, insert it to its full depth in the ramrod channel of your gunstock and use the front end cap itself to gauge where to trim your ramrod so there's enough wood to fit all the way up inside it.

You'll also use this end cap to mark the depth of the required rebating to seat it on the end of the rod. Do this by putting the cap over the side of the rod with the front flush with the muzzle. Holding it there, mark your rebating line along the rear of the cap with a sharp pencil. Complete shaving the rod diameter and fitting the front cap just like the rear cap.

*Unless the broken rod is an antique, forget about gluing it. A glued rod isn't safe to use.*

## Matching Finish

When the epoxy is dry, you can sand the wood smooth with progressively finer sandpaper (150-, 220-, 320-grit) and polish the metal ends if you desire. Once sanded, you can stain the wood to match your gunstock. Water based stains work best. I made my own iron stain by dissolving rusty nails in apple cider vinegar in a vented jar. Over the course of a few months, the metal was bare and the liquid a dark brown. The more coats applied, the darker the finish. Being water based, it takes a little time to dry.

When the stain dried, I knocked off the raised grain on the wood with some 000 steel wool and sealed the rod. You can use several applications of linseed oil for this, rubbed in every day over the course of a week. Tung oil works even

The finished new ramrod cost less than $5 and required just about an hour of shop time to make. Not bad!

better with fewer applications and I did this rod with some Birchwood Casey Genuine Oil, which is essentially a tung oil. After rubbing in three coats, I had a nice protective surface finish.

In my observation, the .32- and .36-caliber rifles seem to build up fouling faster than the big calibers. Be conscious of this if you are shooting guns of several calibers on the range and try to remember not

to use .50 caliber loading force on those slender ramrods.

Make things easier on yourself, just order some Hickory rods ahead of time so they'll be on hand when you need them.

*For more info:*
*www.dixiegunworks.com,*
*www.birchwoodcasey.com*

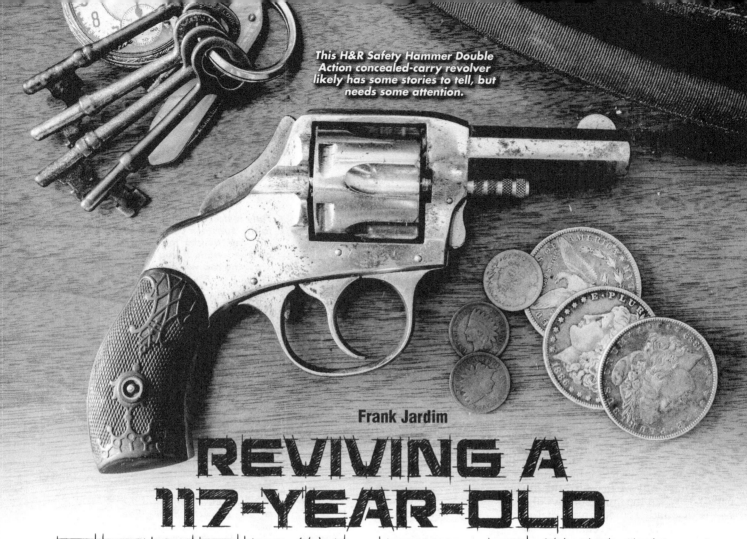

This H&R Safety Hammer Double Action concealed-carry revolver likely has some stories to tell, but needs some attention.

Frank Jardim

# REVIVING A 117-YEAR-OLD CONCEALED CARRY REVOLVER

## New life for an H&R Safety Hammer Double Action.

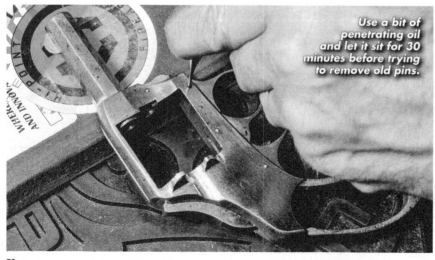

Use a bit of penetrating oil and let it sit for 30 minutes before trying to remove old pins.

**N**othing quite removes anxiety over a gunsmithing project than working on an inexpensive firearm. Such is the case with my 117-year-old Harrington & Richardson Safety Hammer Double-Action Revolver. This was the concealed carry version of H&R's American Double Action, one of America's most popular handguns you've probably never heard of. Production began in 1884, ended during World War II and spanned the black and smokeless powder eras. H&R made over 850,000 American Doubles, mostly in .32 and .38 calibers. They cost a little over *a dollar* through the early 20th century, putting them within reach of working people looking for a reliable, easy-to-shoot and decently made weapon for self-defense.

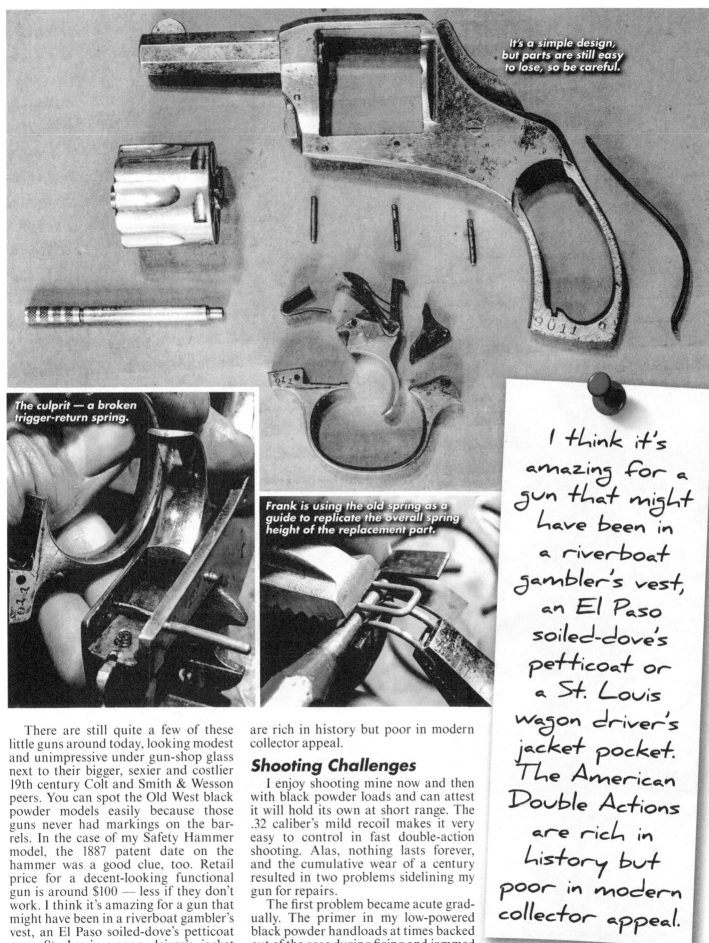

It's a simple design, but parts are still easy to lose, so be careful.

The culprit — a broken trigger-return spring.

Frank is using the old spring as a guide to replicate the overall spring height of the replacement part.

I think it's amazing for a gun that might have been in a riverboat gambler's vest, an El Paso soiled-dove's petticoat or a St. Louis wagon driver's jacket pocket. The American Double Actions are rich in history but poor in modern collector appeal.

There are still quite a few of these little guns around today, looking modest and unimpressive under gun-shop glass next to their bigger, sexier and costlier 19th century Colt and Smith & Wesson peers. You can spot the Old West black powder models easily because those guns never had markings on the barrels. In the case of my Safety Hammer model, the 1887 patent date on the hammer was a good clue, too. Retail price for a decent-looking functional gun is around $100 — less if they don't work. I think it's amazing for a gun that might have been in a riverboat gambler's vest, an El Paso soiled-dove's petticoat or a St. Louis wagon driver's jacket pocket. The American Double Actions are rich in history but poor in modern collector appeal.

## Shooting Challenges

I enjoy shooting mine now and then with black powder loads and can attest it will hold its own at short range. The .32 caliber's mild recoil makes it very easy to control in fast double-action shooting. Alas, nothing lasts forever, and the cumulative wear of a century resulted in two problems sidelining my gun for repairs.

The first problem became acute gradually. The primer in my low-powered black powder handloads at times backed out of the case during firing and jammed the cylinder against the recoil shield.

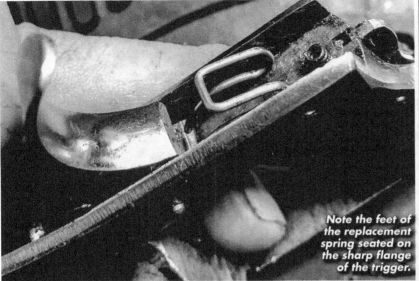

Note the feet of the replacement spring seated on the sharp flange of the trigger.

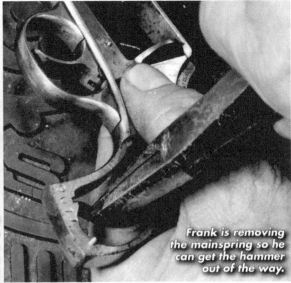

Frank is removing the mainspring so he can get the hammer out of the way.

You might break off a screw head with a gunsmith screwdriver, but you won't "bowtie" the screw slot.

Frank is using a Real Avid hollow-ground gunsmith screwdriver to remove the hammer pivot screw without damage.

The correct trigger parts orientation.

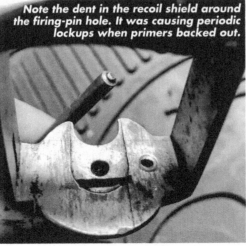

Note the dent in the recoil shield around the firing-pin hole. It was causing periodic lockups when primers backed out.

This didn't happen with original (vintage black powder) cartridges from some reason. I could minimize the primer protrusion on my ammunition, but the problem persisted. My conclusion was the depression in the recoil shield around the firing pin hole had finally gotten deep enough to anchor a fired case with even the slightest primer protrusion.

The second problem announced itself abruptly when the trigger failed to return forward after a double-action pull.

## Cost Effective Guns — And Fixes

Fortunately, both common problems have cost-effective solutions. Numrich Arms carries plenty of parts for old H&Rs, including modern replacement trigger-return springs. My cost, delivered, was less than $10. The primer-grabbing, action-jamming dent in my recoil shield required some thought and minor metal working, but no capital outlay. During the repair process, I gained some insight, and a greater level of respect, for the production practices H&R used to make these guns. The company provided solid quality for the money.

The American Double Action pistols were designed for economy and efficiency of manufacture. Their one-piece solid frames were cast from malleable iron, with the interior cavities already in place. There are only two screws in the whole gun: One holds on the grips and the other provides the pivot point for the hammer. The barrel is threaded into the frame, but everything else is pinned in.

## Preparation

These guns don't have a lot of parts, but try not to make the project bigger than it needs to be by carelessly losing or breaking them. Prepare your

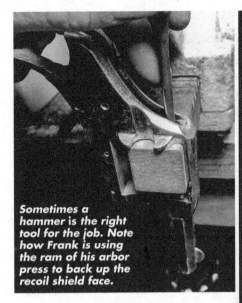

Sometimes a hammer is the right tool for the job. Note how Frank is using the ram of his arbor press to back up the recoil shield face.

While it still shows its age and hard-earned wisdom, the recoil shield is now fully functional again.

work area so little pieces don't roll off into oblivion.

To replace the trigger-return spring, only the trigger guard needs to come off and it's held on with just two pins directly above the front and rear legs of the guard. Since I also planned to repair the depression in the recoil shield around the firing pin hole, I needed to go further and empty the frame from the trigger backward. This included unpinning the trigger, hand and lifter assembly and removing the mainspring and hammer.

The grips are an old-fashioned Bakelite-type hard plastic that is brittle and prone to chipping. *Use great care in removing them.* They are held in the correct position by a pin through the bottom rear of the grip frame. This plastic doesn't flex, so gently wiggle them off the pin with a razor blade or some other thin, broad object. A screwdriver tip is too thick for this job. Once you have the grips off, put them out of harm's way so you don't drop and break them. If they are already broken, you can get new replacements from Vintage Gun Grips for less than $20 plus shipping. They have a vast mold collection and are an excellent resource for rare grips.

## Pin Removal

If the pin heads aren't too heavily burred over, you can get them out easily. Prep them with a drop of penetrating oil and let it work its way in for half an hour before you start. Support the backside of the frame with some non-finish marring material (like the cover of my journal in this case), tap the pins flush against the frame with a brass drift and then drive them all the way out with a 1/16" punch. You can make an expedient brass drift by slipping a spent .22 LR casing over the tip of a standard carpentry flat-point nail punch.

Anchor the trigger guard by partially setting the pins, then drive them all the way into position.

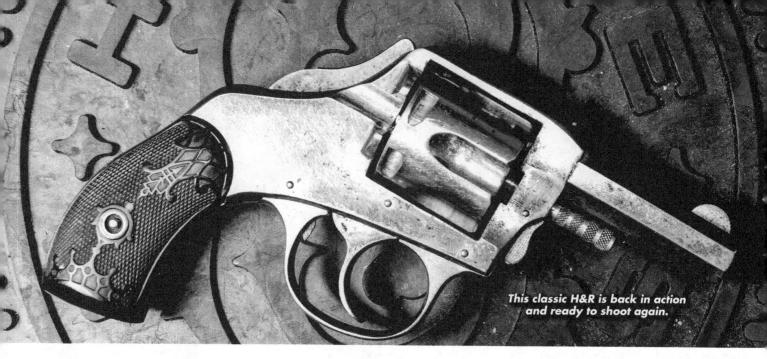

*This classic H&R is back in action and ready to shoot again.*

The pins are straight, not tapered, so they can go in and out in either direction. Tap in the side that looks like it's small enough to pass through the hole without swaging. The iron is soft, and the pins are tiny, so they should yield with light hammer taps. Lay the pins aside so you know which one went where. Keep track of the left and right ends by making a pen mark on the right side of each pin and tape them to a piece of paper with a notation showing the proper hole.

With the front and rear retaining pins out, the trigger guard will drop from its milled slot on the bottom of the frame. The sear and tiny sear coil spring beneath it in the rear leg can fall free. The broken flat trigger-return spring and the tiny cylinder pin latch coil spring in the front of the trigger guard slot may also fall out. If those tiny coil springs don't fall out, take them out immediately so they don't get lost.

Save the broken trigger-return spring! Clean off the two halves and use some super glue to restore it to its original form so it can serve as a model for forming the replacement part. I needed a magnifying glass to get the edges of the break squared.

## Adjusting The New Spring

Comparing the new wire trigger-return spring to the original flat spring, you'll notice the wire spring looks too big to fit. That's because it is. As delivered, it's too tall and too long, so don't try to force it. Compare it to your glued-up original spring and make the adjustment to overall height at the bend and the length of the legs. I squeezed the height of the bend down with a punch as a mandrel and a pair of vice grips. Naturally, this collapsed the feet of the legs of spring too, rendering it a lot less "springy." While I had it in the vice grip jaws, I used pliers to flex the legs up evenly and restore their range of travel. You might have to do this

a couple times until you get the overall height of the spring low enough to install the trigger guard.

Once you have the right spring height, refer again to the original spring and trim the legs of the wire spring to the same length. The ends of the legs are supposed to sit directly on top of the sharp leading edge of the trigger. You can fit the spring in with the legs too long, but if they extend too far over the sharp edge, they'll lever upward off it when the trigger is pulled and jam its rearward motion. Trim with side cutters and then smooth the ends off with a Swiss file so they don't abrade the trigger — the spring is harder metal than the trigger. The forward trigger guard retaining pin hole proved a good reference point for determining the correct spring length. When the bend of the spring came up to the near edge of the front trigger guard pin hole, with its legs sitting on the trigger's leading edge, function was good. Get there and you're ready to put it back together.

## Reassembly

To prepare the frame and trigger guard for reassembly, start by reinstalling the tiny coil springs in their bores. I put a little grease in the hole to hold them in place better. The sear at the rear leg of the trigger guard is held in by the rear pin, so you need to make a slave pin to hold it in place temporarily. My slave pin was the point of a small finishing nail filed smooth so it wouldn't drag in the hole. Finally, pre-insert the tips of your pins in their respective frame holes.

Now here's the tricky part that's easier with an assistant third hand. While holding the frame vertical, place the trigger-return spring in the frame with its legs on the trigger's leading edge, and then press the trigger guard and sear assembly straight down into position. When it seats in the frame slot,

try to push the pins in enough to engage its holes and keep it from popping out.

Then you can turn the gun on its side and tap the pins in until they are fully through the frame. The ends of the pins will stick out a little on each side of the frame. Use pliers to reinstall the mainspring — rounded end under the ledge on the bottom of the hammer — and test the trigger pull. If you adjusted the spring correctly, the trigger should return forward smartly after the hammer falls.

## Repairing The Recoil Shield

As my gun needed further disassembly to fix the dent in the recoil shield, there was no point in putting it all back together just yet. I needed to remove the trigger/hand/lifter assembly and hammer from the frame so I could use punches to drive out the dent from inside the firing-pin hole.

The hammer/hand/lifter assembly is held in by the same pin it pivots on. Remove it by driving out the pin and slipping a punch or some other slender object — like a straightened paper clip — behind the assembly to depress the lifter and hand spring and unhook the lifter from the notch on the hammer. Then you can pull the whole assembly out complete. Getting the hammer out requires removing its pivot screw.

Old screws can be a challenge to get out. Penetrating oil helps, but you'll need a quality gunsmith screwdriver set with hollow ground bits of varying sizes to remove tight screws without damage. The Real Avid Smart Drive 90 set has nine widths of bits, and all the Torx and metric and standard hex bits you're likely to ever need. It might seem like a lot, *but perfect fit is critical.* You want to use the bit that will transfer the most turning force to the screw slot by selecting one that fits tightly and spans as much of the slot as possible. You might break off a screw head with a gunsmith screwdriver, but you won't "bowtie" the screw slot. I got the screw out with no damage at all.

## Hammer Time

With the hammer out of the way, and a heavy square steel bar (the ram of my tipped over arbor press) backing up the face of the recoil shield as an anvil, I could control the direction and isolate the force of my punch blows directly to the back of the dent without stressing and bending another part of the frame. These frames are thin and delicate in the recoil shield area where the cylinder-pin hole and hand go.

I started with a round-tip roll-pin punch to ease out the center, and deepest part of the dent first. I was concerned starting with a flat punch might compress the metal into the firing-pin hole instead of the dent. Two light blows and I switched to a flat-nosed punch for the full diameter of the firing-pin recess. Two more light blows and the dent was gone.

Recalling the seemingly excessive gap between the rear of the cylinder and the recoil shield, I gave it one more tap to extend the dent just slightly outward. I

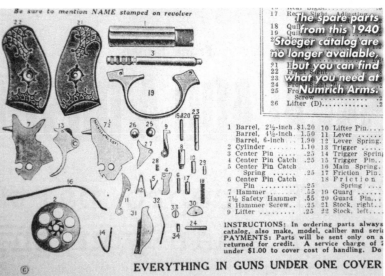

Be sure to mention NAME stamped on revolver

The spare parts from this 1940 Stoeger catalog are no longer available, but you can find what you need at Numrich Arms.

| 1 | Barrel, 2½-inch ..$1.20 | 10 | Lifter Pin.... |
| | Barrel, 4½-inch . 1.50 | 11 | Lever ...... |
| | Barrel, 6-inch .. 1.90 | 12 | Lever Spring. |
| 2 | Cylinder ...... 1.10 | 13 | Trigger ..... |
| 3 | Center Pin ..... .25 | 14 | Trigger Sprin |
| 4 | Center Pin Catch .25 | 15 | Trigger Pin.. |
| 5 | Center Pin Catch | 16 | Main Spring. |
| | Spring ...... .25 | 17 | Friction Pin. |
| 6 | Center Pin Catch | 18 | Friction |
| | Pin .......... .25 | | Spring ... |
| 7 | Hammer ....... .55 | 19 | Guard ...... |
| 7½ | Safety Hammer .55 | 20 | Guard Pin... |
| 8 | Hammer Screw.. .25 | 21 | Stock, right.. |
| 9 | Lifter ......... .25 | 22 | Stock, left... |

INSTRUCTIONS: In ordering parts always catalog, also make, model, caliber and seri PAYMENTS: Parts will be sent only on a returned for credit. A service charge of 3 under $1.00 to cover cost of handling. Do

EVERYTHING IN GUNS UNDER ONE COVER

did all this cold with light hammer strikes. I cleaned and greased the inside of the frame and reinstalled the hammer to check the firing pin clearance through the hole. To my delight, it swung back and forth through the hole with no frame contact.

Before reinstalling the trigger/ hand/lifter assembly, clean and grease it and check if the hand spring is correctly positioned.

The hand is attached to its spring, but not to the trigger. If it falls off during removal, as it is apt to do, you have to

ensure you position the horizontal leg of the hand spring so it exerts pressure on the lifter and pushes it rearward toward the hammer. That spring keeps the lifter in contact with the hammer so it can lift it during the double-action trigger pull. When installing the trigger/hand/lifter assembly, you must depress the lifter slightly (use the bent paper clip again) so it can get into its notch in the hammer. Otherwise you can't insert the assembly deep enough to be pinned in place.

With both repairs complete, this pistol is fully shootable again — at least until something else breaks. Eventually I'll be writing another DIY repair story, and I'm fine with that. I don't let it frustrate me, and neither should you. Learning how to fix them is part of the experience of shooting vintage guns. When you get down to it, no machines that old owe any of us 21st century people a thing.

*For more info: www.gunpartscorp.com, www.realavid.com, www.vintagegungrips.com*

Frank Jardim

# ARISAKA! ADD A DUST COVER

## Fitting repro parts is easier than you think.

I've had a Japanese World War II Type 38 training rifle patiently leaning in the corner of my office for the past decade. While browsing Arisaka parts at Sarco, I realized it was time to finish the incomplete.

These interesting trainers were designed to fire blanks, so they show variation in their manufacture and overall appearance. Some, like mine, are virtual clones of the standard service rifle. Other makers clearly took a more liberal approach to the specifications. Restoring them can be challenging because none appear to use standard military parts.

Sarco's reproduction Type 38 dust cover is a high-quality part, but due to variances in training rifles, you still may need to custom fit it.

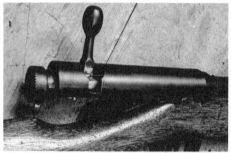

The correctly fitted cover lays on top of, and moves parallel to, the bolt body.

Once the top slot fits the bolt boss, you can install the bolt and dust cover into the receiver to check the fit of the lower slot. Frank needed to remove 0.025" from the front edge.

A perfect fit in less than 10 minutes: The bolt and cover slide smoothly together with no binding.

The cover's upper slot needs to be enlarged slightly to fit over the bolt handle boss.

Some, like mine, are virtual clones of the standard service rifle. Other makers clearly took a more liberal approach to the specifications. Restoring them can be challenging because none appear to use standard military parts.

They're also not particularly valuable so you can often find them in the $100 to $150 range. Original Arisaka parts are getting pricey so it doesn't make sense to use too many to restore a training gun selling for a third of the price of a real rifle. Reproduction parts are a better idea, and Sarco's $20 reproduction dust cover was a perfect investment to install on my $80 trainer.

Even on a stock military gun, you should expect reproduction parts to require some fitting. On a trainer, you might have to do more. My reproduction cover mated to the receiver slots perfectly, but I did have to adjust the bolt handle slot.

## Check The Fit

To install a dust cover, first remove the rifle bolt from the receiver. Then slip the bolt handle through the hole in the cover. Supporting the cover by gripping the bolt handle, align the folded top and bottom edges of the cover in the upper and lower slots along the length of the receiver — the bottom one is covered by the stock. Now push it forward until you can fit the front of the bolt back into the receiver. Once the bolt is re-engaged in the receiver, the whole assembly should slide smoothly forward, and the bolt handle should swing down fully to lock up the action.

## Dust Cover Slot Fitting

The most common fitting issue is the size of the slot in the dust cover where the square bolt handle boss moves up and down when the action is opened and closed. In this case, the slot was about 0.015" narrower than the bolt handle boss. This prevented the cover from laying parallel to the bolt body. When you push the bolt forward, the cover binds after a couple inches of travel.

To fix this, take a fine mill bastard file and shave the front edge of the upper slot in the cover. You might be able to shave a little off the back side too, but the reinforcing lug riveted there probably won't allow much room. Test fit the bolt boss after every few file strokes until it's an easy sliding fit. Don't mess with the lower part of the slot just yet.

## Bolt Operation Fitting

The next step is to install the bolt and cover and evaluate how much metal needs to be shaved off the dust cover's lower slot to allow the bolt to fully close. Once installed, it was obvious a lot more metal needed to be shaved off the front edge because the front of the bolt handle boss hung up solidly on front edge of the lower slot.

Removing the bolt and cover several times for filing and test fitting, I ultimately shaved off about 0.025" before the bolt handle boss slipped smoothly through the lower dust cover slot and into battery. I actually removed much less metal than I initially thought necessary.

The lesson here is: When you're trying to fit a part, test the fit more often than you think you should. It's easier to take metal away than it is to add it.

Considering the variance in trainer rifle specifications, my reproduction part fitting job was easy. Just don't be surprised if you have to break out the files with your project.

*For more info:*
*www.sarcoinc.com,*
*Ph: (610) 250-3960*

You'll also want to measure the bolt.

Measure the slot to see how much metal to remove. It shouldn't require much.

Hold the file square with the slot and be careful not to cut into the top flat of the slot with the narrow edge of the file. Be sure to check the fit often!

**Greg Derr**

# LOCTITE: BY THE NUMBERS

## More than just thread-lockers.

Loctite is an often-used adhesive in the gunsmith trade. It can secure threads to a variety of degree of permanence. Selecting the formula working best for your application can be critical. A sight adjustment going awry during a match is one thing. But an essential pin holding a trigger in place failing during a defensive shooting could be life-threatening. Assuring you're using the right "locking" product could honestly be the difference between life and death.

Most often, Loctite or a similar product is used to set a screw in position after an adjustment or installation is made. In part like a sight or trigger mechanism it prevents a screw or pin from moving during vibration and stress caused by shooting and running the action.

Even lowly grip screws prone to backing out can benefit from one of the low-adhesion thread lockers, like #222 "Purple" Loctite. It will hold the screw in place easily in this situation, yet will release with a bit of torque from a screwdriver.

### Color Meanings

I like to break it down into colors, since different Loctite products are color-coded. For instance, as we said, "Purple" (#222) is low strength and can also be used on metals like aluminum or brass. It's handy for eyeglass screws, sights, wristwatches and any light-duty screw less than 1/4" in diameter.

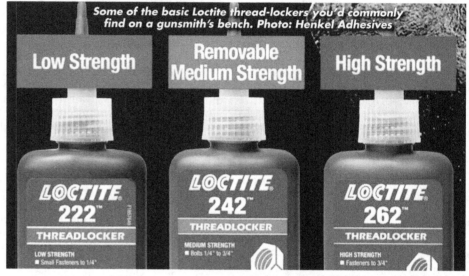
Some of the basic Loctite thread-lockers you'd commonly find on a gunsmith's bench. Photo: Henkel Adhesives

**Low Strength** — **LOCTITE 222™ THREADLOCKER** LOW STRENGTH ■ Small Fasteners to 1/4"

**Removable Medium Strength** — **LOCTITE 242™ THREADLOCKER** MEDIUM STRENGTH ■ Bolts 1/4" to 3/4"

**High Strength** — **LOCTITE 262™ THREADLOCKER** HIGH STRENGTH ■ Fasteners to 3/4"

Loctite #242 or "Blue" comes in many forms (stick and tape too) but gunsmiths will likely use the liquid form. Its "medium" strength means it's great for stock bolts, sights, side-plate screws or anywhere you want something to stay put. It can be removed fairly easily by the tool that tightened it to begin with.

Loctite #277 or "Red" is higher strength. Think trigger over-travel screws, action parts needing to be secured in place once set or a cylinder screw. Some like to use it on 1911 grip bushings to keep them from turning out when the grip screws are removed.

### Tips

To ensure Loctite really works I first degrease the parts to be set. A squirt of break cleaner to clean the parts, then I use a small torch or a butane BBQ lighter to sweat off any cleaner. The Loctite should be used sparingly, just a dab is enough. They even offer a gel stick applicator which won't spill. Now screw the parts together with light tension, the adhesive will work without over tightening.

In the event you want to remove a screw I use the same method for most screws, with or without Loctite. Using the proper sized "gunsmith" screwdriver, Allen key or Torx bit, try to lightly turn the screw. If I feel resistance, I add a little

*Loctite #243 is a bit "brawnier" than standard blue #242 and is also more oil resistant. This one is marked in German because it was bought online from Europe! But the number is always the same.*

muscle. But if it still won't move I apply heat to the screw.

You can use either a small handheld butane torch or a soldering iron placed on the screw head. The heat will soften the Loctite, allowing it to break free without damaging the head. The key here is feeling the screw slowly break free and not buggering the fastener.

When in doubt, a drop of Loctite will never hurt and might just keep a gun running. If you're a gunsmith, this also translates into a happy customer!

*For more info:*
*www.henkel-adhesives.com*

**Various Loctite products Greg keeps handy on his bench. Each one does a specific job so knowing their features helps you to select the correct product. The Henkel website explains them all clearly.**

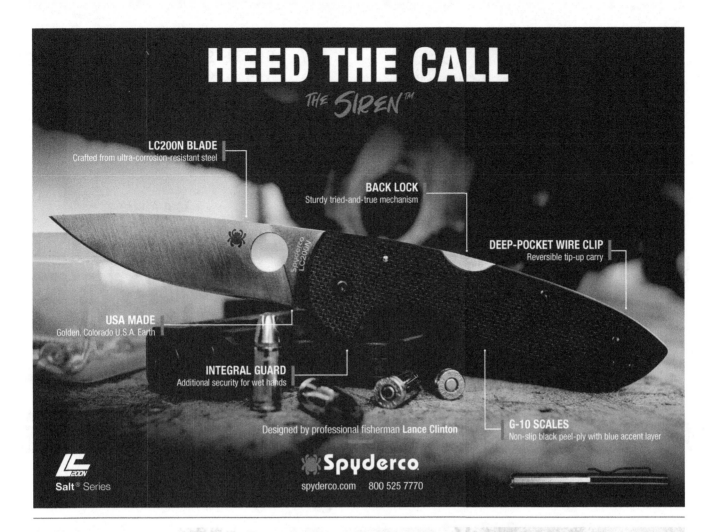

I've enjoyed the matte finish on the top of the slide — no glare when sighting in bright conditions.

"A man's got to know his limitations."

*Detective Harry Callahan,* Magnum Force

**Tom McHale**

# HOW I DESTROYED — AND RESURRECTED — A WALTHER PPK/S

## And things you shouldn't do — ever ...

This now carry-ready pistol pairs nicely with a leather DeSantis IWB holster.

One benefit of the professional rework by Cylinder & Slide is this old PPK/S feeds modern ammunition, like this Black Hills HoneyBadger, flawlessly.

I'm pretty sure Dirty Harry delivered a subtle message to aspiring hobby gunsmiths. It's good advice because sometimes you gain the most valuable experience by learning what *not* to do. If the cost of such a life lesson is a butchered gun and subsequent "can you fix this" visit to a competent gunsmith, chalk it up to education expense.

Let's rewind to a time long ago and not so far away, when I knew even less than I do now. I'll just say my hubris was only surpassed by my ignorance and leave it at that. I urge you to remember there may have been a time when you did something equally stupid, so please be gentle — I'm baring my soul in the interest of higher learning.

As a freshly minted gun owner, I got a bug up my butt to buy an old Walther. Money was tight, so I was looking for deals on the auction boards. One caught my eye: "Gunsmith Special! Interarms Walther PPK/S!" It arrived rough. I figured it had been through a couple of wars and at least three seasons of "Desperate Housewives of Possum Kingdom, S.C." It lacked grips, ejected magazines randomly when firing and only cocked the hammer when cycling on odd-num-

bered days. The finish resembled the interior of a construction dumpster.

### Now What?

All of those seemed surmountable problems to an expert like me with precisely zero experience working on guns. I bought some wood grips and new magazines, looked for anything broken, reassembled the pistol and took it to the range for reliability testing. I wanted to carry this 007 classic, so I had to make sure it fed self-defense ammo without fail. In case you didn't know, that stuff is expensive. A few magazines in, I figured out this pistol couldn't feed three rounds in a row.

No worries. Maybe it was just "ammo sensitive" being an old gun and all. Fast forward to another expensive trip to the gun store and a return to the range with different, although equally abusive on the wallet ammo. The result? Same problem. So, I tried again. And again. Not only did I prove the definition of insanity, retrying the same failed strategy hoping for a different outcome, I burned through second and third mortgages with my ammo bills.

Finally, I got smart and took it to a gunsmith. Sounding supremely confident to a noob like me, the counterman

The original ad photo, in all its un-retouched glory. Tom wanted you to see the "gunsmith special" as he saw it advertised.

Note the muzzle crown. It's gotten some wear and tear in the 15 years since the custom work, but this project was always intended to create a working gun, not a safe queen.

The beautifully radiused trigger made all the difference on this pistol. It now shoots like a finely tuned revolver in DA mode.

informed me, "These old Walthers are finicky about the magazine lip profile. We see it all the time." After making some adjustments, he returned the gun. Still no love. I'll spare the details, but I made repeat visits to this local 'smith, and many others, and received nothing but a bucket of fail for my efforts. With the benefit of hindsight, I now see those local "gunsmiths" were guys just like me who thought they knew more than their experience supported.

## Power Tools

Enter the Dremel. Having bought and adjusted somewhere north of 13,512 Walther magazines to no avail, I was now confident the problem emanated from the feed ramp. I'd been reading about the importance of "polished feed ramps" so I buffed the snot out of this one using a felt Dremel bit and some grocery store metal polish. While it looked great, the pistol still shot with the same success rate as monkeys in a Food Network baking competition.

No worries.

I surmised I needed to bevel the feed ramp just a hair to ease feeding of modern hollowpoint bullets. The fact the pistol didn't even feed Cor-Bon Pow'R Ball ammo, which not only have a round nose, but a slick polymer one, eluded my logic.

I broke out the Dremel, and I might have used, let's just say, "aggressive" bits on the feed ramp. And I learned. If you practice dry-firing at home, you know not to keep the firearm and ammo in the same room. For safety. There's a lesser known apothegm, and I'm taking full credit for it. *Don't allow those orange and green Dremel bits having the texture of bricks and cinder blocks in the same county as your firearms.* You're welcome.

If you want to use a Dremel tool, knock yourself out. Just make sure the bit has the letters F, E, L and T in its name. Needless to say, the results were

about as good as the first iteration of the Affordable Healthcare Act website.

So, let's recap. I didn't learn the importance of knowing my limitations after spending eight or 10 figures on premium ammo for testing, working through every crank gunsmith in town, depleting the national Walther PPK/S magazine supply, polishing like no one's business and finally, performing steel liposuction. Yes, I can be stubborn occasionally. It was time to suck up my pride and call for help — professional help.

## The Pros

Enter the Cylinder & Slide shop. I'd seen their ads and read volumes about their pistol artistry for years in *American Handgunner*. There were two roadblocks to seeking help. The first was pride. I overcame that easily enough since I was mailing the gun to them. I didn't have to endure a face-to-face walk of shame with my bag-o-parts. While I didn't exactly lie outright, I might have implied the guy I bought this pistol from "sure messed it up."

The second was cost. The pistol in question was worth maybe a couple hundred bucks at the time — before I started "improvements." From a resale perspective, doing a custom job didn't make fiscal sense. I rationalized by telling myself I would make this a personal keeper — a cool and historical gun finely tuned for everyday use with modern ammunition while looking like a million bucks.

The pros at Cylinder & Slide opened my eyes, not only to what was required to fix this little pistol, but to possibilities to make it better. See what happens when you listen to the experts?

Before quality custom work, my not-very-professionally installed wooden grips had a tendency to move around with each shot because there's a single grip screw passing through the frame holding both panels in place by friction

alone. A glass bedding job on the back of each panel to match the steel cutouts solved the slipping problem once and for all. Good idea guys!

As for metal work, they, umm, repaired the damage "some guy" did to the feed ramp. It's now slick, gouge-free, feeding any .380 ACP ammo I care to supply — without fail ever. That's valuable, but the nifty work was apparent in the extras my Cylinder & Slide consultant recommended. Note the radius work on the trigger face. Sure, this is a preference decision, but that polished and rounded trigger face changes the feel of the double-action press dramatically. It now operates more like a finely tuned revolver.

## Live And Learn ...

A few other improvements rounded out this custom job. The gun gurus at C&S suggested, and received my enthusiastic approval for, a re-bluing job, so the frame and slab sides of the slide are mirror finished. The curved sections of the slide now sport a matte surface, reducing glare. Since the gun was broken down for all the other work, I decided to have C&S polish all internal surfaces. Last, but not least, I had the barrel re-crowned with an 11-degree bevel because part of its "gunsmith special" heritage was a beat-up muzzle.

So, what does all this have to do with DIY gunsmithing? Simple. Good judgment comes from experience, and a lot of that comes from bad judgment. If you can minimize the cost of bad judgment by knowing your limitations, all the better.

Enjoy your DIY gunsmithing endeavors, just proceed with caution. If you're embarking on a learning journey, start with the basics. There are several beginner-friendly DIYs in this issue. Those projects are a great place to start! 🔫

*For more info:*
*www.cylinder-slide.com,*
*Ph: (800) 448-1713*

**David Freeman**

# GUNSMITHING WITH A DREMEL?

## Disaster in the making? Not if you use it right.

I read on an internet forum the three worst enemies of guns were rust, politicians and the Dremel tool. Since it was on the internet it has to be true, right? Sure, it was meant as a joke, but there is some truth to it. We get impatient at times, and therein lies the temptation to use a tool capable of speeding up whatever job we're trying to get done. My dad used to tell me speed was the enemy of craftsmanship. He said it to me often because I've always been impatient when it comes to getting a job done.

*Different-sized collets are used with certain accessories.*

### A Versatile Tool

Since the Dremel is so versatile and inexpensive, it seems as universal in a tool repertoire as a set of sockets or drill bits. Somehow, I've wound up with two of them and so many accessories I use one of those plastic tubs from Walmart to store them.

One reason I get in trouble with the Dremel is I'm not always sure what accessory to use for what job. Something I have learned is no matter what the accessory, you've got to be careful when you use it. And I do mean careful because that little speed demon can eat away metal, plastic or wood faster than the Blue Angels can sneak up behind you at an airshow.

The accessories come in so many shapes and sizes I found myself looking online for a *Dremel Tool For Dummies* book but, alas, didn't find one. I did find a handy chart on Dremel's website (www.

dremel.com) listing all the accessories and their usage. The site also has lots of "How-To" videos. Sadly, none of them are related to guns.

### Understanding Accessories

A key to working with a Dremel is to understand collets and mandrels. Collets come in four sizes — 1/8", 3/32", 1/32" and 1/16". The 1/8" collet ships with all the Dremel tools, but you can get a set with all four sizes. The purpose of the collet is to tighten around the shaft of whatever accessory you're using. One situation where you're likely to need

*David uses two Dremels in his gunsmithing projects. The cordless 7300 is handy for quick touchups, while the multispeed 3000 is good for cutting and other projects requiring more speed.*

There seems to be no end to accessories for the Dremel, some universal and some packaged by project type such as cutting, polishing, sanding, etc.

The EZ Lock Mandrel makes changing accessories quick and easy.

David used these tools to clean up a bad weld on one of his shotguns.

different collets is when using a drill — those often have smaller diameter shafts.

Mandrels are the shafts for various accessories, and they come in a variety of sizes and types. I particularly like the EZ Lock Mandrel you can use with sawing and sanding discs. The screw mandrel is designed for use with felt polishing tips and discs that wear out fast and need to be changed often. Then there are the drum mandrels for sanding bands.

Most of the accessories for a Dremel tool are designed to remove material. This is, as I said before, where you can get into trouble. Say you want to remove just a little material, such as a spot of rust, or maybe you're trying to strip a gun for re-bluing and some stubborn blue material from the old job just won't come off. The temptation to use the Dremel is great, but from experience I can tell you once you get the little devil turning and touch it to your sacred firearm — with certain accessories — it will immediately take off more than you intended. The Dremel takes away, but it never gives back.

## Gunsmithing In Action

There are some gunsmithing tasks for which no tool is better. An example from my experience involves a JW-2000 Chinese-made, double-barrel shotgun commonly called a coach gun. This shotgun was a cheapy that came through my store some years ago. Although the gun seemed to be substantially made, one part of it was exhibiting horrible workmanship — so bad we didn't put the gun in inventory. Instead, I took it home with the idea of cleaning it up someday.

The rib was bead welded, or more likely soldered, with no thought of cosmetic appeal. All along the rib there was excess beading in some places and gaps in others. I put a screwdriver in one gap and pried, and soon I was able to pull off the entire rib. None of the weld stuck to the barrels. As it turned out, it was an aluminum rib attached to steel barrels.

I took my time trimming the edges of the rib, even cutting and filing the weld off in places. When I had it in presentable condition, I attached it to the barrels using J-B Weld. Before the J-B Weld compound hardened, I used a wet cloth to wipe down the joints and smooth them as best I could, but there was still some beading. Once hardened, I used a pointed aluminum oxide abrasive wheel on my Dremel to grind off the high beads. A bit of judicious touch-up with a Dremel sanding disc made it presentable. I used Birchwood Casey Blue & Rust Remover to strip the entire barrel and re-blued it with Birchwood Casey Super Blue.

Cutting a wooden plug to shape and sanding it to blend in with the stock is a great example of the Dremel's use on a gunsmithing project.

Don't like the tang on the front of your pistol's trigger guard? Some shooters have been known to cut it off with a Dremel using a cutting disc.

The Dremel rotary sanding accessory can be used to increase the trigger guard undercut on GLOCKs and other polymer pistols.

Another project where the Dremel excelled involved two old shotguns I restored. Both had rusted barrels and actions, and the stocks were cracked with chunks of wood missing. I used the Dremel for squaring off the broken edges of the stocks and for cutting wooden plugs to replace the broken areas. Then I used it for sanding after gluing the wood plugs and filling around them with plastic wood.

The Dremel's wire brush was perfect for cleaning rust off some hard-to-get-to action parts. I did not use it on the barrel or action to speed up the removal of rust and old bluing (what little there was) because I didn't want to scar it. After trimming the Pachmayr Grind-to-Fit Recoil Pads I added to the shotguns with my grinder. I used an aluminum oxide grinding disc on the Dremel to do the final dressing.

## Recovering From An Oops!

No Dremel article would be complete without mentioning a screw up — and how to recover from a big mistake. When Remington issued the R1 1911s, they were beautiful. I started using a Commander-sized R1 as a daily carry gun. It wasn't long before the bluing wore thin. Every place where it contacted my leather holster showed bare metal. I tried something I'd never done before and used DuraCoat DuraBlue Spray-on Bluing to make it beautiful again. I loved how the results looked initially, but it wasn't long before it began to chip. Yea, I know I'm hard on guns.

Here's where the Dremel and I screwed up. I determined to totally strip the R1 and blue it again with Birchwood Casey Super Blue. I treated it with Blue & Rust Remover and started working with steel wool, but there were a few spots I couldn't strip to bare metal.

I figured a quick touch with a Dremel sanding disc would do the trick. It was just a touch, but it gouged my slide with some ugly pitting. I tried cleaning up those scratches with Dremel polishing pads and the included compound. I tried polishing with Flitz and I tried it with Mothers, both commonly used to polish guns.

After hours and hours of sanding with 600-grit sandpaper, I was almost, but not quite, back to a smooth, pit-free slide. I didn't get the scratches fully removed until I tried a product called Rejuvenate Stainless Steel Scratch Eraser. It's designed for kitchen appliances, but did a good job on my gun.

One brief touch with the wrong accessory on my Dremel caused me a lot of extra work.

## What Else Can You Do With A Dremel?

You can polish stainless steel. In fact, you can do a bang-up beautiful job of

This Remington R1 slide shows an example of damage caused by using a Dremel incorrectly or with the wrong accessory.

A Dremel kit may be just the thing for your gunsmithing projects.

If you intend to polish some action parts such as feed ramps, seers, etc., you might consider mounting your Dremel in a vise and using it more like a rotary wheel than a hand tool.

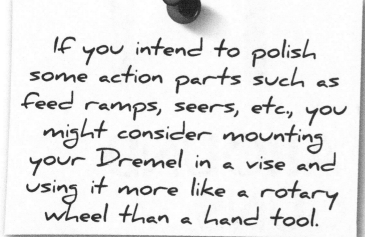

Lots of hand sanding and this Rejuvenate Stainless Steel Scratch Eraser Kit helped David recover from damage he did to his Remington R1 slide using his Dremel incorrectly.

polishing if you're careful. Use Dremel's polishing compound, Flitz or Mothers. Just start with a very small section of the gun, maybe one normally covered by a grip panel, until you get the hang of it. Dremel has polishing pads of various sizes, and you can buy add-on kits just for polishing so you don't run out of pads.

If you intend to polish some action parts such as feed ramps, seers, etc., you might consider mounting your Dremel in a vise and using it more like a rotary wheel than a hand tool. This will allow you to be more judicious with how much contact the part is making to the tool.

The Dremel is also good for drilling small holes. If you're into fabricating at all, the Dremel's cutting discs are just the ticket. You can use them to cut metal to make small parts, or to cut out a slide for installing optics, even shorten a barrel. I do a lot of wood cutting with my Dremel for small jobs, including working on stocks as I described earlier.

If you want a smoother, more pronounced undercut on your GLOCK's trigger guard, you can make the change with careful use of a rotary sanding bit with your Dremel. Finish it off with emery cloth or 2,000-grit sandpaper. If you have an early Springfield XD or a CZ-P07 — or any polymer gun — with a tang on the bottom front of the trigger guard you don't want, use a cutting disc with the Dremel to cut it off. Then smooth it with sandpaper. These are easy adjustments if you've got a steady hand and don't go too fast.

Whatever you do, it's a good idea to practice first on junkers before messing up your valued firearms. It doesn't have to be a gun. Make an adjustable crescent wrench pretty. Customize a bayonet or machete. Get really good with the tool and understand what its numerous accessories will do for you before trying them on an expensive gun.

If you become proficient, maybe you can be the one to write the *Dremel Tool For Dummies* book.

*For more info:*
*www.dremel.com,*
*Ph: (800) 437-3635;*
*www.birchwoodcasey.com,*
*Ph: (877) 269-8490*

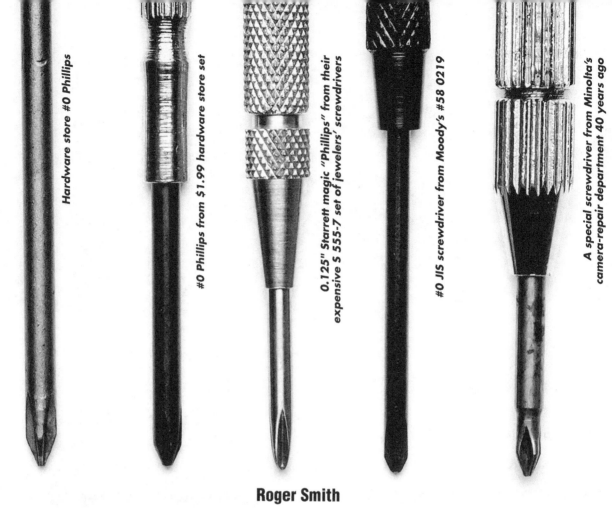

Hardware store #0 Phillips

#0 Phillips from $1.99 hardware store set

0.125" Starrett magic "Phillips" from their expensive S 555-7 set of jewelers' screwdrivers

#0 JIS screwdriver from Moody's #58 0219

A special screwdriver from Minolta's camera-repair department 40 years ago

**Roger Smith**

# TOOLING AROUND WITH GUNS

## Gunsmith tools you need to do quality work.

**Bunged-up screw heads on this poor old Marlin seriously devalued it. Roger bought it anyway. At least it shoots well.**

Editor Roy wrote a great article about repairing "Bunged-Up Screw Heads" (*The Insider, American Handgunner*, May/June 2017). Even better: Don't damage them in the first place. *Don't go near a gun with common household screwdrivers.* Those garage tools are wedge-shaped in two directions — when you look at them from the broad flat side, and also from the edge.

They're always a very poor fit, putting all the torque on the very top edge of the slot, and nothing any further down. Under pressure, the wedge shape forces the blade up and out, widening and burring the edges of the slot as it comes out. Worse is using one too small

for the slot to start. If you try to use one big enough to fill the slot of a screw head flush with the surface, the wedge shape at the sides frequently carves the edges of the hole from flat to a bevel.

Instead, use what we call hollow ground screwdrivers or screwdriver bits, which also have straight sides. Choose the correct thickness and it will fit the screw slot clear to the bottom, greatly reducing the risk of damage to the screw. Use one slightly less than full width, especially with oval head screws, because it's too easy for a bit to slide slightly in the slot as you twist it and gouge the edge of the screw hole.

Hardware store sets with handle and bits are better than nothing, but few of them are the correct size for guns unless

The takedown screw on this Marlin .22 has a bunged-up head and the screw hole on the left is chewed out around the edge from using common household screwdrivers.

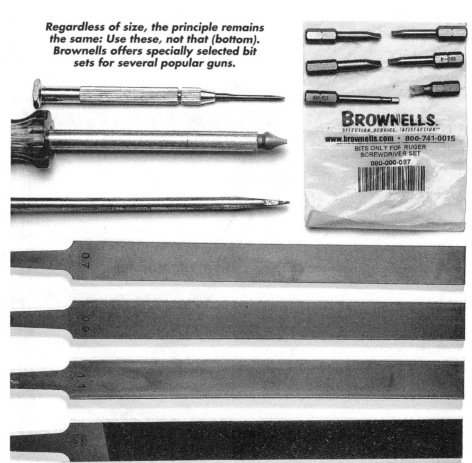

Regardless of size, the principle remains the same: Use these, not that (bottom). Brownells offers specially selected bit sets for several popular guns.

Screw-slotting or screw-head files (top three) by Friedrich Dick are thin to match small screw slots, to allow cutting the slot deeper, but not wider. They run nearly $40 each, but there's no substitute. Equaling files to square up the slot sides and base (bottom) come in sizes to match the slotting files.

you custom grind them with a small stone in your electric drill. Specialized gunsmithing sets are available all over the internet these days, from basic $20 sets on up. And up.

## Beyond Butched-Up Slotted Screws

Do yourself a big fat educational favor and spend $5 for the Brownells catalog. Because of space limitations, this article has to be an "Introduction to Gun Tools 101." The tool sections of the Brownells catalog will advance your education through Tools 102, 103 and beyond. One of the best things I have ever done screwdriver-wise was to supplement my basic B-Square set with specially selected bit sets for Marlin lever actions and for Ruger and Colt revolvers from Brownells. They offer other gun-specific sets as well.

## Another Phillips?

We all know about Phillips-head screws, right? You may never see one in a gun, but did you ever try to replace the battery in an Asian-made electronics gizmo? Did you destroy the cross-point head of the tiny screw and have to give up on it? Or strip out a small screw head on your Japanese motorcycle? That's because they're not Phillips-head screws, but rather a pattern called JIS, for Japanese Industrial Standard. JIS screwdrivers will work in Phillips heads, but not the other way around. I like the JIS drivers made in the USA by Moody.

## Needle Files Aren't All The Same

If a straight-slotted screw head is bunged up badly enough, it will probably need its slot cut deeper to be able to remove it with a proper bit. Regular needle files are usually too thick for gun screws. Don't try to do it with a hacksaw blade. You need special thin screw slotting, or screw-head files. They range in sizes from #1 at 0.012" to #11 at 0.043" thick. They run nearly $40 each and are fragile, but there is no suitable substitute.

They cut only on the narrow edge, so you can't accidentally widen the slot. You may need to follow up with an equally expensive same-sized equaling file to get nice straight sides and a flat

Top view of thin screw-head files, compared to a needle file (far right).

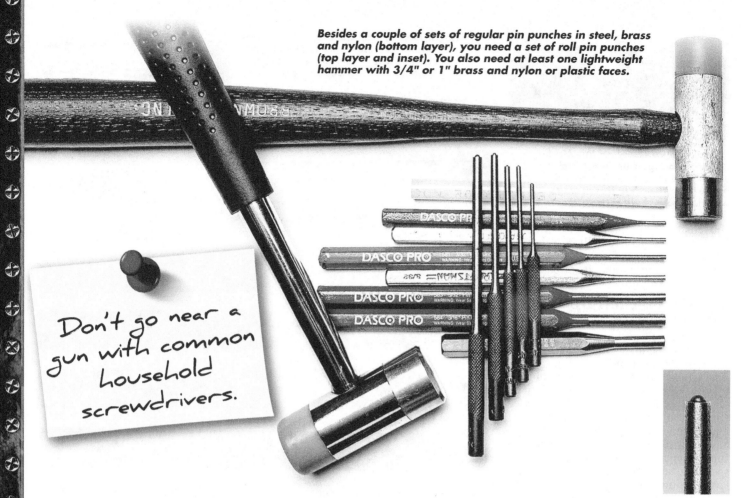

Besides a couple of sets of regular pin punches in steel, brass and nylon (bottom layer), you need a set of roll pin punches (top layer and inset). You also need at least one lightweight hammer with 3/4" or 1" brass and nylon or plastic faces.

*Don't go near a gun with common household screwdrivers.*

bottom. Don't mistakenly buy slitting files. They have a diamond-shaped profile and cut on all sides.

Flat, round and triangular needle files are darn near indispensable, but popularly priced sets give you no clue to the coarseness of their cut. They all seem to be made in China nowadays, including the pricey ($51 MSRP) Nicholson brand #42030 Hobby File Set. My very old, inexpensive set of Great Neck files made in Italy has given me many years of reliable service. Besides the Nicholsons, I bought brand new sets of Great Neck, K&S and Tekton just for this article. Beats me whose files are

the best nowadays; only time and accidental destructive testing will tell.

Standard length for needle files seems to be 5 1/2" and all brands seem to be about 0.050" thick. The proper names for flat files are: Equaling — cuts on all four sides; Hand — has one safe edge and pillar — with two safe edges. There are also sets of miniature needle files available, 4 1/2" long and 0.036" thick. The flat file in my mini set is a pillar file.

High-dollar needle files from Grobet, Vallorbe and Friedrich Dick come in a choice of cuts from coarser #0 to the fine #6 cut. Like connoisseurs everywhere, those who buy them usually say

they'll never go back. *Sigh* … someday, maybe …

## Punches And More Punches

Like screwdrivers, it's difficult to have too many pin punches in the sizes you use most often. You need at least two sets. Sometimes you need to keep a part aligned with two holes while you fiddle diddle with another piece. And when one bends or breaks, it's always when the stores are closed.

Use a punch one size smaller than the pin you're trying to drive. Spin the tips of one set of punches against some emery cloth or paper to slightly round off the sharp edge. This will help it slip into the hole instead of dinging the edge when the punch slips. If a steel punch slips while driving a pin into your gun, you'll wish you had some brass and nylon punches. Steel pin punches can also be used to peen or swage holes smaller on purpose. For roll pins, buy a set of special roll pin punches. If you use standard pin punches on roll pins, you deserve what's going to happen.

Brass and nylon punches are also great for drifting sights to avoid dinging the steel barrel, damaging the sight or enlarging a recalcitrant dovetail foot and binding it even tighter in the slot.

There is an amazing variety of specialized gunsmithing punches in the Brownells catalog, like the ones for SIGs, various special sight punches and

This pillar file has two cutting surfaces. It's great for corners where only one edge needs work.

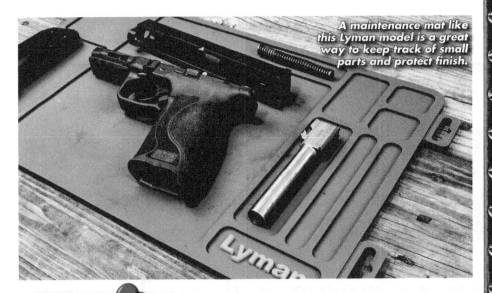

A maintenance mat like this Lyman model is a great way to keep track of small parts and protect finish.

*Buy the right ones for whatever your gun needs, or your buddies will call you Dumb Schmuck.*

those for domed pins in S&W revolvers. Don't make do. Buy the right ones for whatever your gun needs, or your buddies will call you Dumb Schmuck.

### Hammers And Patience

Don't be a cheapskate here. Leave the steel hammers alone, except for special circumstances. One miss with a steel hammer, and you'll be making a very long face. Double Dumb Schmuck.

Buy a small nylon or plastic and brass double-faced hammer from Brownells or Wheeler. The 1" diameter seems to be the most popular, but I also have the lighter 3/4" diameter and a bigger one as well. So many jobs need only a gentle tap. Start light and small, and if more force is needed, don't swing harder. You lose control that way. Increase the weight of the hammer as needed. Swing carefully with full control and let the hammer's weight do the work.

Use the right tools for the job, and you can proudly show off your work. Screw things up with improper tools, and you'll have to work hard to hide your sins from view. Money spent on proper tools is money well spent.

*For more info: www.safariland.com, www.brownells.com, www.dick.delenl, www.graceusatools.com, www.greatnecksaw.com, www.grobetusa.com, www.ksmetals.com, www.moodytools.com, www.nicholsontool.com, www.tekton.com, www.vallorbe.comlen, www.btibrands.com*

Nylon punches are handy for light tapping of parts and they won't harm metal. They do wear quickly, so buy a supply.

**David Freeman**

# GET THAT $50 BEATER BACK IN THE FIELD

## Bringing a pair of wall hanger discards back to life.

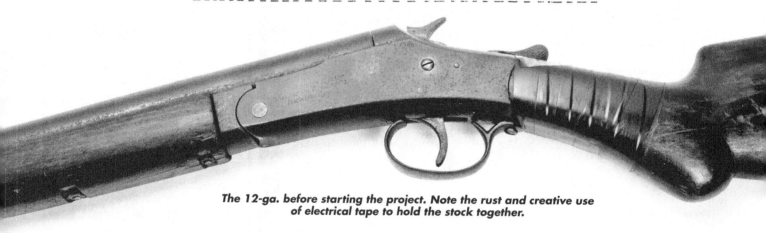

*The 12-ga. before starting the project. Note the rust and creative use of electrical tape to hold the stock together.*

**T**here are two of them — a .410 and a 12-gauge — so worn I don't even consider them real guns.

The .410 was my first gun, given to me by my father when I was seven. I knew nothing about it at the time except it had been my father's gun. I hunted squirrels with it until getting his Winchester Model 12 16-ga. when I was 11. The .410 was then relegated to a closet.

We discovered the 12-ga. at my grandfather's house after he passed away, many years after my dad gave me the .410. It was the same brand with some slight differences, but I always thought of them as father and son guns. Blue Book and other firearm guides indicate they're worth around $50, so I never paid them any attention.

I did take the .410 apart and completed a little sanding on the stock when I took a gunsmith course a few years back. I work with a bunch of guys who are always tinkering with guns, so I got an urge to do some DIY projects myself. The old Crescent shotguns were perfect for the task because they needed operational repair, metalwork and woodwork.

## Starting Point

The finish on both guns was brown patina mixed with rust. Someone had wrapped electrical tape around the stock where it joined the action on both guns. When I removed the tape, I discovered cracking and missing chunks on both stocks. On the 12-ga., the regular screws holding the forearm to the metal locking piece were gone. The holes had been bored out, wide flat notches cut from the wood and replacement bolts and nuts held the pieces together.

The actions were simple, flat mainspring affairs, but the firing pins were worn and the screw and two roll pins holding the .410 action parts together were missing. Numrich Gun Parts had a decent selection of parts for old Crescent firearms, but because there were no model numbers or serial numbers to determine a year of manufacture, getting the right parts was just a guessing game. Fortunately, none of these parts was expensive.

I got nearly everything I needed, though I did fabricate a pin for the trigger on one of them from a drill bit. I measured the barrel lengths — 30" for the 12-ga., and 26" for the .410. There were no markings on the barrels for choke, so I measured the bores and found the .410 to be Improved Cylinder and the 12-gauge Full Choke.

## Task At Hand

After complete disassembly, two separate areas needed work. On the metal, I needed to remove rust and redo bluing. The wood required patching and refinishing. I worked them in tandem since there was always some drying/curing time for the type of work I had to do in both areas.

I set out to strip all the metal using Birchwood Casey's Blue & Rust remover. The plan was to re-blue them using Birchwood Casey's Super Blue. Between the various steps of the bluing project, I turned my attention to the stocks.

The wood from both guns was soft and crumbly where it joined with the action, and each stock had chunks missing — evidence of oil from years of cleaning seeping

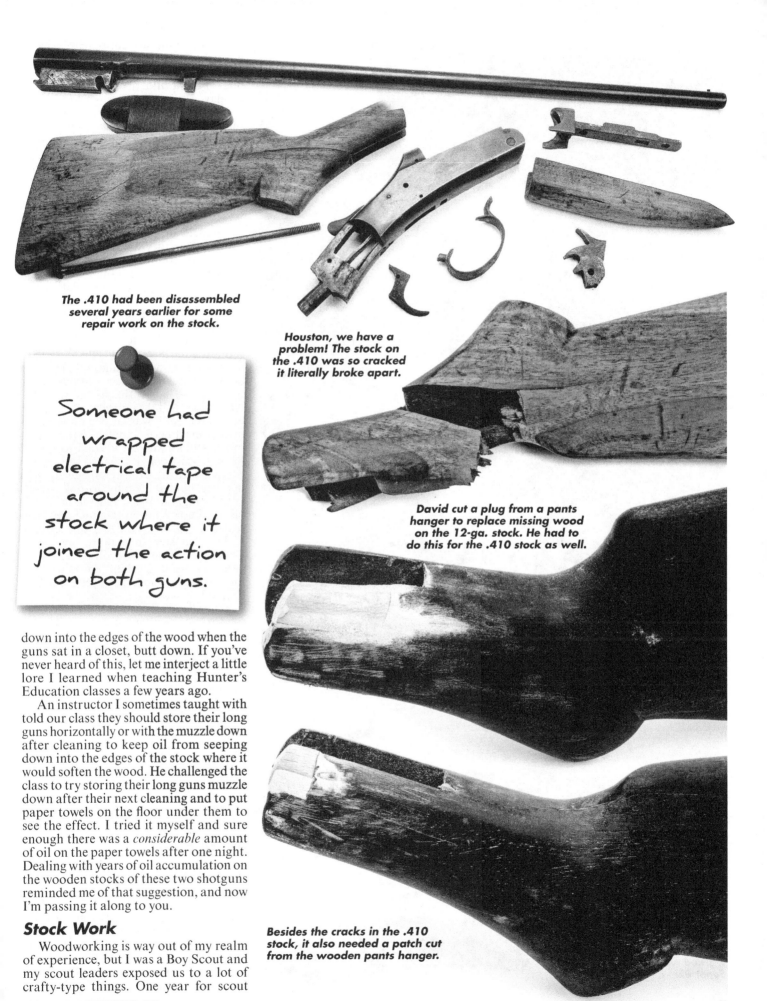

*The .410 had been disassembled several years earlier for some repair work on the stock.*

*Houston, we have a problem! The stock on the .410 was so cracked it literally broke apart.*

Someone had wrapped electrical tape around the stock where it joined the action on both guns.

*David cut a plug from a pants hanger to replace missing wood on the 12-ga. stock. He had to do this for the .410 stock as well.*

down into the edges of the wood when the guns sat in a closet, butt down. If you've never heard of this, let me interject a little lore I learned when teaching Hunter's Education classes a few years ago.

An instructor I sometimes taught with told our class they should store their long guns horizontally or with the muzzle down after cleaning to keep oil from seeping down into the edges of the stock where it would soften the wood. He challenged the class to try storing their long guns muzzle down after their next cleaning and to put paper towels on the floor under them to see the effect. I tried it myself and sure enough there was a *considerable* amount of oil on the paper towels after one night. Dealing with years of oil accumulation on the wooden stocks of these two shotguns reminded me of that suggestion, and now I'm passing it along to you.

## Stock Work

Woodworking is way out of my realm of experience, but I was a Boy Scout and my scout leaders exposed us to a lot of crafty-type things. One year for scout

*Besides the cracks in the .410 stock, it also needed a patch cut from the wooden pants hanger.*

David plugged the 12-ga. forearm holes to re-drill for standard screws.

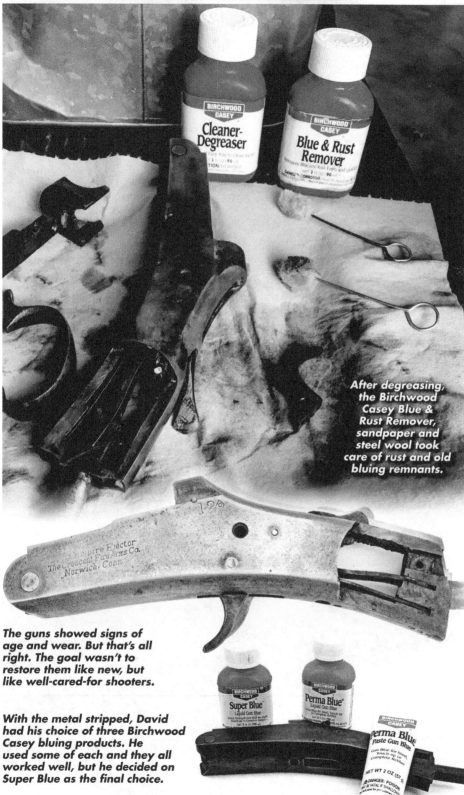

After degreasing, the Birchwood Casey Blue & Rust Remover, sandpaper and steel wool took care of rust and old bluing remnants.

The guns showed signs of age and wear. But that's all right. The goal wasn't to restore them like new, but like well-cared-for shooters.

With the metal stripped, David had his choice of three Birchwood Casey bluing products. He used some of each and they all worked well, but he decided on Super Blue as the final choice.

week we built an entire campsite in miniature for display in the window of a department store selling scouting supplies. I did a little of the carving for the display; I think just enough to earn the woodcarving merit badge, but that was the end of such experiences.

I determined to patch those wood stocks and make it look like they'd never had missing chunks. I started with some shims we had around the house for leveling furniture and such. They were pine, so they shaped easily. Elmer's Wood Glue held the plugs in place, and I patched around them with plastic wood. When they were dry, I sanded the patches smooth and stained them with Minwax penetrating stain.

They looked pretty good, but when I reassembled the guns, the plugs on both of them fell out. I admit I was disappointed and not sure where to begin again. Then it occurred to me the stocks were made from walnut, a hardwood. I located a strip of hardwood in the most unusual place, the floor of my closet. It was a wooden strip from a pants hanger that had come apart. Not only was it the correct thickness for my needs, but it was curved on the ends in an almost perfect match to the curves in my stocks where I needed to install the patches. I cut and shaped the needed patches with my Dremel tool, glued them in place, pinned them by drilling a small hole through the patch and into the stock, inserted a roll pin in the hole and then sealed it with glue. I did this for each gun.

The last step in making the stocks whole was to install recoil pads. I tried one from Numrich that indicated it was for a hammer model Crescent shotgun. It didn't fit.

I found my solution at MidwayUSA in the form of two Pachmayr Decelerator Ultra-Light Grind-to-Fit recoil pads. Following Pachmayr's instructions, I filled in the existing holes in the stock, then drilled 1/8" fresh holes for the screws that came with the pads. The replacement pads were approximately 1/2" wider than the stock all around. I applied blue masking tape to protect the stock and used my grinder with an 80-grit zirconia grinding wheel to trim them to size. Not being the world's greatest craftsman, I dinged them a little, but by using 240-grit sandpaper followed by a coat of Armor All Protectant, I made them look presentable and certainly functional.

## Metal Blues

I've always been pleased with how well Birchwood Casey's cold blue products work. These two shotguns are so worn that when stripped they didn't have the best surface for re-bluing. Between the worn metal and the broken stocks, I adjusted to the fact this would not be a "make them like new" project, and I started hoping for something along the lines of "well-used but cared-for working guns."

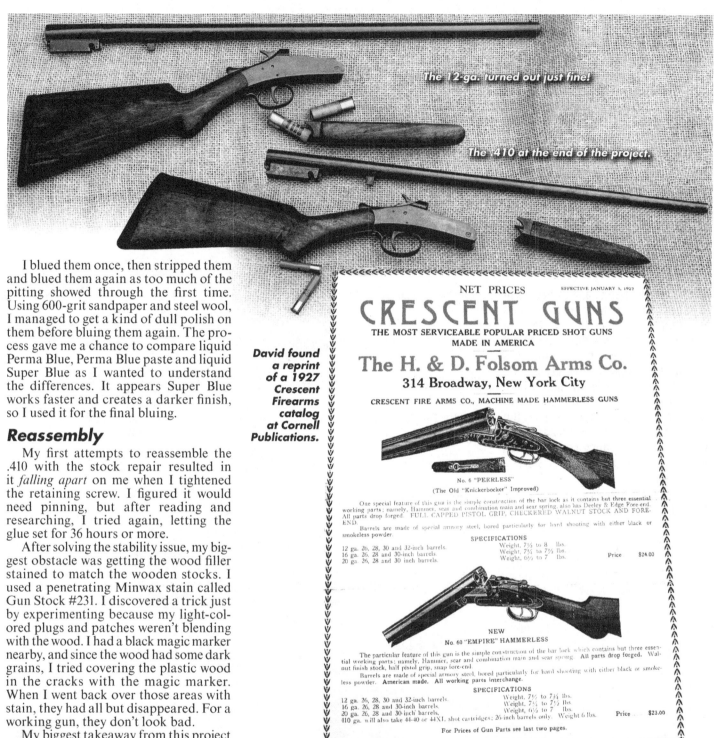

The 12-ga. turned out just fine!

The .410 at the end of the project.

I blued them once, then stripped them and blued them again as too much of the pitting showed through the first time. Using 600-grit sandpaper and steel wool, I managed to get a kind of dull polish on them before bluing them again. The process gave me a chance to compare liquid Perma Blue, Perma Blue paste and liquid Super Blue as I wanted to understand the differences. It appears Super Blue works faster and creates a darker finish, so I used it for the final bluing.

## Reassembly

My first attempts to reassemble the .410 with the stock repair resulted in it *falling apart* on me when I tightened the retaining screw. I figured it would need pinning, but after reading and researching, I tried again, letting the glue set for 36 hours or more.

After solving the stability issue, my biggest obstacle was getting the wood filler stained to match the wooden stocks. I used a penetrating Minwax stain called Gun Stock #231. I discovered a trick just by experimenting because my light-colored plugs and patches weren't blending with the wood. I had a black magic marker nearby, and since the wood had some dark grains, I tried covering the plastic wood in the cracks with the magic marker. When I went back over those areas with stain, they had all but disappeared. For a working gun, they don't look bad.

My biggest takeaway from this project was the new skills I learned. I've never worked with wood like this project required. I learned how to research and find sources of obsolete parts, most of which came from Numrich. I learned a bit about the history of Crescent Firearms Company, and I found a 1927 catalog of their products through Cornell Publications.

As best I can match them, it appears these two shotguns sold for $9.60 in 1927 dollars, putting them at about $140 each in today's dollars. Bottom line: I turned two junkers into working firearms.

*For more info: www.gunpartscorp.com, www.birchwoodcasey.com, www.cornellpubs.com*

*David found a reprint of a 1927 Crescent Firearms catalog at Cornell Publications.*

NET PRICES    EFFECTIVE JANUARY 3, 1927

# CRESCENT GUNS

### THE MOST SERVICEABLE POPULAR PRICED SHOT GUNS MADE IN AMERICA

## The H. & D. Folsom Arms Co.

### 314 Broadway, New York City

CRESCENT FIRE ARMS CO., MACHINE MADE HAMMERLESS GUNS

**No. 6 "PEERLESS"**
(The Old "Knickerbocker" Improved)

One special feature of this gun is the simple construction of the bar lock as it contains but three essential working parts; namely, Hammer, sear and combination main and sear spring, also has Deeley & Edge Fore-end. All parts drop forged. FULL CAPPED PISTOL GRIP, CHECKERED WALNUT STOCK AND FORE-END.
Barrels are made of special armory steel, bored particularly for hard shooting with either black or smokeless powder.

SPECIFICATIONS

| | |
|---|---|
| 12 ga. 26, 28, 30 and 32-inch barrels. | Weight, 7½ to 8 lbs. |
| 16 ga. 26, 28 and 30-inch barrels. | Weight, 7¼ to 7½ lbs. |
| 20 ga. 26, 28 and 30 inch barrels. | Weight, 6½ to 7 lbs. |

Price    $24.00

**NEW**
**No. 60 "EMPIRE" HAMMERLESS**

The particular feature of this gun is the simple construction of the bar lock which contains but three essential working parts; namely, Hammer, sear and combination main and sear spring. All parts drop forged. Walnut finish stock, half pistol grip, snap fore-end.
Barrels are made of special armory steel, bored particularly for hard shooting with either black or smokeless powder. **American made. All working parts interchange.**

SPECIFICATIONS

| | |
|---|---|
| 12 ga. 26, 28, 30 and 32-inch barrels. | Weight, 7½ to 7¾ lbs. |
| 16 ga. 26, 28 and 30-inch barrels. | Weight, 7¼ to 7½ lbs. |
| 20 ga. 26, 28 and 30-inch barrels. | Weight, 6¼ to 7 lbs. |
| 410 ga. will also take 44-40 or 44XL shot cartridges; 26-inch barrels only. Weight 6 lbs. | |

Price    $23.00

For Prices of Gun Parts see last two pages.

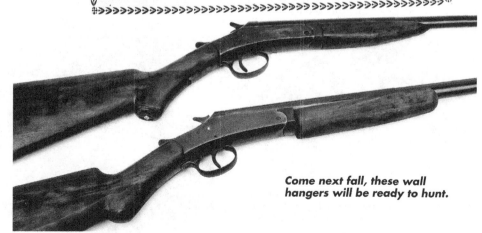

*Come next fall, these wall hangers will be ready to hunt.*

Garrett M. Baugher

# GRIP MAKING DIY:

## Precious metal or wood — it doesn't really matter.

I've never seen a factory grip panel I'd label anything more than "adequate." I get it, you have to play to the middle and please the masses, meeting a price-point, but this doesn't mean you're stuck with what you've got. We all like to take our guns and make them our own. While it would be easier to troll the internet with your credit card and magically make fancy custom grips show up at your door — I hereby offer some options.

Given the choice to go big or go home I rarely choose to go home — mostly 'cause my wife is waiting with her honey-dos, and gun stuff is more fun. Often, when I swing for the fence like this I end up biting off more than I can chew. But it's where the magic happens! I'm just crazy that way I guess. So pay attention, dust off your hands and ramp up the can-do attitude here. You honestly can do this.

### What's It Take?

Sure, our samples are fancy sterling silver. But almost the entire process is the same if you're using wood, horn, synthetic or some other exotic material. And believe it or not you probably already have all the tools and skills you need to do the job. You don't have to be

a professional jeweler to hit a homer here, friend. Anyone with basic tool skills can do this.

Power tools and specialty equipment do make the job easier. But don't shy away if all you've got are files, sandpaper, a drill and a good supply of elbow grease.

### Getting Started

Choose your weapon, as it were, and source your materials. In my experience eBay is a gold mine for blanks cut to size specifically for making all sorts of grips, in just about any material you want. You won't find ivory, but you can find some pretty darn good synthetics mirroring the old world appeal. I like to measure the factory grip to be sure whatever wood or crazy other stuff I'm ordering will fit the bill. If

*Garrett made this set of highly figured and stained maple grips using these same techniques — except for the casting part!*

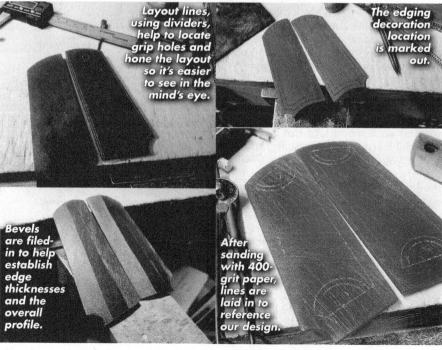

*Almost the entire project can be com-pleted with a file, calipers, dividers, a scribe, a factory set of grips and some various grits of sand paper. A power buffer is useful, as well as a drill press.*

*Layout lines, using dividers, help to locate grip holes and hone the layout so it's easier to see in the mind's eye.*

*The edging decoration location is marked out.*

*Bevels are filed-in to help establish edge thicknesses and the overall profile.*

*After sanding with 400-grit paper, lines are laid in to reference our design.*

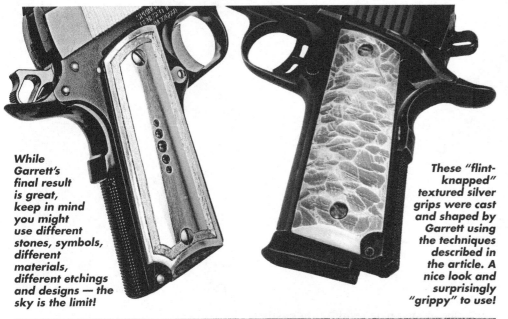

While Garrett's final result is great, keep in mind you might use different stones, symbols, different materials, different etchings and designs — the sky is the limit!

These "flint-knapped" textured silver grips were cast and shaped by Garrett using the techniques described in the article. A nice look and surprisingly "grippy" to use!

Once the single piece of wax is profiled and cut in two, the backs are flattened and made coplanar with the front. The project is beginning to "look" like what it's to become.

Paring down the wax to a useable size is helpful when laying out the grip outline. The casting wax works with cutting tools easily.

Dividers — using the factory grips as reference — are used to scribe a reference line for thickness on the edges of the grip panels.

you measure twice, you won't even have to cut once!

While I have made grips for other guns, 1911 grips are my favorite. They're flat-backed, so you don't have to worry about matching some crazy contour to ensure a tight fit. Simple is good when you're starting out.

Since I wanted to "go big" I'll be carving wax for a casting here. But the carving process is almost identical for wood and you can apply the same skills. In fact, most tools made for wood also work wax wonderfully. Don't be afraid to use what you have. The best and most powerful tool for the job is your creativity.

I love working wax because it welcomes so much more imagination with so much less effort than other mediums. I can use an old wood-carving knife to whittle the wax surface and create, say, a flint-knapped texture. Or I can sand them smooth before casting so later I can polish them to a brilliant shine — or anything in between.

Another benefit to wax is it's so cheap it's almost free. You can pick up a block big enough for five sets of grips at www.riogrande.com somewhere in the neighborhood of $15–$20. I buy the Matt wax brand. It carves and machines really well while also remaining flexible and forgiving. So don't be afraid of messing up.

## Roughing It

I'm not talking "sleeping on a rock here" but roughing out what you're going to build. Grab your gun, grip blanks and a pencil or sharp scribe. Take the grips off the gun and orient the grip on the workpiece. I find it much easier to use a factory or sample grip as a starting point and build to suit from there.

I lop off a big hunk of wax to become our model for casting. Since our grips mirror each other I only need one piece. While I'm at it I also cut it twice as thick, plus a smidge, as one finished grip. More on this in a second.

I lay the sample on the wax and trace the outline into the work with a sharp scribe. It's at this point modifications can be made. I like the grip edge to land

just shy of the corner of the flats on the pistol, so I choose to make mine wider, but do what suits you. When you're satisfied with your outline it's time to remove all the material "that isn't the grip." Like the old timer said, when asked how he knows how to carve a cigar-store Indian statue: "Easy, son, just cut off everything that doesn't look like an Indian."

A small hand saw makes quick work of the big chunks, and a coarse file brings it to final size. I check for square often to ensure everything is even.

Remember how we left it extra thick? Using dividers or calipers I scribe a center line on the edges, run my saw down the line and presto — two mirroring grip panels. Easy peasy.

## Lose Some Weight

If I were working wood or anything that would be my final material I'd pause on shaping to drill holes for bushings and screws. Again, the sample grip is mighty handy for locating the holes to be drilled. It's always easier to drill into a flat surface as opposed to a curved one.

*Rough castings are usually covered in oxidation and extra material to be polished off, as well as buttons to be removed. Looks scary but it's not, honest!*

One unfortunate result of the casting process is shrinkage. When the metal is poured into the mold it has to be liquid, obviously. But as it cools and solidifies it contracts, resulting in the finished casting being ever so slightly smaller than the wax model.

The first time I made silver grips I drilled holes before casting — I'd forgotten about shrinkage. This resulted in frustration and wallering-out the holes to accept the bushings. But my daddy didn't raise no dummy! I'm not going to make the mistake again, and neither should you.

After filing, sanding or milling the back of the grip flat and parallel with the opposing surface, it's time to keep shaping. We have a lot of extra material and this wax won't shape itself. I scribe along both long sides to denote how thick I want the edges of the grips to be, then using a wax file at a shallow angle (any coarse file will work) I file a bevel about a third of the way into the surface of the wax model. Wash, rinse, repeat for the other side.

The result is a faceted surface. The middle surface is still flat and parallel to the back while the adjoining surfaces slant downward toward the edges, terminating at the thickness line we established earlier. Now all that's left to do is file off the corners of the facets and blend everything together, making the final rounded profile. This is really where it starts to take shape. Wax — like wood — responds well to scraping. I have an old wood-carving knife I use to scrape the heavy file marks out of the surface. I take it one optional step further and sand the wax with 400-grit paper. This isn't necessary at this point but remember, any marks in the wax will be in the casting so a smoother finish now means less work later.

## Getting Creative

Almost anything a person can imagine can be done in wax. There are some lim-

*The "almost" final result is a set of silver grips — cast, shaped, fitted and polished by Garrett. Believe it or not, this is well within the DIY skills of most people and the same skill set can be used to make grips from wood or other material.*

itations here but for the most part any carving, engraving or texturing will work. As a jeweler, I happened to have some synthetic rubies lying around from my old jewelry store days, so let's incorporate those. A border-texture would be a nice contrast to a high polish as well.

I use dividers to outline a border, then using a round graver I deepen the lines. If we were to cast these as they are they would be extremely heavy, and in silver, heavy equals expensive. I used a 5mm ball burr to relieve the back of the grips making sure to leave the perimeter flat so it will lay flat when on the pistol. After the ball burr I move to a rounded scraper made from an old spoon handle. Remember, no fancy tools required!

## Casting

Casting can be quite a bear and a bit of a crap shoot at times. If you're attempting this at home I would recommend finding a casting house or talking to a local jeweler who has equipment and

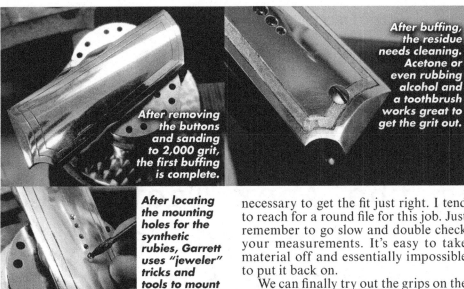

**After removing the buttons and sanding to 2,000 grit, the first buffing is complete.**

**After buffing, the residue needs cleaning. Acetone or even rubbing alcohol and a toothbrush works great to get the grit out.**

**After locating the mounting holes for the synthetic rubies, Garrett uses "jeweler" tricks and tools to mount the stones.**

experience in casting precious metals. Casting equipment can be very expensive and getting good results takes lots of time, patience, troubleshooting and dialing in of all variables involved.

Trust me when I say you'll want to farm out this part. But some simple advice from the caster will help you to craft the wax mold so you're still doing the creative part. If that's the road you choose to take you'll still have plenty of work ahead.

I'm lucky enough to have access to good casting equipment, and just enough experience to get by. But enough about casting. Let's wrap this sucker up.

## Making It Shiny

Casting leaves a bulbous tumor of metal called a button sticking off the piece. It's ugly, but useful. Holding grips so slim for finishing can cause tremendous frustration and hand cramps. So I clamp the button in a sturdy bench vise to hold the work in place as I file off any little extra bits and sand up to 2,000 grit. Using a hacksaw, I get rid of the button and can file and polish the real estate it used to occupy.

I like to do what I call a preliminary polish on the buffer at this stage. This will show any scratches or pits still needing to be sanded out. In drilling and stone-setting the metal will pick up light scratches anyway. So I don't get too attached to my surface finish right now.

After careful measurements of my 1911 I can select drills and locate where holes need to be in the grips, and it's off to the drill press we go. Drilling silver is a snap, and it feels much like drilling aluminum. After drilling, some adjustments might be

necessary to get the fit just right. I tend to reach for a round file for this job. Just remember to go slow and double check your measurements. It's easy to take material off and essentially impossible to put it back on.

We can finally try out the grips on the pistol — and my, oh my, are they pretty! But don't get too tied-up admiring your work as there's more to do.

I examine the surface and sand out any scratches before going back to the buffer for the second round of polishing. It's at this stage I have to repress my inner giddy schoolgirl. I just get so excited to see them finished!

After applying some texture and flush-setting the stones, it's finally time for the very last polish. I work up through heavy, medium and fine polishing compounds on progressively finer buffing wheels. After a bath in the ultrasonic cleaner and several blasts from the steam cleaner, the grips are complete! I drop them on my Range Officer and couldn't be happier with the result.

## The Afterglow!

The new grips sure dress up the old gun, but I felt they might be better suited on a gun with a richer finish. Until one can be found I'll sit back admiring what I've created, reflecting on the fun I had in the process. I hope you can see how this same basic set of operations also work to create grips from other materials.

Every time I make a new set of grips I learn something in the process. This makes the next set even better. It's not an overly difficult task, and you can knock out a set of wood grips on a Saturday afternoon. If you have a power sander, it's even easier. It's a relaxed way to have fun, be creative and make all your range buddies jealous.

"Huh? You made those? No way!"

Yes way. 🔫

*For more info:*
*www.riogrande.com*

**The stones are set, the final buffing applied and the edging texture is done. The grips are now complete!**

**David Freeman**

# UPGRADE YOUR TRIGGER

## Installing the Apex Tactical Flat-Faced Forward Set Sear & Trigger Kit.

David installed the Apex Tactical Forward Set Trigger Kit in this Smith & Wesson VTAC M&P.

**S**everal years ago, I installed an Apex Tactical Duty/Carry Action Enhancement Kit in my Viking Tactical M&P. The kit reduces overtravel, smoothes trigger pull and keeps a safe 5- to 5.5-lb. trigger pull weight. A benefit of the installation was the elimination of a characteristic slight *sideways movement* in the M&P's muzzle as the trigger breaks.

If you have an M&P and are unaware of this little quirk, make sure your gun is unloaded, then cock it by racking the slide. Put the bottom of the muzzle flat on the top of a table so the front of the trigger guard is up against the table edge. Now watch the muzzle carefully as you pull the trigger. Chances are you'll see the tiniest little wiggle of the muzzle as the trigger breaks. At least I did, and the Apex trigger kit fixed it.

### Apex Tactical Flat-Faced Forward Set Sear & Trigger Kit

Pleased with the results of that first Apex installation, I was eager to try a newer kit offered by Apex Tactical — the Flat-Faced Forward Set Sear & Trigger Kit for the M&P. Although I have several M&Ps the Viking Tactical is my favorite with its Flat Dark Earth color scheme. I figured the red-trigger kit would enhance its appearance and performance. The kit is available in other colors if you prefer something different.

Designed to work in any Smith & Wesson M&P model pistol in a centerfire caliber, the Apex Flat-Faced Forward Set Trigger Kit mimics a 1911 trigger. It reduces trigger pre-travel and over-travel and lowers pull weight to between 3 and 4 lbs. depending on the trigger spring used. Although the trigger feels like a 1911 trigger when you're shooting, it has a center-mounted pivoting safety.

The Flat-Faced Forward Set Sear & Trigger Kit comes with two little bags of small parts in addition to the trigger. The spring kit includes both 3- and 4-lb. trigger-return springs, a sear spring and a reset-assist mechanism spring that is not applicable to my model of the M&P.

### Easy Installation?

Apex suggests installation of this kit might be something you would want a competent gunsmith to do. I'm not a gunsmith, but I took a gunsmithing course a few years back and have practical experience. I've also got a great reference library and a son who is mechanically inclined, has great dexterity and can usually bail me out if I get in trouble. With these confidence builders, I dove in. As it turns out, Apex Tactical's instructional videos made the job easy, but it involves practically every action component in the gun.

### Do You Have What It Takes?

If you have a non-marring hammer, a punch set and a pair of needle-nose pliers, that's all you really need. I used a Range Maxx pistol cleaning mat for the

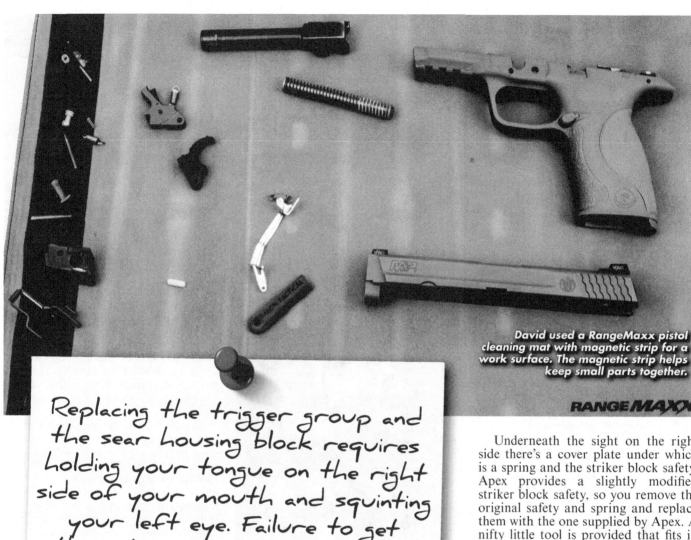

David used a RangeMaxx pistol cleaning mat with magnetic strip for a work surface. The magnetic strip helps keep small parts together.

**RANGEMAXX**

Replacing the trigger group and the sear housing block requires holding your tongue on the right side of your mouth and squinting your left eye. Failure to get these two facial configurations correct will result in undue frustration in properly inserting the tight-fitting components while keeping various pins from sliding this way or that.

installation because it has a soft, textured surface to protect the gun's finish and a magnetic strip along the side for keeping small parts together.

The Apex kit I got included the red-anodized, flat-faced forward set trigger, a forward set sear, an ultimate striker block kit and a forward set spring kit. Two tools were included in the kit — a yellow polymer slave pin to help with aligning the trigger pivot pin when installing the trigger group and a Talon Tactical Tool for holding the striker block and spring in place during rear sight reinstallation.

Watching the videos walked me right through the process, but I want to give you an overview to help you decide

if this is something you want to do to your M&P. My goal is to tell you what's involved in the process, but *you'll want to use Apex's video tutorials* to learn how to do it.

### Striker Block Replacement

Let's start with the striker block replacement. To get to it you'll need to remove the slide from the gun, then remove the rear sight. There's a set screw holding the rear sight in place you must loosen before removing the sight. With the set screw removed, drive the sight out of its groove from left to right. You'll need a non-marring punch and hammer to encourage it to start moving.

Underneath the sight on the right side there's a cover plate under which is a spring and the striker block safety. Apex provides a slightly modified striker block safety, so you remove the original safety and spring and replace them with the one supplied by Apex. A nifty little tool is provided that fits in the groove and covers the plate holding it all together while you slide the sight back in, line it up and tighten it down. That's it for the slide.

### Strip To The Frame

Like I mentioned, everything will be removed from the frame. There are two groups of parts — the trigger group and the sear housing block assembly. To remove both groups, you'll drive out roll pins. Once the groups are removed from the frame, you'll disassemble the components of each group and reassemble them with the new components from the kit. Starting with the trigger group, replace the trigger and the trigger-return spring, reconnect the trigger bar and reinstall the trigger group, which includes the slide locking mechanisms and the locking block that holds the trigger group in place.

Then it's time to remove the sear block so you can replace the sear and sear spring to match the shorter stroke of the trigger. The sear housing block assembly will vary in configuration depending on whether there is an external safety on the gun. Regardless, what you will be doing is removing and replacing the sear and the sear spring before reinstalling the sear housing block in the gun.

**Installation of the kit involves removing the trigger and sear groups from the frame — easy to do with a simple punch.**

**Removal of the trigger group and block is the first step with the frame.**

**The new Apex trigger with existing trigger bar installed.**

**The kit includes this tool to hold the striker block spring and cap when reinstalling the rear sight.**

**The Apex flat trigger is almost vertical and although hinged, feels like a 1911 trigger when shooting.**

**David used a Lyman Trigger Pull gauge to check the pull with both the light spring and duty spring that came with the kit.**

None of these actions is particularly difficult, but they do require some manual dexterity. The magnetic strip on the Range Maxx pad helped me keep up with the small parts. If you don't have one of these, I recommend some method of preventing the tiny parts and springs from falling on the floor because they tend to jump around a bit.

Replacing the trigger group and the sear housing block requires holding your tongue on the right side of your mouth and squinting your left eye. Failure to get these two facial configurations correct will result in undue frustration in properly inserting the tight-fitting components while keeping various pins from sliding this way or that.

## Video Learning

When you've followed the Apex video instructions, you'll have a working gun. If by some slight chance you don't, call them for help. As you put the various parts back together, function check them along the way.

Function checking is easy, but I couldn't wait to get to the range for some real testing. First, I installed the 3-lb. spring and used my Lyman trigger pull gauge to verify the trigger pull. Before going to the range, I swapped it with the 4-lb. spring since I'll likely be carrying this gun from time to time as my PDW.

Frankly, my fingers, which probably haven't been calibrated in several years, can't tell the difference between 3 and 4 lbs. The take-up is 1/4" or less and you can hardly feel the break it's so easy. As advertised, it feels like a good 1911 trigger. The pivoting trigger safety is so light you hardly notice its operation.

With everything back together and a few dry-fire tests for operation, I was anxious for some live-fire testing. Since I had removed and reinstalled the rear sight, I used a Firefield Universal

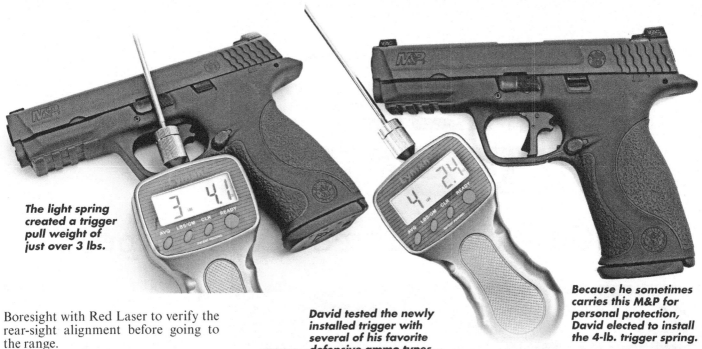

*The light spring created a trigger pull weight of just over 3 lbs.*

*David tested the newly installed trigger with several of his favorite defensive ammo types.*

*Because he sometimes carries this M&P for personal protection, David elected to install the 4-lb. trigger spring.*

Boresight with Red Laser to verify the rear-sight alignment before going to the range.

Hornady recently sent me two new 9mm loads for testing — a 124-gr. Custom XTP load and a 147-gr. Subsonic XTP load. I also included two of my favorite 9mm defensive loads — Inceptor 9mm +P 65-gr. ARX and Speer 124-gr. Gold Dot Personal Protection. With the targets at 10 yards, I fired 5-shot groups using each of these loads. The tightest groups came from the Speer Gold Dot ammo, with the Hornady Subsonic 147-gr. load close behind. All four loads provided decent defensive accuracy, and operation of the M&P was delightful. I shoot 1911s a lot and the Apex Forward Set Trigger mimics the 1911 trigger as advertised.

While writing this article, the VTAC M&P with its new Apex Tactical was on the desk beside me. I kept looking at it and feeling quite a bit of satisfaction knowing the red trigger which is obviously not stock, and several other performance enhancing parts were installed by me. This gun not only works but is uniquely mine.

## Should You Try It?

One advantage of doing one of these upgrades is when you get through you will thoroughly understand your pistol's mechanical operation. That should make you a better shooter, though it won't replace the fundamentals of stance, grip, breathing, aiming, trigger control and follow-through. Apex Tactical has kits for all the M&P models as well as action enhancement and trigger kits for GLOCKs, SIGs, FN and CZ products. I recently learned their GLOCK Gen 5 Forward Set Trigger Kit also works on the new .22-caliber G44. That might be a project I'll try some day. The typical cost for one of these kits is in the $125–$175 range.

*For more info: www.apextactical.com*

*The best grouping at 10 yards came from the perennial favorite Speer Gold Dot 124-gr. load (above). Hornady's new 147-gr. Subsonic load produced several groupings like this one at 10 yards (left).*

Roy Huntington

# FROM THE BENCH:

## HS Custom's First .38 Super!

The "Tri-Cut" slide Dusty created from the Nighthawk Custom base slide. After a lot of "set-up" time with indicators, Dusty took a deep breath and began cutting. I think the results are fetching.

The slide is "bushing-less" meaning the barrel is indexed with a tapered fit into the end of the slide. To do this, the barrel is threaded and a Chambers Custom Coned Sleeve installed and turned down on the lathe. The slide internal diameter measures 0.7025" and the cone is fit to 0.702" so everything locks up like that bank vault you always hear about! Here's Dusty's set-up to start on the muzzle of the barrel assembly.

The first cut begins to establish a square face at the muzzle, critical for accuracy.

Here's where Dusty adds the convex "crown" protecting the actual chamfer cut from dings and banging around.

Ta-Da! Note the neat fit of all the bits. This arrangement also requires a special recoil spring guide rod assembly. Don't you think that Tri-Cut looks great?

I've had the pleasure of helping a young veteran build his custom gunsmithing business over the past couple of years. Now, Dustin "Dusty" Housel is open for business. I wanted to show you what time, energy and great tool skills can accomplish in a short time. As of right now, Dusty is backlogged a good six months on custom 1911 work — and this gun I'm going to share with you is one of the reasons.

We're sharing this success story to help motivate you to trust yourself and your dreams when it comes to pistolsmithing and building custom guns. Dusty had a dream, then worked toward it. But first, for a bit of backstory on Dusty read this article I did on his first "official" build. https://americanhandgunner.com/dustys-1911/

### A Tri-Cut

This particular gun is what's called a "full-build" meaning creating a gun from a series of un-fitted parts. This one happens to include some custom-made pieces Dusty built using his lathe and mill in his shop — as well as careful hand work. In this case, the gun started out as a Nighthawk Custom un-fitted frame and slide. The customer wanted a "COO"-sized gun — a Commander slide on an Officer's ACP frame — in .38 Super, no less. And, he wanted the slide cut in a special way, called a "Tri-Cut." Unlike a conventionally shaped 1911 slide, this one has heavy angular cuts in the top of the slide, giving it a unique sort of "triangle" top. Since this build, Caspian now offers slides with the "Tri-Cut" treatment already done.

Dusty did plenty of careful set-up in his big mill and nailed it on this first slide cut. He admitted it was scary — but was pleased with the result. He also made the front and rear sights to fit the special cuts he made for them. Amazing work for someone

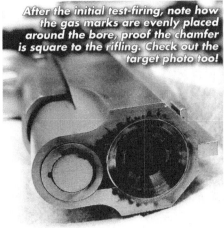

After the initial test-firing, note how the gas marks are evenly placed around the bore, proof the chamfer is square to the rifling. Check out the target photo too!

Dusty built a custom rear sight for this .38 Super. Here it is in the rough form while he checks fit. It will eventually be profiled and the final cuts made. This was made from bar stock steel.

The gun isn't quite finished yet as slide serrations need to be added and final detail work completed. But at 25 yards on an icy cold 20-degree windy day, 1" or so isn't too bad! There are five shots in those four holes! Amazingly enough, Dusty's sight dimensions were almost spot on right off the bat. The upper target was for fun. We moved in to 10 yards and tried to shoot around the center green spot. Almost got it right! This gun ended up amazingly accurate, and the straight trigger and crisp break helped matters.

who didn't own a mill or lathe a year ago!

The pictures show various stages of the build but not all of them. The "fire control" parts (trigger, hammer, disconnector, etc.) all need fitting, grip safety fit and blended/tuned, and a hundred other details all need to be sorted out, blended and tuned to work together. Dusty usually does test-firing once the build is complete, but not cosmetically finished.

## Final Fitting

If there's any tweaking to be done, he does it after the test-firing so the final fit and finish isn't compromised. When things meet Dusty's approval, the final hand finish gets done. That's where tool marks are smoothed out, flats are made flat again, checkering finished, French borders added — basically getting the gun to the point it's ready to be sent out for the final finish to be applied.

Once everything is dialed in "just right" it gets a final cleaning in preparation for the finish. Finish options include Cerakote, classic bluing, hard chrome, Black Nitride (which is what this gun is getting from Nighthawk Custom) and lots of other options.

Check out the pictures to see a bit of what goes into something like this. I often help Dusty do the final shooting/sighting in on his builds and I have to say, this one shot like a laser beam! Check out the 25-yard target, on a 20-degree, blowy day!

If you have questions about building your own custom 1911, touch base with Dusty. I know he'd be happy to answer some questions. And who knows, you may decide to have one built just for you! A "Hat's Off" to Dusty for taking his dream from an idea in my garage — to a working shop!

A teaser photo of another gun nearing completion at the time of this article. A "Commander" 1911 in .45 ACP, this one has had extensive precision welding done to it (frame rails, mag well, etc.), French Borders (note the thin line at the top of the slide, just before it rounds over), flat trigger, bevel slide bottom and more. The front sight is incomplete and Dusty has final machining to do to it yet — also plenty of polishing ahead!

I was able to get Dusty to send over a picture of the Commander build since he just got it back from final finish as we were about to put this to bed. Note the front sight (blued with gold bead installed now), fancy grips and grip screws, French Border and checkering, among many custom touches. The flat trigger looks swell and feel great too. It's done — and ready to return to his customer!

*For more info:*
*www.hs-custom.com,*
*Ph: (620) 704-1646,*
*email: hscustom34@gmail.com*

Ray Fleck

# A SIG SIGHT MOUNT

## Using simple tools to solve DIY problems.

The repurposed Picatinny mount came with the ROMEO5 sight. The green taping goop makes for less broken taps. Ray didn't have access to his milling machine so he did this build the hard way!

25 YARD OFF HAND

1 3/4 W/O FLY

Black Hills HoneyBadger ammo has less recoil than normal 230-gr. ammo so Ray didn't suffer vertical stringing during test shooting. He managed respectable accuracy even with the one flyer. The "homemade" red dot mount actually worked! Cobbling something like this together might let you see if it makes a difference for you in a certain or oddball gun. Then, if so, you could try to find a factory-manufactured mounting system if available. Either way, DIY projects like this are both fun and satisfying.

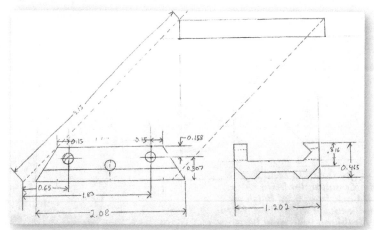

While observing the finished contraption, a friend of Ray's (another engineer) commented it was a neat and simple solution. He is mostly correct; but even a simple project like this will cause less angst if you do the math and make drawings before you start. This drawing is two times life size. The effort to make this drawing to scale saved Ray from making any parts over.

As I get old and my carcass slowly falls apart, I seek out accommodations for hitting the target. Easy "assists" are better sights, better grips and a better trigger. I acquired this SIG P220 when I could still see — a long time ago — and put the Hogue grips on promptly. A few years ago I upgraded the sights to "LPA Sights" and this was a step up from the glow in the dark sights the gun came with. Now my groups are opening up — again. The next assist for old eyes is a red dot sight. I have the slide-mounted sort of red dot on other guns, but I wanted to test the bridge mount idea. Being frugal, and not liking aspects of the bridge mounts on the market, I decided I would just build one.

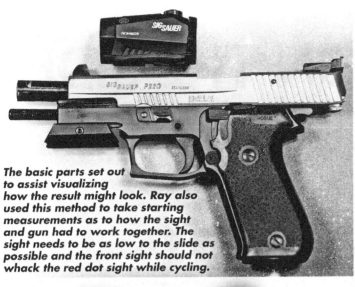

The basic parts set out to assist visualizing how the result might look. Ray also used this method to take starting measurements as to how the sight and gun had to work together. The sight needs to be as low to the slide as possible and the front sight should not whack the red dot sight while cycling.

The top plate is 0.25" thick. Ray used #6-32 screws as #8 screws were too big. This sort of free hand work requires diligence to achieve straight holes. Each hole was drilled and then tapped through the side plate to maintain alignment. A clearance hole was then drilled (carefully) through just the side plate and a screw was tightened down after the hole was taped. Drilling and taping were repeated for each hole in sequence. It was cold in Ray's garage!

The side plates were cut with a hacksaw and "milled" to size with a belt grinder. Drilling the side plate along with the Picatinny rail mount in one go assured accurate alignment. The holes were drilled with an 8-32 tap drill bit — not a clearance bit. After the left plate was done, Ray clamped the right plate to it and used the holes from the left plate as a template for drilling the holes on the right plate. The hole in the plate was then used as a drill guide for the next screw hole. Ray threaded each hole before drilling the next hole. Screws do not get in the way of drilling like the clamp.

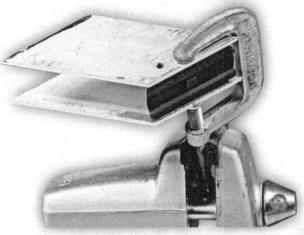

Mount assembled: Note the screws on the right plate are still long — the belt grinder worked well to adjust the screw length.

According to Ray, the set-up is finished for "testing" but he'll need to run a lot more ammo through the gun before he decides if he likes it or not. If he does, he'll clean it up and get rid of the pointy bits.

The target with holes made by Black Hills HoneyBadger ammo is testimony the mount and sight are a good shooter assist. At 25 yards with the LPS iron sights the group would have been 2–3 times as big. The all-copper alloy bullet (135 gr.) in HoneyBadger has good terminal performance with less recoil than a traditional 230-gr. .45 bullet. Less recoil is demonstrated by less vertical stringing compared to the SIG 230-gr. ammo. The SIG ammo is great ammo, and so is the red dot sight I use from them, but a lighter bullet may help you to shoot better, so give it a try.

My first thought on the vertical stringing was something was loose in the mount. Lots of ammo later I was confident the only loose screws were mine. My wrist, arm and shoulder no longer like recoil and it shows up as vertical stringing. Inconsistent grip/control will cause vertical strings too.

The design of my homemade mount works well, and it points naturally even though it's higher above the bore than a slide-mounted red dot. The only modification to make would be to move the sight a bit forward if you make one. It's too close to the ejection port and the back of the sight collects splattered lube. Let's show you how I did it with a step-by-step look.

*For more info:*
*www.black-hills.com,*
*www.sigsauer.com*

Jeremy D. Clough

# BARBECUE ON THE SIDE

## Building a compact carry M1911 with a touch of old-school style.

The combination of selective polish, fire blue and the silver-inlaid grips combine to bring this compact .45 into the barbecue gun tradition. Under the shine is a serious concealed carry pistol.

Wilson Combat provided the compact slide and receiver. Jeremy lapped in the trigger until it would "flow" back and forth under its own weight.

There has to be a slight step between the feed ramps in the barrel and the receiver. Also note the as-machined finish on the frame ramp.

Every build starts with a vision of what you want the finished product to be. Candidly, this one took me a while. Wilson Combat sent me a slide, receiver and barrel for use in a pair of barrel-fitting articles. After fitting the barrel, I never finished the gun and it rested at ease in the safe for several years. In time, my vision coalesced to turning the compact receiver and slide into a barbecue gun — a carry pistol dressed up nicely enough to display at a social gathering. Of course, before you can make it pretty, you have to build it, so we'll start there.

The frame feed ramp after being polished. Take care not to change the angle of the ramp when polishing it.

Jeremy used a hammer/sear/disconnect set from Novak's, then used a Power sear and hammer jig to stone the breakaway angle on the nose of the sear and cut the hammer hooks to the correct depth.

*In time, the vision coalesced of turning the compact receiver and 4" slide into a barbecue gun — a carry pistol dressed up nicely enough to display at a social gathering.*

To checker the original housing, Jeremy used a Marvel checkering jig to lay out the horizontal lines with a 20 LPI checkering file.

The beavertail radius on a frame is usually oversized, so Jeremy "marked and moved" to find where to remove material. The sides of the contact pad also needed fitting where they contact the frame.

## First Steps: Barrel And Trigger

I fit the barrel using the John Miller hard-fit technique I was taught at Novak's: file-fit and lap the barrel hood and upper lugs, then the lower lugs, which are cut with a milling cutter inserted through the slide-stop hole. I used a mix of several different barrel fitting tools and a fine Swiss pillar file — you can find all of those at Brownells. Fitting a coned barrel, like the short one for this compact pistol, is similar to the usual process except you must fit the lockup area at the muzzle at the same time as the hood and upper lugs, instead

Jeremy used files and sandpaper backed with a hard oak dowel to blend the top of the beavertail with the frame and the heel of the slide.

After the lines were blended, Jeremy cut a matching bevel on the top of the frame and beavertail using a fine file, then finished it with sandpaper and a fine abrasive wheel.

Not bad — but it can get a lot better. The blue is Dykem marking fluid, useful for showing low spots.

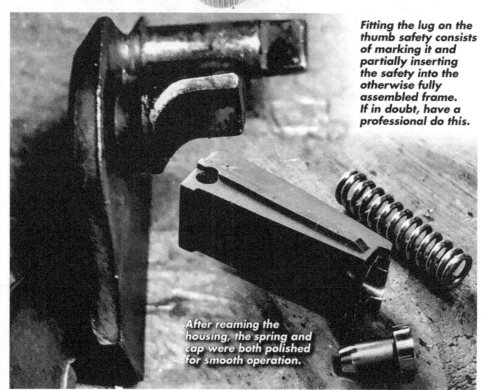

To fit the top of the beavertail, Jeremy used this tool from Harrison Designs that locks the beavertail in the upward position.

Fitting the lug on the thumb safety consists of marking it and partially inserting the safety into the otherwise fully assembled frame. If in doubt, have a professional do this.

After reaming the housing, the spring and cap were both polished for smooth operation.

of last, which is how I was taught to fit bushings.

The first operation on the frame was to fit the long, solid aluminum trigger I ordered from Wilson. As a general principle it makes sense to break all sharp corners on a part prior to fitting it, otherwise you may get a false fit that will quickly wear away, leaving your part loose. With this in mind, I used the pillar file to break all four corners on the trigger shoe, and small needle files (followed by backed sandpaper) to go all the way around the trigger bow to ensure it wouldn't bind on anything in the raceway.

The broach that cuts the raceway will eventually get dull, starting at the corners, so a slight bevel on the trigger bow is cheap insurance against a less-than perfect raceway. Mark the wear areas of the trigger with either Dykem or a Sharpie and once you start to push the trigger shoe into place, you'll see where the material needs to be removed. Once it's fully seated, put some lapping compound (such as Brownells' 600-grit garnet compound) on the trigger shoe, then install the sear spring and mainspring housing to put pressure against the trigger and lap the trigger in. After you're done and have removed the compound, you should be able to put the trigger in the raceway and have it "flow" back and forth under its own weight.

## Action Work

Working toward the back of the gun, I assembled the magazine catch (I used a machined one provided by EGW) and lapped it into place to make sure it mated smoothly with the frame. Word to the wise: I polish springs and the holes in which they ride, but the wise man will not flatten and polish the end of the mag-catch spring, as it will let the mag-catch lock rotate and lock up. Ask me how I know.

With the mainspring housing, spring, cap and retainer installed, Jeremy used a file backed with sandpaper to bring the frame and housing to a single flat plane.

These aircraft spring clamps were helpful for holding small parts during bead blasting.

For the lockwork, I used a hammer/sear/disconnect set from Novak's, and used a Power sear and hammer jig to stone the breakaway angle on the nose of the sear and to cut the hammer hooks to the correct depth. The general rule of thumb is they should never be less than 0.018" — and assuming you can still get a crisp trigger break, more is better. No matter what, the sear should fully engage the hammer hooks using either Dykem or a Sharpie to verify.

While skeletonized M1911 hammers have been popular since the days of Steve Nastoff, the extra weight of the original rowel-style hammer makes it hit just a little harder, adding a bit of insurance should lint or other debris accumulate near the firing pin, as it does with carry guns.

The frame came with a beavertail, and the rear-frame ears had already been radiused. This, however, is the beginning of the fitting process. The radius is usually a little oversized, which requires marking it and moving the beavertail back and forth until a bright spot appears and shows you where to remove material with either a file or 220-grit sandpaper.

The sides of the contact pad also need fitting where they contact the frame, as does the leg of the safety that interferes with the rear movement of the trigger (the actual "safety" part). I used a file to fit the leg, making sure the trigger would clear it when pushed in and wouldn't when the safety is in the outward position.

When you fit the safety leg and have the sear spring, trigger, beavertail and mainspring housing in place, you should be able to depress the grip safety, pull the trigger and hold it back and release first the grip safety then the trigger. If both the grip safety and trigger spring back when you release the trigger, you're done, but if the trigger hangs up on the leg of the safety,

EGW supplied a keyed reverse plug drilled for a guide rod, providing a cleaner, closed look. The keyed part required minor fitting to ensure it didn't interfere with the barrel fit.

Novak's welded the front dovetail and re-machined the slide for their Glow Dome front sight. The Novak front also uses a roll pin to prevent sight movement.

This adjustable Novak rear fits the same dovetail as the fixed version and has a tritium bar, avoiding the problems inherent in having two tritium dots on the rear.

You can install and remove grip screw bushings with a regular screwdriver, but you're also likely to destroy them in the process. Use this bushing driver from Brownells instead.

Unless you want them to come off the gun every time you remove the grips, you should stake the bushings in place with an 1/8" punch and staking tool.

Handmade Grips creates outstanding pistol grips with silver or gold-colored metal inlays. They made this set with the heraldic design that's Jeremy's personal logo.

Many grips will require some degree of fitting. Jeremy serrated a grip screw, so it recut the front hole cleanly.

you've got more work to do. After it was fit and functional, there was very little work required to fit the "grip" part of the safety to the frame, but, like the trigger and other parts, I lapped it in to ensure smooth operation.

## Safety First!

For aesthetic reasons, I picked a Wilson ambidextrous safety because the lines of the thumb-contact pad mimic the original Swenson ambi, which, when combined with a well-fit beavertail, creates an attractive S-curve visual. Although the plate part of the safety did not need any fitting (as they often do with particularly high-cut beavertails such as the Ed Brown), I still beveled all corners on both sides.

Fitting the lug on the safety consists of marking it and partially inserting the safety into the otherwise fully assembled frame and moving it until you can get a wear mark where it contacts the sear. Carefully remove material until it locks the sear in place and you can move it up and down with thumb pressure. The hammer should not move when you engage or disengage the safety.

## Mainspring Housing And Beavertail

The mainspring housing provided an unusual number of hours' work. Other than blending it, the MSH is usually a drop-in thing. However, I decided I couldn't live without an arched one, and they are surprisingly hard to find for an Officer's-size receiver. I resorted to purchasing a used Colt one from Numrich Gun Parts.

Unfortunately, the hole for the mainspring cavity was significantly undersize and the hole for the retaining pin was drilled incorrectly. All three holes had to be reamed by hand, which took more time. I also had to polish the mainspring cavity afterward, but I would have done it anyway.

To checker the housing, originally serrated at 20 lines per inch (LPI), I installed it in the frame and used a Marvel checkering jig to lay out the horizontal lines with a 20 LPI checkering file, then chased each individual line with a triangular riffling file.

Beveling the sharp edges on a gun is mandatory for a carry pistol; blending the individual parts, though, while not absolutely required for the gun to be useful, is an element of craftsmanship that shouldn't be ignored. With the mainspring housing fit and installed (along with its spring, cap and retainer) and providing pressure on the hammer and strut, I used sandpaper backed with a file to bring the frame and housing to a single flat plane.

Similarly, I blended the top of the beavertail with the frame and the heel

of the slide (including the extractor and ejector) using fine files followed by sandpaper backed with a hard-oak dowel. Generally, the bottom of the beavertail — where it contacts your hand — is fit in the depressed position, and can be taped into place for that part of the work.

You should fit the top of the beavertail while the safety is in the opposite, upward position. I held it in place using a neat little tool from Harrison Designs that fits into the trigger raceway and uses a hex screw to lock the beavertail up.

## Guide Rod

I wound up with two separate recoil systems: I purchased one from Wilson and EGW provided one identical to their 4" Kimber system. Both used a 22-lb. flat wire recoil spring riding on a 0.250" guide rod. The Wilson rod stops just a little shy of the muzzle and is tapered near the end so it can be removed without tools, long an irritation of using a full-length guide rod. The one-piece EGW rod is drilled for the usual paperclip.

Faced with the choice of easy takedown, which leaves the front of the gun open to debris, or a closed front harder to take apart, I chose the EGW full-length system — your mileage may vary. EGW also supplied a keyed reverse plug drilled for a guide rod, providing a cleaner, closed look.

## Final Tuning And Polishing

Once the gun was fit and assembled, the parts took a trip through the solvent tank to get all the grit and lapping compound out. Then it was time for final tuning, including polishing the chamber and feed ramps on both barrel and frame and final shaping of the extractor hook. It'll feed my preferred 230-gr. JHP load from Black Hills as well as empty brass.

Satisfied it worked, I bead blasted all the parts with a fine 800-grit media, then lightly polished the slide flats at 600 grit and shipped the big chunks of the gun to my alma mater, Novak's .45 Shop, for bluing. I kept the controls and pins to nitre blue them.

While the gun was at Novak's, I asked them to weld up the front dovetail cut and re-machine the slide for a Novak front. Besides using a different dovetail dimension, the Novak front is held in place with a roll pin to keep the sight from drifting in its dovetail should it shoot loose.

They also installed a bright Glow Dome tritium front and an adjustable rear that has the same low profile as the famous LoMount rear and fits the same dovetail. The M1911 industry has broadly adopted the Novak rear sight

Mike "Doc" Barranti's Ranger holster is a faithful interpretation of the Brill-style holster designed at the request of the Texas Rangers almost 100 years ago. Barranti also included a matching black mag pouch stamped with the same basketweave pattern used on original Brill holsters.

cut, so the rear of my slide was already correctly machined. The rear has a tritium bar, avoiding both the possibility of major misalignment with three dots, as well as keeping the extra brightness of two dots on the rear from drawing your eye first to the rear sight instead of the front where it belongs.

## Fire Blue Elegance

The nitre ("fire blue") bluing was used on the earliest M1911 pistols and is usually seen on retro, pre-A1-style guns. I'd been inspired by a Powder River Precision Hi-Power, where the otherwise matte-black carry pistol had polished and fire blued pins that added a classy, subtle touch. I did a light, selective polish in places like the edge of the thumb pads on the safety levers prior to bluing to create more contrast.

## Grips Make The Gun

Of course, the grips also make the gun, so I reached out to Handmade Grips. They create some outstanding pistol grips with silver or gold-colored metal inlays. After sending them an image of the heraldic design I've used for many years as a personal logo, they sent me a pair of laser-checkered wooden grips with my logo inlaid in each side. While the end result was a little different from what I had imagined, it's cool enough it doesn't matter. Pricing is more reasonable than you would think, as was turnaround time.

Many grips will require some degree of fitting, and these were no exception, as the screw holes were just a bit too close. I used a file as a scraper to relieve the rear of the grip panels, as well as sandpaper on a round needle file.

Once the grips would seat in place on their bushings, I took a grip screw and used a 40 LPI checkering file to serrate all the way around the screw head so when I screwed it in place, it would cut a clean relief for the screw head. The grips are held in place

with a set of Mil-Tac's practical grip screws combining a hex with a slot so there's more than one way to remove or install them.

## Ready For The BBQ

And now we get to the holster. Since the whole idea of the barbecue gun is a bit of a Western thing, I reached out to Mike "Doc" Barranti who crafted one of his Ranger holsters as well as a matching spare-mag pouch. Appropriately named, the Ranger is a faithful interpretation of the Brill-style holster designed at the request of the Texas Rangers almost 100 years ago. Minor modifications make it sit a bit higher on the belt, so it's more practical for modern carry. Although tan usually shows off stamping better, I chose black, and the result is breathtaking: beautifully crafted, with white stitching and a smooth tan lining.

It's the sort of thing that would look exceptional displayed at a barbecue … and just as good concealed beneath a jacket.

*For more info:*
*www.barrantileather.com,*
*www.black-hills.com,*
*www.brownells.com,*
*www.egwguns.com,*
*www.handmadegrips.com,*
*www.mil-tac.com,*
*www.gunpartscorp.com,*
*www.novaksights.com,*
*www.wilsoncombat.com*

Word to the wise: I polish springs and the holes in which they ride, but the wise man will not flatten and polish the end of the mag-catch spring, as that will let the mag-catch lock rotate and lock up. Ask me how I know.

Roy Huntington

# TOOL OF A THOUSAND USES!

## A shop-made scribe.

This simple scribe was inspired by YouTuber "Clickspring" — you really need to check out his amazingly well done videos. With simple tools like a small mill and lathe, he's built a complicated mechanical clock and all the tools needed to build it. The videos are simply a delight to watch. One of his first tools was a cleanly designed metal-tipped scribe and it immediately struck me I needed one. I had always used "whatever was laying around" but since making this one, I find it's in constant use in my shop. It's also a great, easy-to-make gift for your friends who are DIY people.

As a long time hobby gunsmith and general "project" guy, I'm fortunate I have a small lathe and mill courtesy of Grizzly Tools. A project like this can be easily done on a very small bench top lathe like the ones sold by Grizzly, Harbor Freight and other companies. In a pinch you could probably get by with a decent drill too if you don't ask too much of it — and use files. You don't need a mill or drill press, but if you decide to drill a cross-hold for a hook or a hanger it would be handy. If you wanted to create a hex shape, then a mill would be needed. To keep things simple here, we'll just use the lathe.

### Raw Goods

Since you're only limited by your imagination, now's the time to decide the materials you need. I chose brass, but keep in mind copper, aluminum, bronze or even mild steel, Damascus, etc., would work just fine. I like a bit of "heft" in the scribe so brass, copper or steel seems to just "feel" better than aluminum. You can find plenty of options to buy metals on-line at places like eBay, Amazon and others.

Roy has made scribes out of copper, brass, aluminum, mild steel — even Damascus stock. You're only limited by your imagination.

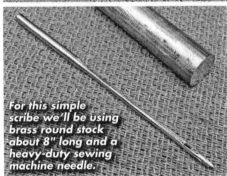

For this simple scribe we'll be using brass round stock about 8" long and a heavy-duty sewing machine needle.

Since this is a custom project, you can fit the diameter to your hand. Mine is about 0.38" and I find the weight and thickness to be comfy. A pencil is about 0.27" give or take to give you some reference. I find thinner models — I've made some 0.25" ones — tend to be a bit fiddly and hard to hold. The one in the pictures here has a brass body about 5" long and I have a shorter one about 3.5" which is handy for detailed work.

I've even made some up to 0.5" thick for some ham-handed machinists I know and they love them. I made one for a welder friend with a piece of 0.25" sharpened drill rod as the point, and the brass body was about 10" long and a full 0.5" in diameter. He keeps it on a lanyard around his neck and tells me it's in constant use. He laughed and said it also scares people away!

You'll also need some old sewing machine needles. You can scrounge 'em or simply buy a small package at a sewing store. Get some heavy-duty ones though. The size is up to you — but a nail isn't hard enough.

### First Steps

Okay, making sure you've got your shop or safety glasses on, the first step is to do some simple preliminary machining to face the end opposite the point. Sort of follow along with the photos on all this. You could also leave

Roy's fortunate to have a medium-sized Grizzly lathe so the first step is true things up in the 3-jaw chuck in preparation for some turning operations.

Roy turned one end to be the "butt" end, opposite the scribe point, lending a bit of eye candy with some light stepped cuts. He later changed his mind on this design.

A center drill goes into a chuck in the tailstock of the lathe. This "center-drills" a small starter hole in the end of the work in the three-jaw chuck.

the raw stock long, cut and fit the scribe end, then cut and dress the tail. But if you put knurling into it at the scribe end you'd risk messing it up, hence the reason I cleaned up the back end first. You can do anything you want, but this is simply how I made this one.

Swapping ends in the chuck, I squared the face, then installed a center drill in the tailstock chuck. This allows you to drill a small "starter" hole for a bigger drill bit. Use cutting fluid to keep things going smoothly.

Next up, measure your needles and find a drill bit offering a very snug fit. In my case, the shank of the needle was 0.098" so I chose a Number 39 drill measuring 0.099". That 0.001" difference will allow some Loctite or glue to hold things nicely. You can fudge up or down according to your needle size.

When you drill, just keep in mind how deep you need to go to hold the shank. A 0.5" deep hole is plenty and gives the glue a good place to grab. If you ever need to change the scribe, you can heat the joint with a propane torch for a few seconds and the Loctite or Super Glue will release neatly.

## Shaping

I like to use a simple measuring tool to assure my turning tool in the lathe is at center of the stock. I align the tool's

tip with a taper in the tail stock, then adjust the tool holder until the tip of the cutter is right at the pointer of the measuring tool. It takes the guesswork out and keeps a job moving along nicely.

You'll find standard High Speed Steel cutting bits will cut brass much better than carbide, but either will work if all you have is carbide. You'll likely need to do a bit more final polish if you're using carbide though.

All we're looking to do at this point is to turn some graduated steps into the scribe end to give a bit of taper to please the eye or to choke up on if you're doing precision work. You can shape yours according to your own artistic eye.

Once the steps are turned, a file — use carefully, please — will blend and smooth the step transitions a tad. This is just to make it look nice and you could sure leave them as stronger steps if you like.

## Knurling

Many people are afraid of this next step and even those owning hobby lathes tend to stay away from knurling. But to me, it adds so much versatility and looks to a project, it pays to just dive right in and try it. The concept is the hardened "knurling" wheels are pressed against the work (brass, copper, steel, whatever) and as the work turns the wheels form a

The center drill touches the work, leaving a neat starting point for a drill so it doesn't wander around.

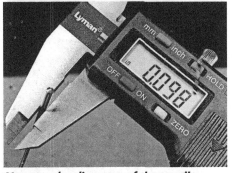

Measure the diameter of the needle you're going to use for your scribe. This one was 0.098" but they vary and the exact size doesn't really matter. Roy found getting heavy duty sewing machine or leather-working needles worked best.

There are "numbered" drill sets machinists use. Roy found the Number 39 drill was 0.099" allowing for a slip-fit for the needle, and room to glue.

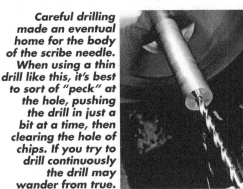

Careful drilling made an eventual home for the body of the scribe needle. When using a thin drill like this, it's best to sort of "peck" at the hole, pushing the drill in just a bit at a time, then clearing the hole of chips. If you try to drill continuously the drill may wander from true.

A special height/scribe gauge allows fast truing of the cutting tool to fit the work you're going to turn.

High-speed tool steel cutters cut brass cleanly. Here, Roy makes a few stepped cuts at the scribe end to give the end some shape.

A single-cut file works great for smoothing and shaping on the lathe. Here the steps are softened some, mostly just for looks. It's "half-art, half-function!"

Knurling lends a handsome gripping surface and really helps to make the look of the scribe pop.

Roy uses a cut-off tool here to nip off the butt end. It's not a mistake — it's a small "design change."

While "parting" can cause some anxiety for many, practice soon shows it's easy to do. You just need to be brave and go for it. It's much more accurate than using a hacksaw too.

A Dremel cut-off wheel makes short work of shortening a heavy duty sewing needle. You could also touch the needle to the edge of a grinding wheel and then break it off. The tip then needs re-sharpening using a belt sander, grinding wheel or even a sharpening stone.

Just about any glue like those from the Loctite brand or Super Glue will hold the scribe needle just fine. It can be removed by applying torch heat if you need to make a change.

Some simple tools and raw materials can soon turn into a handy shop-made scribe for your bench. Note the circular rings on the scribe body for a non-slip grip.

Here Roy used his scribe to start layout on a small shop-made hammer he's going to mill. Note the Dykem layout fluid and clear lines made by the scribe.

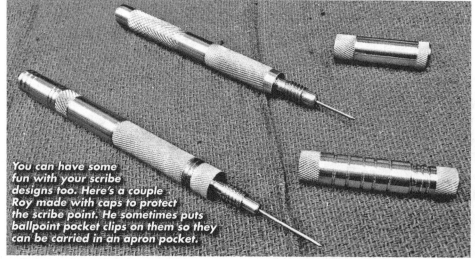

You can have some fun with your scribe designs too. Here's a couple Roy made with caps to protect the scribe point. He sometimes puts ballpoint pocket clips on them so they can be carried in an apron pocket.

raised diamond pattern in the material. There are some tricks though.

A knurling wheel will only deliver a clean, complete knurl on specific diameters of stock. Too small or too big and the knurl will overlap. But there will be specific steps in size where whatever knurling tool you have will leave full, complete diamond points. While there are mathematics you can use to compute it, it's also fun to just try it on different diameters until you find the sweet spots. And even what I'd call "poor" knurling is often good enough for hobby jobs.

Keep in mind too you're not cutting the material, but swedging it (pushing it around) to form the diamonds. So you want lubricating fluid while you do it (like WD40) not cutting fluid like you'd use to drill a hole. You want the knurling tool to be able to slip over the surface as it molds it. I honestly didn't learn that until recently and it explained why my old knurls were sharp and nasty at times — I used cutting fluid. Duh.

The knurling lends a firm purchase to the scribe, especially if your fingers are oily or greasy. Plus it just looks good and ramps any DIY project into the "professional" level.

While we're here, let's talk about "parting off." That's the way you cut a piece of round stock in the lathe, separating it from the main raw material. In this case, I ended up not quite happy with the butt end so parted it off and re-machined it. A thin cutting tool is pressed into the work by the cross-feed, eventually parting the stock. It can be very precise and handy but can also be a disaster. Like knurling, some people are intimidated by the process, but watch some videos online and you'll soon figure out how to do it.

I also used the parting tool to cut a series of light round cuts along the main body of the scribe. It's for looks, and also gives you some purchase when holding it at different points along the body.

## Final Steps

If you're using sewing machine needles the point end will have a small hole for the thread. I like to cut it off using a cut-off wheel in a Dremel. You can then use the side of the cut-off wheel to dress the point, or use a belt sander, stone wheel or anything handy. I've also used a diamond hone bench stone.

Cutting off the end also allows you to custom tailor the length of the scribe. At first I thought a shorter, stubbier scribe length would be best but soon found a longer one reaches into screw holes to pick out debris, can reach along taller stock, and you can even use it for a rough measure of the depth of holes you drill. So the longer option is best.

Once you assure the pin body fits into the drilled hole, you can secure it. I've found any of the various Loctite-type products or Super Glues work fine. No need to solder it, and the glue method allows fast and easy removal. The thinner glues will "wick" into the hole nicely too.

When the part is in the lathe would be the time to do any polishing. I generally use various grits of wet-or-dry paper, stopping around the 320 grit. It leaves a sort of handsome matte finish. But you could certainly shine things up to a mirror gloss if you want. Keep in mind the brass will tarnish, which I think is cool as it makes your tool look like you actually use it.

## You Can Do It

Once the glue sets you can put your new scribe to work. It resides right at my hand on my workbench. I use it for scribing metal after laying Dykem layout fluid down, probing the unknown in a wooden rifle stock, picking out splinters, poking gunk out of an empty case's primer hole and a hundred other jobs. When I showed my wife Suzi the first one I had made, she smiled, saying, "Why thank you. I'm sure I can use this for all sorts of things."

This is a great first lathe project and helps you to build skills you can put to use down the road making firing pins, gun parts and other needed tools like assembly pins, etc. There's a distinct sense of satisfaction when someone is visiting and they comment, "Hey, that's a sweet scribe. Where'd you buy it?"

"Why, I made it on my lathe," you can say off-handedly. Just be prepared for a rush of "Can you make me one too!" pleadings.

And use caution on who you show that first one to. Just sayin'.

*For more info:*
*www.grizzlytool.com,*
*www.harborfreight.com*

**Roy Huntington**

# A REVOLVER EJECTOR-ROD WRENCH

## Banish buggered-up knurling!

*The raw stock was 2" in diameter so it was turned down to 1.5" per the drawing. Leave enough raw stock to be held in the chuck's jaws.*

I f you work on revolvers you know unscrewing the ejector rod can be an iffy proposition at times. First, you can't recall if it's "lefty-loosey" or "righty-tighty" since the threads reversed in 1961 for S&W revolvers. Today, they are "left-hand" threads — while prior to 1961, they were "right-hand." Regardless, aside from tightening when you should be loosening or the other way around, that little rod is tough to get ahold of without destroying the fine knurling on the end.

*A simple drawing in a gunsmithing tips book caught Roy's eye. The result is this nifty ejector rod wrench, handy on anyone's bench.*

*A center hole is drilled in the lathe using a chuck and drill bit held in the lathe tail stock. This assures the hole is well-centered. The other visible hole was done on the mill.*

People try using hard leather under plier jaws and it mostly leaves leather crud in the now-ruined knurling. I've tried lead sheeting, copper and even a sort of hard rubber. Sometimes, if the rod wasn't screwed-in too tightly, it worked. But often I still ended up with buggered-up knurling. Sometimes you can chuck the rod in a vise lined with hard wood jaw protectors, allowing you to grab along the length of the rod. But even that doesn't always work.

After drilling, the part was set-up for knurling. This texture allows fingers to get a firm grasp on the wrench to turn the ejector rod to loosen or tighten it.

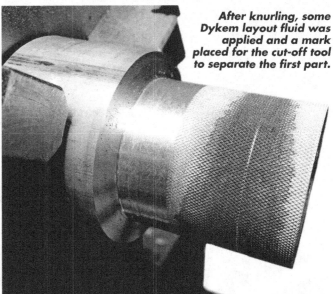

After knurling, some Dykem layout fluid was applied and a mark placed for the cut-off tool to separate the first part.

Using his medium-sized mill Roy drilled the needed secondary hole for a channel he later milled.

The lathe parting tool sort of "slices" off the part and is "usually" neater than using a hacksaw!

To hold the cut parts in the lathe, Roy stacked washers behind it. This allowed him to use the lathe to do a bit of final finishing on the edges and chamfer the holes cleanly.

One tool cut and ready for final machine work. The one behind it has the second hole drilled through too, it's just hiding behind the first part. Roy will part that second one off as well.

The secret ingredient? A simple shop-made "wrench" crafted out of aluminum.

Aluminum is flexible enough to work with this design, and soft enough not to mar the relatively soft steel of the ejector rod knurling. While it may look on the complicated side, it's not and could actually be made using a hacksaw, some files, a hand drill and a tap or two. I used my lathe and milling machine because,

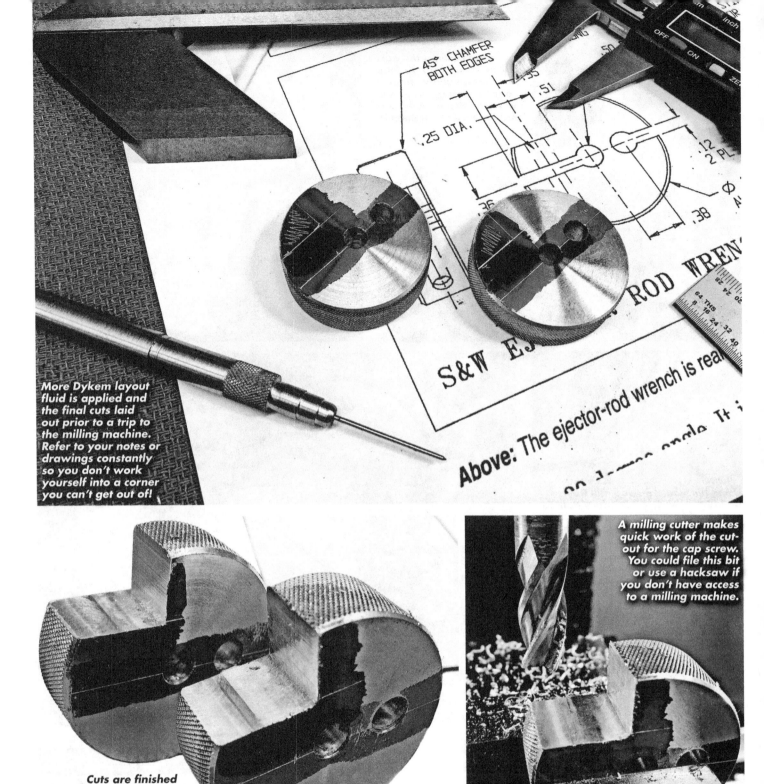

45° CHAMFER BOTH EDGES

.25 DIA.

.51

.55

.12 2 PL

.38

More Dykem layout fluid is applied and the final cuts laid out prior to a trip to the milling machine. Refer to your notes or drawings constantly so you don't work yourself into a corner you can't get out of!

S&W EJ... ROD WREN...

**Above:** The ejector-rod wrench is rea...

A milling cutter makes quick work of the cut-out for the cap screw. You could file this bit or use a hacksaw if you don't have access to a milling machine.

Cuts are finished and the parts are ready for the relief channels to be milled.

well … I have them. Could you buy a tool like this? You bet. But why, when you can make one — and have a good time doing it?

## Starting Out

I used a drawing I found in an old gunsmithing tips book I have as the basic design of the wrench. You can easily make it from slightly smaller stock or bigger, but I think aluminum is the

best material for sure. I found some nice 2" aluminum round stock on eBay for about $10. It was a foot long so gives me plenty for more projects down the line. I also rounded up some cap bolts and washers I had on-hand, following what was recommended in the drawing.

I parted off about a 5" length of the round stock, chucked it up and turned it to diameter. After taking it out of the chuck, I laid out some lines using Dykem

blue layout fluid to find the secondary holes and channels to cut. Using my mill as a drill press, I drilled the end hole for one of the channels, re-chucked it and drilled the center hole in the lathe. It's easy to find dead center that way.

Keep in mind this isn't really a precision tool so these measurements can be within a few thousandths of an inch without causing any undue concern. Follow the drawing to get basic dimen-

At this point the holes for the bolts need to be drilled and tapped, the edges smoothed and the flats taken to a 220-grit finish just to look good.

A quick test use before final polish and cleanup showed the clamps worked just fine. Note how the ejector rod end slips into the center hole, then as the bolt is tightened the aluminum relief channels allow the tool to flex, clamping down so the rod can be turned.

Clamping onto a flat aluminum plate allowed Roy to cut through the bottom of the part to make the channels through-and-through.

sions but feel free to adjust to suit the materials you have on-hand.

## More Lathe Work

While the stock was in the lathe, I ran some knurling over it to give fingers purchase on the round body of the wrench to turn the ejector rod. If you don't have a lathe, you could file some cross hatching or even just raise some surface burrs to do the same thing.

I used Dykem to mark a cut-off line (I wanted to make two wrenches at least) and parted the end one off. The parting tool had to stick out a bit far so I took my time. Once the cut was off, I cleaned up the face of the remaining stock for another cut-off. When I drilled the holes, I made sure to drill deeply enough to pass through the second wrench material too. No use having to re-do the layouts for the second one.

Inserting a scribe or, in this case, simply a handy Allen wrench, into the center hole allows you to catch the part when it falls off. This sure beats using a hacksaw, trust me.

## More Layout

At the bench I put more Dykem (handy stuff) and laid out the channels I needed to mill. You could also use a simple Sharpie-type marker to color the surfaces. I decided to mill the cut-outs for the bolt heads first. If you don't have a mill, some careful hacksaw work (or a roughing file) would form the same cut. You will find a jeweler's saw can really deliver some amazingly fine cuts. I've often used one to profile cut a hammer or gun part from a flat piece of steel.

*Roy ended up making one more tool for a total of three from the original cut of the raw stock. The original stock diameter was 2" and was turned to about 1.5" for the tool.*

They work surprisingly fast and have a very thin kerf. There are loads of them on eBay which are fine, old German models for around $30 or so.

## Careful Mill Work

Chucking the disc in the milling vise was easy since both sides were flat at this point. Since this isn't a high-precision tool, I just eyeballed the layout lines, assuring the vertical one was aligned with the side of the milling cutter. I ran the quill down to the bottom line and zeroed the depth gauge on the mill. As I cut, once I got to zero I knew I was deep enough. You could also just eyeball it if you like. Once you start to make cuts like this it's exciting to see a part start to magically appear from the raw stock.

My milling machine is what I'd call "medium" sized, with a one horsepower motor. Consequently I take light cuts even in aluminum and use plenty of cutting fluid when cutting steel. A spray of air now and again will keep chips clear and the cuts cleaner. Aluminum is sort of grabby and tends to collect on the cutter's edges so keeping things clean helps the cut along. For around $800 to $1,200 you can get a benchtop mill able to do this sort of work, along with sight dovetails and other light-duty milling. Awfully handy in the home shop! Ditto for the lathe.

At this point we need to lay out the bolt holes to drill and eventually tap, and mill the channels to allow the wrench to "flex" in order to grab the ejector rod as the cap screw is tightened. A step at a time, and soon you're finished.

At the mill, I clamped the parts onto a piece of flat aluminum stock

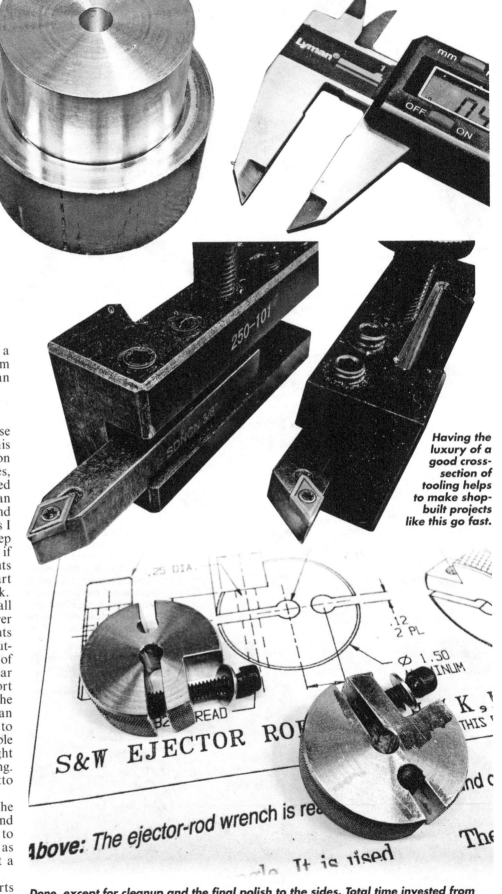

*Having the luxury of a good cross-section of tooling helps to make shop-built projects like this go fast.*

*Done, except for cleanup and the final polish to the sides. Total time invested from raw stock to a test use was about two hours.*

and cut the channels using an appropriately sized milling cutter. This way I can cut right through the bottom of the part into the base metal of the flat stock. Slow and steady wins the race. Remember, those channels could have been cut using a hacksaw, power hacksaw or even filed if you had some patience!

## Last Touches

I drilled then tapped the bolt holes using the mill as a drill press again. I tapped the holes freehand, clamping the parts in my bench vise since it's easy that way and there's enough precision for this, even tapping by hand. Then I ran a very fine file over all the edges to de-burr things, and put a 220-grit final finish on the flats just to pretty things up.

*A set of simple steel lettering stamps allowed Roy to put his friend's name on one for a gift. There's nothing like a shop-made tool as a gift for a friend who appreciates such things.*

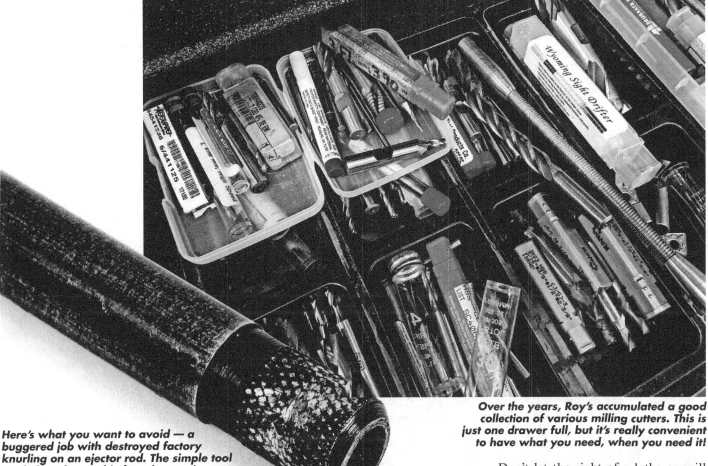

*Here's what you want to avoid — a buggered job with destroyed factory knurling on an ejector rod. The simple tool made here keeps this from happening.*

*Over the years, Roy's accumulated a good collection of various milling cutters. This is just one drawer full, but it's really convenient to have what you need, when you need it!*

I've found tools like this get battered but at least initially they look nice.

A bit of acetone or rubbing alcohol will remove the Dykem and degrease things. Then a final wipe and a drop or two of oil on the threads of the bolt and it's time to try things out. You'll need to do a bit of experimenting to discover how hard you need to tighten the bolt but you'll soon find a sweet spot between "not hard enough" and "too hard." The channel cuts allow the aluminum to flex as you tighten the bolt, clamping around the ejector rod.

## Final Thoughts

I ended up making three tools and sort of had an assembly line going. I gave one to Tiger McKee (see his Model 10 build in this Special Edition) and one to my friend Dusty (see his .38 Super build here too). Note the simple lettering stamp to make it a personal gift.

Don't let the sight of a lathe or mill make you think you can't do this stuff easily at your own bench. I spent many years turning out gunsmithing jobs, projects and building tools as I needed them, all done with hand tools like files, hacksaws, sanding paper, hand taps and dies and various grits of stones for shaping and polishing. I still use many of the tools I made 40 or more years ago when I was first starting out.

The best thing to do? Just do it.

*For more info:*
*www.grizzlytools.com*

Roy Huntington

# UPGRADING A STOCK 1911

## Nighthawk Custom's 'Drop-In' parts assure success!

*Nighthawk Custom's Vice President 1911 shows off some of their remarkable machined parts. Most are available to the DIY home gunsmith too.*

Whether your heart lies in upgrading an existing 1911 you have, or a complete build from scratch, starting with quality parts is a must. I've seen too many botched jobs by amateurs and professionals trying to "make do" with inferior or just plain crappy parts. Barrels, hammers, triggers, sears, ejectors, extractors, mainspring housing and all the other small bits and pieces all play critical roles in how a gun fits and runs. Trying to save a bit of money on a build or improvement is not only a silly waste of time and money — it can also be unsafe.

Those boxes of gun-show used and worn parts, or even "new" cheaply made knockoffs are hard to resist. I know because I've failed to resist them myself. But I honestly can't think of a single instance where buying a knockoff, imported, or cast "who-knows-what-it-is" metal part ever paid off in the long run. It's almost invariably followed up with the purchase of the better part you should have bought initially. I speak from loads of experience on this, trust me.

Equate it to the $5 socket set — another hard-to-resist purchase. "But I may only need it once." Exactly, and that's why you need to buy a good one or risk the busted knuckles when the

cheap socket splits or the wrench slips on the pot-metal ratchet. Do I make my point here?

### Choices

While many makers offer high-quality aftermarket parts for your favorite 1911, I wanted to specifically address the exceptional new line offered by well-known custom shop Nighthawk Custom, from Berryville, Ark. They're made of solid steel, with the grade and specific type dependent on the part. You won't find Metal Injection Molded (MIM) parts here.

From slides and frames, barrels of all sorts, bushings, safeties, sights, triggers, guide rods and plugs, pin sets, sears and other action parts, even grip screws and bushings, Nighthawk has it all. I've used virtually all of their parts in guns I've built personally and have never had a single issue with anything — ever. While their mainstream machined parts are marvelous, there's one new offering I'm especially enthused about, and it's perfect for any 1911 shooter — an instant upgrade to the trigger pull of your existing 1911.

### Drop-In Trigger System!

Custom pistolsmith Mark Dye has worked with Nighthawk to finalize his design of an amazing, completely modular, drop-in trigger unit. The result is a chassis-based system containing the hammer, sear, disconnector and spring dropping right into your factory-stock 1911. It uses the existing hammer and sear/disconnector pins due to the clever

*Nighthawk Custom's new line of "drop-in" all-steel machined parts are flawlessly executed, ready to upgrade your existing gun — or be a part of a full build. Some fitting may be needed depending on the gun.*

"hollow" pins in the unit. The key here is the fact the drop-in system allows the hammer/sear/disconnector relationship to be rock solid, so a reliable 3.75–4-lb. trigger pull is assured. It can be used on a new build, but excels in upgrading an existing gun.

The actual swap takes about three minutes and can be done by anyone who can detail-strip a 1911. You can also install the kits in several guns so you have the same press in each. The system is machined from 416 bar stock and can be had in a silver stainless look or black Nitride. It works with 1911 Series 70, Series 80, 2011 models as well as the "Swartz" safety-style. The unit also comes with an unusual looking single-pronged spring replacing the stock three-pronged sear spring, since the drop-in unit has its own internal spring for the sear. The replacement spring just controls the grip safety. The unit is CA-legal too.

The average cost of a full-custom trigger job (with parts) can easily hit the $350 mark, not counting the wait, shipping the gun and risking it getting lost or stolen in transit. If you're comfortable detail-stripping your own 1911 — or can build a gun from fitted parts but are uncomfortable with fitting action parts — this is the way to go. I tried my test

*The Nighthawk Drop-In Trigger System is just that, completely drop-in. It's a chassis system with the sear, hammer, disconnector and spring in one assembly — an amazing breakthrough for any 1911 owner.*

*The rise of suppressor popularity means changes to the classic 1911 design to accommodate them. Nighhawk's new "drop-in" parts include pre-threaded barrels.*

unit in five different 1911s from Ruger, Springfield, Colt, a custom one and even one from Armscor and the Drop-In Trigger System worked fine. Nighthawk does say "minimal gunsmithing skills" are necessary, but so far I didn't need to do any additional work to get mine to function safely. The MSRP is just $299.

I invite you to study Nighthawk's offerings as you contemplate an upgrade to your favorite 1911 — or a full custom build!

*For more info: www.nighthawkcustom. com, Ph: (877) 268-4867, info@nighthawkcustom.com*

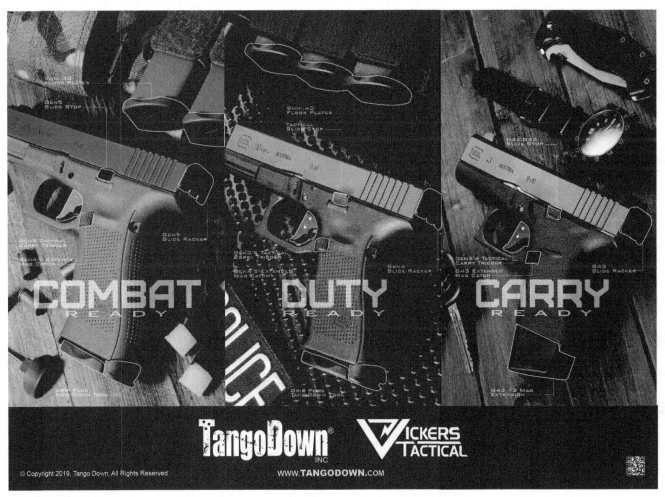

# NEW PRODUCTS ›››››

## ACE CLYDE — BRASS
GiantMouse Knives

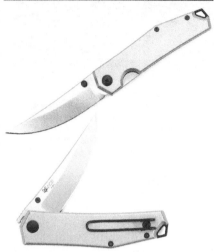

The Clyde is a mix of Scandinavian, Japanese and Persian influences. GiantMouse introduced it as an EDC knife but is now offered as the *ACE Clyde — Brass*. The knife comes with a slim, pointy and slightly upswept 3" blade made of M390 steel with a stonewash finish. But it's the brass handle that steals the show. Brass takes on a beautiful patina over time, with each knife developing its own unique look. So the more it's used, the better it looks. The ACE Clyde — Brass has an OAL of 6.97" and features bronze washers in its pivot mechanism. For more info: *www.giantmouse.com*

## GUN TOOL CORE — AR15
Real Avid

Real Avid's Gun Tool CORE — AR15 is all about core AR15 function. It's designed to keep AR15s up and running in the field or at the range. The CORE will work fine on a gun bench but it's meant to solve problems wherever the gun is used. Easy to carry, the CORE easily secures to MOLLE straps or a belt. The unique but practical design packs six tools into a folding metal frame. It features a bolt scraper, carrier and firing pin scrapers, cord cutter and bottle opener, bolt override and scope turret adjuster, takedown punch and A2 front sight adjuster. For more info: (800) 286- 0567, *www.realavid.com*

## ALUMINUM SLIP-JOINT FOLDERS
Bear & Son Cutlery

The *Aluminum Slip-Joint Folders* from Bear & Son Cutlery are lightweight pocketknives. They have aluminum handles that fit in pockets or purses and can even hang on key chains. Offered with 1.5" or 2.375" blades, the pocketknives include a taperground drop-point blade made from high-carbon stainless steel. Handles are made of aluminum. OAL is 4.25" or 6.5". For more info: (256) 435-2227, *www.bearandsoncutlery.com*

## RIO BRAVO LEVER-ACTION RIMFIRE
Rossi

The *Rio Bravo* is Rossi's new .22 LR long gun. Based on the company's popular line of R92 lever-action firearms, the Rio Bravo features a German beechwood or black polymer forearm and stock with polished black metal finish. It is well-suited for small-game hunting, adventurous target shooting, around-the-farm pest control and also for youth training. Up to 15 rounds of .22 LR can be fed into the magazine tube. Traditional buckhorn sights are on the wood model; the synthetic model has fiber optic sights with the rear sight adjustable for precise zero. For more info: (229) 515-8707, *www.rossiusa.com*

## PROFESSIONAL GUN CLEANING MASTER KIT
RamRodz

The *Professional Gun Cleaning Master Kit* from RamRodz includes caliber-specific swabs and brushes that match bores ranging from .22 to .45 caliber, as well as 12- and 20-ga. The case features four layers including 550 precision tools, brushes, a pull-through cable, interlocking claw tweezers, accessories and a new biodegradable lubricating oil and cleaning solution. The kit also comes with a Hypalon chemical-resistant cleaning mat, removable work tray and industrial-strength bore-cleaning swabs. For more info: (855) 486-7922, *www.ramrodz.com*

## THE SHOTBLOCK
ShotBlock

*The ShotBlock* is a new gun accessory that stops a gun from being loaded and provides anti-corrosion benefits while in storage. It thus aims to avoid the accidental discharge of a firearm. It ensures a bullet cannot be loaded into full breech. An easy-to-use indicator that slides into the barrel of the firearm, The ShotBlock allows a manufacturer to ship firearms to the retailer protected from loading a live round yet offers a customer the chance to safely hold and manipulate the firearm. For more info: *www.theshotblock.com*

## SIDE-SLIDE PISTOL AMMO BOX
### MTM Case-Gard

The *Side-Slide Pistol Ammo Box* gives quick "bulk access" to cartridges. Users can also "tip out" the exact amount of ammo needed. Depress the one-touch release to slide the top of the lid to the desired amount of ammo required and tilt the box. The transparent clear blue or clear green design allows visible inventorying without the need to open the box. Stack them in the safe, in a range bag, or on the shooting bench for an organized workspace. Available in 9mm or .45 ACP sizes, the new MTM Side-Slide Pistol Ammo Box makes ammo management easy. For more info: (800) 543-0548, *www.mtmcase-gard.com*

## SHIKRA FOLDER
### Ontario Knife Co.

The *Shikra Folder* from Ontario Knife Co. has a 3.2" stainless steel blade with a 55-57 HRC rating and a beveled taper to a fine tip. The versatile knife has a slotted spine by the grip for delicate work when opened to its full 7.4" length. The handle is linen Micarta on one side and full titanium on the other. This reduces the weight while providing excellent grip, even in wet conditions. A belt-clip helps secure the knife when not in use. For more info: (800) 222-5233, *www.ontarioknife.com*

## DELUXE WETLAND SEAT
### ALPS OutdoorZ

ALPS OutdoorZ expands its waterfowl line with the *Deluxe Wetland Seat*. It is for use in marshlands, flooded timber and water-covered or saturated ground where typical hunting seats are not feasible. With a height-adjustable, vertical support made of lightweight yet rigid aluminum, the Deluxe Wetland Seat inserts into the ground with a wedged post end. Support arms on sides of the seat post pivot 90 degrees to prevent sinking into soft soil. Seat height can be adjusted from 24" to 34" to accommodate a range of shooters. For more info: (800) 344-2577, *www.alpsoutdoorz.com*

## DEFENDER 856
### Taurus

Taurus has released the *Defender 856* revolver. Based on the original Taurus 856, the Defender 856 features a factory-installed front sight post with an integrated tritium vial for quick sight picture acquisition even in low light. Chambered for .38 Special +P ammo, the Defender 856 boasts a 6-round capacity and DA/SA action with a transfer bar safety. The barrel length is 3", making it short enough for deep concealed carry while delivering a sight radius for accuracy at distances beyond the personal space zone. The longer 3" barrel (vs. 2" barrels) also delivers increased muzzle velocity for more decisive terminal performance. The Defender 856 debuts in four standard models with ergonomic, no-slip Hogue rubber grips for maximum recoil absorption. For more info: (800) 327-3776, *www.taurususa.com*

## DENALI CHEST HOLSTER
### Diamond D Outdoors

Designed and tested in Alaska, the *Denali Chest Holster* is built to withstand challenging weather conditions. It is offered in 10 sizes depending on your type of gun and barrel length. With an innovative strap system and adjustable retention strap, the Denali Chest Holster is worn tight on your chest for one-handed, quick and easy drawing of your firearm. It is made of 1050 Ballistic weave exterior with high-density foam between two layers for increased strength. For more info: *www.diamonddoutdoors.com*

## BLUE GUARDIAN
### Fiocchi

Fiocchi introduces the *Blue Guardian* series of lead-free defense and training ammo for LE as well as personal defense. The new ammo is offered in three versions: 1) Blue Guardian FR — for high-volume training with lead-free and frangible ballistically matched bullets in .380, 9mm Luger, .40 S&W, .45 ACP and more; 2) Blue Guardian HP — for duty use and personal/home protection where ricochet is a concern in hard structures; and 3) Blue Guardian SC – for optimal penetration, weight retention and terminal performance in soft tissue. For more info: (417) 725-4118, *www.fiocchiusa.com*

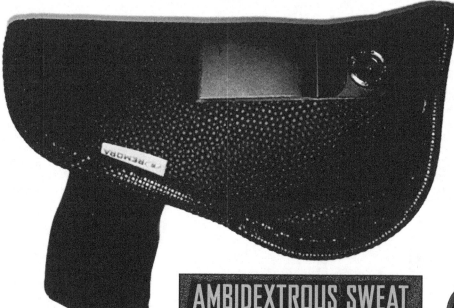

The *DIY Special Edition* is giving away a 1911 from Rock Island Armory — the *Rock Standard FS – 45ACP!* It's just the thing you'd want during this difficult time. Built on RIA's traditional classic 70 series design, the Rock Standard FS offers top-quality production and engineering standards. Chambered in .45 ACP with a 5" button rifled barrel with a full-length guide rod, the pistol's smooth, angled, snag-free style allows for a quick draw when needed. OAL is 8.56"; weight 2.49 lbs. empty (2.87 lbs. loaded); length of twist 1:16". The frame and slide are finished with a parkerized matte coating. Other features include dovetail-mounted front- and fixed rear-sights and checkered rubber grips. Like all Rock Island 1911s, the Rock Standard FS comes with a crisp factory 4- to 6-lb. trigger. A perfect "base" gun to start your own custom 1911 build too!

When you win this giveaway package, you can carry your new Rock Standard FS – 45ACP in the *Remora Ambidextrous Sweat Shield 2-in-1 Holster.* It's a combination of two of Remora's holster styles that keeps body oils and sweat away from the gun while also protecting the user from "hammer gouge" or similar irritations. Use the holster's swivel clip for IWB carry; the no-clip option for IWB, pocket, purse carry and more.

Streamlight's 1,000-lumen ProTac HL-X is a tactical handheld flashlight that can be recharged through an 18650 USB battery with integrated micro USB port or with two CR123A lithium batteries. The multi-fuel innovation ensures you'll have a beam whenever it's needed.

This prize package is a gift you will surely appreciate! Join the giveaway by clicking on www.americanhandgunner.com/giveaways or by mailing a post card! Here's hoping you win! —*Jazz Jimenez*

**PROTAC HL-X**

Maker: Streamlight
(800) 523-7488
www.streamlight.com

Value: $157.50

**ENTER ONLINE:**
www.americanhandgunner.com

**ENTRY DEADLINE:**
**September 2, 2020**

# CUSTOM GUNSMITH DIRECTORY

For those of us who want something "just right" and like their handguns personalized to their specific needs — or just something "purty!" — then a top-notch custom gunsmith is your best option. But how do you find the artisan fitting your needs? The following is a detailed listing of some of the best custom gun-smiths and gun makers out there today. So, take a look and get going on your next great project! Special thanks to the American Pistolsmiths Guild for help in compiling this listing. Some information may have changed by press time.

**Alpha Precision**
Jim Stroh
3238 Della Slaton Rd.
Comer, GA 30629
**(706) 783-2131**
jim@alphaprecisioninc.com

**Art Enterprises**
Alan Tillman
1702 Barbara St.
Austin, TX 78757
**(512) 454-9328**
artent@austin.rr.com

**AT Custom Gunwork**
Alan Tanaka
17924 South Hobart Blvd.
Gardena, CA 90248
**(310) 327-2721**

**Bar-Sto Precision Machine**
Irv Stone, Jr.
3571 Hansen Ave.
Sturgis, SD 57785
**(605) 720-4000**
barsto@eee.org

**Ben Van Dyke**
29000 Highway V
Smithville, MO 65350
**(660) 281-4155**

**Better Firearms Design**
Clifford H. Benjamin
1032 Ridgewood Ave.
Daytona Beach, FL 32117
**(386) 523-6590**
**www.betterfirearmsdesign.com**

**Caspian Arms**
Gary Smith
75 Cal Foster Dr.
Wolcott, VT 05680
**(802) 472-5217**

**Colby Brandon**
P.O. Box 755
Fort Davis, TX 79734
**(432) 466-4843 or
(432) 426-2791**
ocotillo.outfitting@hotmail.com

**Curtis Custom Shop**
Michael Curtis
212 Wren St. North
Martinsburg, WV 25401
**(304) 267-1984**

**Cylinder & Slide, Inc.**
William Laughridge
245 East 4th St.
Fremont, NE 68025
**(402) 721-4277**
wrl@cylinder-slide.com
**www.cylinder-slide.com**

**D&L Sports, Inc.**
Dave Lauck
P.O. Box 4843
Chino Valley, AZ 86323
**(928) 636-1726**
dlsports@cableone.net
**www.dlsports.com**

**Defensive Creations**
Dave Laubert
253 Maplewood Dr.
Alliance, OH 44601
**(330) 823-6906**
dave@defensivecreations.com
**www.defensivecreations.com**

**Derr Precision**
Greg Derr
25 Rockwood Rd., #2
Marshfield, MA 02050
**(781) 834-3225**
greg@derrprecision.com
**www.derrprecision.com**

**Doug Turnbull Restorations, Inc.**
Doug Turnbull
6680 Route 5 & 20
P.O. Box 571
Bloomfield, NY 14469-0471
**(585) 657-6338**
turnbullrest@mindspring.com
**www.turnbullrestoration.com**

**Ed Brown Products**
Ed Brown
43825 Muldrow Trail
P.O. Box 492
Perry, MO 63462
**(573) 565-3261**
**www.edbrown.com**

**Engineered Revolvers
& Semiautomatics**
James (Jerry) C. Keefer, Jr.
2330 Goodluck Rd.
Maidens, VA 23102
**(804) 357-1344**
keefer45@msn.com

**Gun Craft, Inc.**
Kim Stroud
1601 6th St. SE
Ruskin, FL 33570
**(813) 645-3828**
bjones258@tampabayrr.com

**Harrison Design**
John Harrison
4313 White Hickory Ln.
Kennesaw, GA 30152
**(770) 419-3476**
john@harrisoncustom.com
**www.harrisoncustom.com**

**Heinie Specialty Products**
Richard Heinie
301 Oak St.
Quincy, IL 62301
**(217) 228-9500**
**www.heinie.com**

**Infinity Firearms**
Sandy Strayer
71229 Interstate Hwy 20
Gordon, TX 76453
**(800) 928-1911**
info@sviguns.com
**www.sviguns.com**

**Jeremy Sides**
310 North College Ave.
Geneseo, IL 61254
**(309) 314-4712**
teamrollingrock@hotmail.com

**Jim Garthwaite, Pistolsmith, Inc.**
Jim Garthwaite
12130 State Route 405
Watsontown, PA 17777
**(570) 538-1566**
email@garthwaite.com
**www.garthwaite.com**

**John Yanek Custom Gun Works**
John J. Yanek
5227 Foxcroft Dr.
P.O. Box 222
Schnecksville, PA 18078
**(610) 767-4423**
john@yanekcustom.com

**Kart Precision Barrel Corp.**
Fred Kart
3975 Garner St. SW
Shallotte, NC 28470
**(910) 754-5212**
info@kartbarrel.com
**www.kartbarrel.com**

**Koppco Industries**
Terry Kopp
1105 S. Business Highway 13
Lexington, MO 64067
**(816) 529-1337**

**Kustom Ballistics**
Neil Keller
1684 E 900 N
Decatur, IN 46733
**(260) 724-3065**
kellers@mchsi.com
www.kustom-ballistics.com

**Lucas Machine & Welding**
Les Lucas
27 Ponderosa Dr.
Colona, IL 61241
**(309) 441-6172**

**Mag-Na Port International, Inc.**
Kenneth Kelly
41302 Executive Dr.
Harrison Township, MI 48045-1306
**(586) 469-6727**
email@magnaport.com
www.magnaport.com

**Marvel Custom Guns, Inc.**
Alan Marvel
3922 Madonna Rd.
P.O. Box 168
Jarrettsville, MD 21084-1034
**(410) 557-6545**
almarvel@zoominternet.net
www.marvelcustomguns.com

**Michael Watkins**
1311 Spencer St.
Grinnell, IA 50112
**(800) 741-0015, ext. 5479**
mdwatkins@windstream.net

**Northern Virginia Gun Works**
Robert Garrett
P.O. Box 128
Springfield, VA 22150
**(703) 644-6504**
gunsmith1@aol.com

**Oglesby & Oglesby Gunmakers, Inc.**
William D. Oglesby
744 W. Andrews Rd.
Springfield, IL 62707
**(217) 487-7100**

**Pinnacle High Performance Revolvers**
Mark Hartshorne
130 Penn Am Dr., Suite D-1
Allentown, PA 18951
**(610) 285-4392**
pinhart@ptd.net
www.pinnaclehighperformance.com

**Powder River Precision, Inc.**
Daniel Bachelor
3835 23rd St.
Baker City, OR 97814
**(541) 523-4474**
sales@powderriverprecision.net
www.powderriverprecision.com

**Reeder Custom Guns**
2601 E. 7th Ave.
Flagstaff, AZ 86004
**(928) 527-4100**
gary@reedercustomguns.com
www.reedercustomguns.com

**Sand Burr Gun Ranch**
Ashley Gibbons
2111 E. 350 North
Rochester, IN 46975
**(574) 223-3316**
sandburrgunranch@gmail.com
www.sandburrgunranch.com

**Springfield Custom**
David Williams
420 W. Main St.
Geneseo, IL 61254
**(309) 944-5631**
www.springfield-armory.com/custom/

**SSK Industries**
J. D. Jones
590 Woodvue Ln.
Wintersville, OH 43952
**(740) 264-0176**

**Ten-Ring Precision, Inc.**
Alex Hamilton
1449 Blue Crest Ln.
San Antonio, TX 78232
**(210) 494-3063**
alex@tenring.com
www.tenring.com

**TGF Services**
Richard Fried
24808 Dunnavant Dr.
Gaithersburg, MD 20879
**(301) 253-2789**

**TK Custom**
Tom Kilhoffer
503 N. Church St.
P.O. Box 333
Thomasboro, IL 61866-0333
**(217) 643-2002**
tom@tkcustom.com
www.tkcustom.com

**Tripp Research**
Virgil Tripp
P.O. Box 2240
Bastrop, TX 78602
**(512) 321-9445**
info@trippresearch.com
www.trippresearch.com

**Tussey Custom**
Terry Tussey
24 Moonlight Rd., #A
Carson City, NV 89706
**(775) 246-1533**
ttussey45@aol.com
www.tusseycustom.com

**Wild West Guns**
Jim West
7100 Homer Dr.
Anchorage, AK 99518
**(907) 344-4500**
alaska@wildwestguns.com
www.wildwestguns.com

**Wilson Combat**
Bill Wilson
2452 County Rd. 719
Berryville, AR 72616
**(800) 955-4856**
bill@wilsoncombat.com
www.wilsoncombat.com

*Les Baer's American Handgunner Special Edition 5" 1911 is a collaboration between American Handgunner magazine and Les Baer, with readers' ideas of a "perfect" 1911 tossed into the mix. Available from www.lesbaer.com.*

# American Handgunner DIY

# 2020 RESOURCE GUIDE

## Find out where you can get your own exciting guns and gear!

## BOOKS/PUBLICATIONS

| | | | | |
|---|---|---|---|---|
| **A&J ARMS BOOKSELLERS**<br>2449 N. Orchard Ave.<br>Tucson, AZ 85712<br>**(520) 512-1065**<br>www.ajarmsbooksellers.com | **AVALON FORGE**<br>409 Gun Rd.<br>Baltimore, MD 21227<br>**(410) 242-8431**<br>www.avalonforge.com | **BLUE BOOK PUBLICATIONS, INC.**<br>8009 34th Ave. S. Ste. 250<br>Minneapolis, MN 55425<br>**(800) 877-4867**<br>www.bluebookinc.com | **FMG PUBLICATIONS**<br>13741 Danielson St., Ste. A<br>Poway, CA 92064<br>**(858) 605-0253**<br>www.fmgpublications.com | **F+W PUBLICATIONS**<br>700 E. State St.<br>Iola, WI 54990<br>**(800) 258-0929**<br>www.gundigeststore.com |
| **IDSA BOOKS, LLC**<br>P.O. Box 36114<br>Cincinnati, OH 45236<br>**(513) 985-9112**<br>www.idsabooks.com | **MOWBRAY PUBLISHING**<br>54 E. School St.<br>Woonsocket, RI 02895<br>**(800) 999-4697**<br>www.manatarmsbooks.com | **NORTH CAPE PUBLICATIONS**<br>P.O. Box 1027<br>Tustin, CA 92781<br>**(800) 745-9714**<br>www.northcapepubs.com | **SCHIFFER PUBLISHING**<br>4880 Lower Valley Rd., Rte. 372<br>Atglen, PA 19310<br>**(610) 593-1777**<br>www.schifferbooks.com | **SKYHORSE PUBLISHING, INC.**<br>307 W. 36th St., 11th Floor<br>New York, NY 10018<br>**(212) 643-6816**<br>www.skyhorsepublishing.com |

## BULLETS/RELOADING

| | | | | |
|---|---|---|---|---|
| **BARNES BULLETS**<br>38 N. Frontage Rd.<br>Mona, UT 84645<br>**(800) 574-9200**<br>www.barnesbullets.com | **C&H/4D DIES**<br>P.O. Box 889<br>Mt. Vernon, OH 43050<br>**(740) 397-7214**<br>www.ch4d.com | **BOOMERS BULLET MOULDS**<br>Leo Bumphrey<br>1221 Broder St.<br>Regina, SK S4N 3R3<br>Canada<br>**(306) 522-8760**<br>www.boomersmoulds.com | **FORSTER PRODUCTS**<br>310 E. Lanark Ave.<br>Lanark IL 61046<br>**(815) 493-6360**<br>www.forsterproducts.com | **GRAF & SONS, INC.**<br>4050 S. Clark<br>Mexico, MO 65265<br>**(800) 581-2266**<br>www.grafs.com |
| **HUNTINGTON DIE SPECIALTIES**<br>P.O. Box 991<br>Oroville, CA 95965<br>**(866) 735-6237**<br>www.huntingtons.com | **LEE PRECISION**<br>4275 Hwy. U<br>Hartford, WI 53027<br>**(262) 673-3075**<br>www.leeprecision.com | **LYMAN PRODUCTS**<br>475 Smith St.<br>Middletown, CT 06457<br>**(860) 632-2020**<br>www.lymanproducts.com | **MONTANA BULLET WORKS**<br>7730 Hesper Rd.<br>Billings, MT 59106<br>**(406) 655-8163**<br>www.montanabulletworks.com | **PALMETTO STATE ARMORY**<br>200 Business Park Blvd.<br>Columbia, SC 29203<br>**(803) 240-2347**<br>www.palmettostatearmory.com |
| **PRECISION RELOADING, INC.**<br>1700 W. Cedar Ave. Ste. B<br>Mitchell, SD 57301<br>**(860) 684-7979**<br>www.precisionreloading.com | **RCBS**<br>605 Oro Dam Blvd.<br>Oroville, CA 95965<br>**(800) 553-5000**<br>www.rcbs.com | **REDDING RELOADING EQUIPMENT**<br>1089 Starr Rd.<br>Cortland, NY 13045<br>**(607) 753-3331**<br>www.redding-reloading.com | **SIERRA BULLETS**<br>1400 W. Henry St.<br>Sedalia, MO 65301<br>**(888) 223-3006**<br>www.sierrabullets.com | **SINCLAIR INTERNATIONAL INC.**<br>200 S. Front St.<br>Montezuma, IA 50171<br>**(800) 717-8211**<br>www.sinclairintl.com |
| **SMARTRELOADER PRODUCTS HELVETICA TRADING USA, LLC**<br>701 Lawton Rd.<br>Charlotte, NC 28216<br>**(800) 954-2689**<br>www.smartreloader-usa.com | **STARLINE BRASS**<br>1300 W. Henry<br>Sedalia, MO 65301<br>**(660) 827-6640**<br>www.starlinebrass.com | **SPEER AMMO**<br>229 Snake River Ave.<br>Lewiston, ID 83501<br>**(800) 627-3640**<br>www.speer-bullets.com | **TOP BRASS**<br>10325 Country Rd. 120<br>Salida, CO 81201<br>**(719) 539-7274**<br>www.topbrass-inc.com | **WIDENER'S RELOADING & SHOOTING SUPPLY INC.**<br>P.O. Box 3009 CRS<br>Johnson City, TN 37602<br>**(423) 282-6786**<br>www.wideners.com |

## BLACK POWDER GUNS

| | | | | |
|---|---|---|---|---|
| **BEAUCHAMP & SON FLINTLOCK'S ETC.**<br>160 Rossiter Rd.<br>Richmond, MA 01254<br>**(413) 698-3822**<br>www.flintlocksetc.com | **DIXIE GUN WORKS**<br>1412 W. Reelfoot Ave.<br>Union City, TN 38281<br>**(800) 238-6785**<br>www.dixiegunworks.com | **NAVY ARMS**<br>219 Lawn St.<br>Martinsburg, WV 25401<br>**(304) 262-9870**<br>www.navyarms.com | **S&S FIREARMS**<br>74-11 Myrtle Ave.<br>Glendale, NY 11385<br>**(718) 497-1100**<br>www.ssfirearms.com | **TRADITIONS PERFORMANCE**<br>P.O. Box 776<br>Old Saybrook, CT 06475<br>**(860) 388-4656**<br>www.traditionsfirearms.com |

# LOADED AMMUNITION

| ASYM PRECISION AMMUNITION | BLACK HILLS AMMUNITION | CCI | CORBON DAKOTA AMMO, INC./GLASER, LLC. | DOUBLETAP AMMUNITION |
|---|---|---|---|---|
| Phone: 201-777-1911 | P.O. Box 3090 | 2299 Snake River Ave. | 1311 Industry Rd. | 586 S. Main St. #333 |
| | Rapid City, SD 57709 | Lewiston, ID 83501 | Sturgis, SD 57785 | Cedar City, UT 84720 |
| | (605) 348-5150 | (208) 746-2351 | (800) 626-7266 | (866) 357-1066 |
| www.asymammo.com | www.black-hills.com | www.cci-ammunition.com | www.corbon.com | www.doubletapammo.com |
| FEDERAL CARTRIDGE COMPANY | FIOCCHI AMMUNITION | HORNADY | LANCER SYSTEMS | PMC AMMUNITION |
| 900 Ehlen Dr. | 6930 N. Fremont Rd. | 3625 W. Old Potash Hwy. | 7566 Morris Ct., Ste. 300 | 2257 N. Loop 336 W., Ste. 140-428 |
| Anoka, MN 55303-7503 | Ozark, MO 65721 | Grand Island, NE 68802 | Allenton, PA 18106 | Conroe, TX 77304 |
| (800) 831-0850 | (417) 725-4118 | (800) 338-3220 | (610) 973-2600 | (281) 703-8146 |
| www.federalpremium.com | www.fiocchiusa.com | www.hornady.com | www.lancer-systems.com | www.pmcammo.com |
| REMINGTON ARMS | WILSON COMBAT | WINCHESTER REPEATING ARMS | WINCHESTER AMMUNITION | |
| P.O. Box 700 | 2234 CR 719 | 275 Winchester Ave. | 600 Powder Mill Rd. | |
| Madison, NC 27025 | Berryville, AR 72616 | Morgan, UT 84050 | East Alton, IL 62024 | |
| (800) 243-9700 | (800) 955-4856 | (800) 945-5237 | (618) 258-2000 | |
| www.remington.com | www.wilsoncombat.com | www.winchesterguns.com | www.winchester.com | |

# SHOOTING ACCESSORIES

| BLACK HILLS SHOOTERS SUPPLY | BROWNELLS | BUFFALO ARMS CO. | DIXIE GUN WORKS | G96 |
|---|---|---|---|---|
| P.O. Box 4220 | 200 S. Front St. | 660 Vermeer Ct. | 1412 W. Reelfoot Ave. | 85-5th Ave. Bldg. #6 |
| 2875 S. Creek Dr. | Montezuma, IA 50171 | Ponderay, ID 83852 | Union City, TN 38281 | Paterson, NJ 07524 |
| Rapid City, SD 57709 | (800) 741-0015 | (208) 263-6953 | (800) 238-6785 | (877) 332-0035 |
| (800) 289-2506 | | | | |
| www.bhshooters.com | www.brownells.com | www.buffaloarms.com | www.dixiegunworks.com | www.g96.com |
| HARRIS BIPODS | MIDWAYUSA | OHIO ORDNANCE WORKS | PROLIX | SMITH & ALEXANDER, INC. |
| 999 Broadway | 5875 W. Van Horn Tavern Rd. | 310 Park Dr. | P.O. Box 1466 | P.O. Box 299 |
| Barlow, KY 42024 | Columbia, MO 65203 | Chardon, OH 44024 | West Jordan, UT 84084 | Copeville, TX 75121 |
| (203) 266-6906 | (800) 243-3220 | (440) 285-3481 | (800) 248-5823 | (800) 722-1911 |
| www.harrisbipods.com | www.midwayusa.com | www.ohioordnanceworks.com | www.prolixlubricant.com | www.smithandalexander.com |

# GRIPS/GUNSTOCKS

| ALUMAGRIPS | ALTAMONT COMPANY | BOYD'S GUNSTOCK INDUSTRIES, INC. | DONSON PRODUCTS, INC. | EAGLE GRIPS |
|---|---|---|---|---|
| 2851 N. 34th Pl. | 901 N. Church St. | 25376 403rd Ave. | 329 Cotton Ave. | 460 Randy Rd. |
| Mesa, AZ 85213 | Thomasboro, IL 61878 | Mitchell, SD 57301 | Macon, GA 31201 | Carol Stream, IL 60188 |
| (602) 294-2390 | (800) 626-5774 | (605) 996-5011 | (478) 225-6056 | (800) 323-6144 |
| www.alumagrips.com | www.altamontco.com | www.boydsgunstocks.com | www.dsplaser.com | www.eaglegrips.com |
| GUNSTOCK BLANKS | HERRETT'S STOCKS, INC. | HOGUE | JACK FIRST GUN SHOP | NILL-GRIPS |
| 2017 Pinto Ln. | 169 Madrona St. | P.O. Box 1138 | 1201 Turbine Dr. | In Schlattwiesen 3 |
| Las Vegas, NV 89106 | Twin Falls, ID 83303-0741 | Paso Robles, CA 93447-1138 | Rapid City, SD 57703 | D-72116 Mössingen |
| (702) 382-8470 | (208) 733-1498 | (800) 438-4747 | (605) 343-9544 | Germany |
| www.gunstockblanks.com | www.herrett-stocks.com | www.getgrip.com | www.jackfirstgun.com | www.nill-grips.com |
| NUMRICH GUN PARTS CORP. | PACHMAYR | PEARCE GRIP | TIGER-HUNT | WICKED GRIPS |
| 226 Williams Ln. | 475 Smith St. | P.O. Box 40367 | Box 379 | 9476 Sunrise Ln. |
| West Hurley, NY 12491 | Middletown, CT 06457 | Fort Worth, TX 76140 | Beaverdale, PA 15921 | Davison, MI 48423 |
| (845) 679-4867 | (800) 225-9626 | (800) 390-9420 | (814) 472-5161 | (810) 287-4048 |
| www.gunpartscorp.com | www.pachmayr.com | www.pearcegrip.com | www.gunstockwood.com | www.wickedgrips.com |

# GUN PARTS

| BRAVO COMPANY USA, INC. | BROWNELLS | BUYMILSURP.COM | CHEAPER THAN DIRT | HUBER CONCEPTS |
|---|---|---|---|---|
| P.O. Box 341 | 200 S. Front St. | 8440 Ulmerton Rd. #500 | 2536 N.E. Loop 820 | 322 N. Military Rd. |
| Hartland, WI 53029-0341 | Montezuma, IA 50171 | Largo, FL 33771 | Fort Worth, TX 76106 | Fond du Lac, WI 54935 |
| (877) 272-8626 | (800) 741-0015 | | (888) 750-5234 | (920) 921-9641 |
| www.bravocompanyusa.com | www.brownells.com | www.buymilsurp.com | www.cheaperthandirt.com | www.huberconcepts.com |
| JACK FIRST GUN SHOP | MAG-NA-PORT INTERNATIONAL, INC. | MILITARY GUN SUPPLY | NUMRICH GUN PARTS CORP. | PACIFIC CANVAS & LEATHER |
| 1201 Turbine Dr. | 41302 Executive Dr. | 2901 S. Cravens Rd. | 226 Williams Ln. | P.O. Box 291909 |
| Rapid City, SD 57703 | Harrison Township, MI 48045-1306 | Fort Worth, TX 76119 | West Hurley, NY 12491 | Phelan, CA 92329 |
| (605) 343-9544 | (586) 469-6727 | (817) 457-6000 | (845) 679-4867 | (760) 868-3856 |
| www.jackfirstgun.com | www.magnaport.com | www.militarygunsupply.com | www.gunpartscorp.com | www.pacificcanvasandleather.com |
| RTG PARTS | SARCO, INC. | SPRINGFIELD SPORTERS, INC. | TG INTERNATIONAL | VTI REPLICA GUN PARTS |
| 20783 N. 83rd Ave. #103-235 | 323 Union St. | 2257 Springfield Rd. | P.O. Box 787 | P.O. Box 509 |
| Peoria, AZ 85382 | Stirling, NJ 07980 | Penn Run, PA 15765 | Louisville, TN 37777 | Lakeville, CT 06039 |
| (623) 362-3459 | (908) 647-3800 | (724) 254-2626 | (865) 977-9707 | (860) 435-8068 |
| www.robertrtg.com | www.sarcoinc.com | www.ssporters.com | www.tnguns.com | www.vtigunparts.com |

Made in the USA
Las Vegas, NV
10 March 2023

68702828R00072